Dr. Bob Griffin's *Firestorms of Revival* is dynamite. This solid and scriptural study is molten lava. Griffin's passion for revival in our time is set in an actual locality and marks out the track in very specific terms. In every generation we need a fresh statement on the nature and necessity of spiritual awakening. J. Edwin Orr, Brian Edwards, and Stephen Olford have shared in days gone by. I believe this readable volume will make such a contribution today, and I strongly endorse it. Every church leader in every local church should have a copy.

—Dr. David L. Larsen, Professor Emeritus of Preaching,
Trinity Evangelical Divinity School, Deerfield, Illinois

Grateful as we are for all the dedicated ministries being carried on around the world, we know that everywhere, and especially in our own country, there is a desperate need for a mighty work of the Holy Spirit. So from our hearts we cry, "Will you not revive us again, that your people may rejoice in you?" (Ps. 85:6, NIV).

While some believers are engaging in fervent intercession for a deep-seated widespread spiritual awakening, most of us are moving along in life's usual groove. Not Bob and Connie Griffin! They have been spearheading a Christ-exalting movement in the city of Rockford, Illinois. And here in this soul-stirring book, Bob shares his and Connie's passion. He tells about revivals in years gone by, spelling out the biblical principles that have been powerfully operative in those great stirrings of church and society. Destined to be a classic in its *genre,* this book will prove effective as a personal catalyst to its readers.

—Dr. Vernon Grounds, Chancellor
Denver Seminary

Bob Griffin is a scholar and a student of revival. He has not only read broadly but has also been involved in the excitement, disappointment, enthusiasm, and down to earth human involvement that God uses to bring new life to congregations and communities. This book provides us with much needed insight into God's work in the twenty-first century. Everyone interested in revival will want to read this important contribution.

—Jay Kesler, President Emeritus
Taylor University, Upland, Indiana

Firestorms of Revival is an invigorating demonstration of God's work! Passionately presented by Dr. Griffin, it challenges the church to set herself ablaze with a resurgence of the Holy Spirit, who is capable and willing to move in the hearts of humbled believers everywhere.

—*Christopher R. Frye, MBA*
WQFL Rockford, Program Director

Dr. Bob Griffin chronicles here God's irrefutable promise for health, healing, and revival in our world, our cities, and our lives. Bob documents God's faithfulness to His promise in 2 Chronicles 7:14, identifies commonality in sweeping movements of the Holy Spirit throughout history, and points the way to revival in our own days. Compelling!

—*Rick Kroeger President*
Kroeger International
Consultant, Leadership Network

I have read many books on revival, but none more comprehensive than *Firestorms of Revival*. The historical documentation from the Old Testament to the present is clearly recorded and defined. While it is comprehensive, it is also very concise, as shown in its statement, "Revival will not cross the bridge until unity is well under construction." Dr. Bob brings a beautiful blend of what we can do and what the Holy Spirit will do. This work could well become the textbook on revival. It is the most exhaustive study I have ever read on the subject. I recommend it to everyone.

—*Rev. Dr. Don Lyon, Senior Pastor*
Faith Center
Rockford, Illinois

Have you ever wondered why all those mainline denominations with so many rich traditions and all those highly educated clergy and laity are dying so quickly? After over three decades as a pastor in a mainliner that continues to move so rapidly to the sidelines of influence on American and global cultures, I have found two books which provide the diagnosis and antidote.

The diagnosis comes from Rhonda Hughey's *Desperate for His Presence*. Her thesis is simple: God's presence, not our programs or professional ingenuity, enables individual and corporate growth. The antidote is Bob Griffin's *Firestorms of Revival*, which is the practical as well as erudite review of the biblical, histori-cal, and pneumatic ingredients of revival's recipe. Dr. Griffin, an uncommonly discerning pastor and scholar on the cutting edge of ecclesiastical evolution, has provided the most complete guide for cooperating with our Lord's reviving movements to prepare His bride for His glorious return.

Coming from the mainline experience, I am encouraged and challenged by Dr. Griffin's passion for holiness, spiritual discipline, and authentic ecumenism as personified in Jesus and prescribed in the Bible as the medicine for that which ails churches. If you're looking for the diagnosis and antidote for a church's lethargy, pick up these two books and put them into the hands and hearts of your leadership and membership.

—*Dr. Robert R. Kopp, Pastor*
First Presbyterian Church
Belvidere, Illinois
Author of Praying Like Jesus, Don't Forget This,
God's Top Ten List, Golf in the Real Kingdom, *and*
Fifteen Secrets for Life and Ministry

The most effective way to increase our spiritual appetite and faith for revival is to consider what God has already done. Biblical and historic revivals are plentiful, and we have a responsibility as God's people to prepare ourselves for His visitation in our day! Bob's book is an important tool for considering again God's pat-tern for revival and the Biblical principles by which His presence draws near to desperate people. This book will ignite a fresh fire in your heart and faith to seek God for another spiritual awakening in our nation.

—*Rhonda Hughey, Director*
Fusion Ministries
Author, Desperate for His Presence

Here is a book that will draw you into the lessons learned from great moves of God in history and today. In 1995 my wife and I started a journey to discover what God was doing to awaken His church across our nation. We have had the privilege of visiting over twenty major cities in the USA and have seen firsthand an obvious new move of pastors and marketplace leaders who are beginning to come together across denominational and cultural lines for prayer, church growth by conversion, and social justice. These spiritual leaders are simultaneously beginning to pastor the church of their city that meets in many locations.

In *Firestorms of Revival*, Bob has captured the time-tested principles that better welcome and sustain a historic move of the Holy Spirit over a city. It is practical and inspirational. You will be convicted and uplifted to pick up the torch to light revival fire in this hour. Bob has thoroughly searched the scriptures and history to give us practical and proven principles. Take these steps and apply them. You will be challenged to be resilient and persistent as God brings firestorms to your region.

—*Rev. Tony Danhelka*
Co-founder and President of Riverwoods Christian Center
Chicagoland Cityreacher

Sensitive to the lateness of the hour, Dr. Bob Griffin sees an American church that is divided, underpowered, and yielded to the materialistic and sinful culture of this age—a culture heavily shaped and influenced by Satan, who understands that his time is now very short. Bob knows that only a genuine heaven-sent revival will change the church into a sanctified bride, dressed in white linen, and he has done a masterful job of presenting the common denominators of revivals in the Old Testament period, the New Testament period, and the church age. He has also shown the resulting changes of revival in society, in the economy, in the lives of individual believers, and also in the spiritual life, ministry, and witness of the church.

God has given Bob magnificent insight to His big picture for the ages. Bob's research has been detailed and insightful, and his conclusions are both relevant and uplifting to the gatekeepers and intercessors who stand in the gap before him, praying for America, and saying, "Come quickly, Lord Jesus."

—*Frank Shappert, President*
Shappert Engineering
Chairman of the Board, Rockford Renewal Ministries

FIRESTORMS
OF
REVIVAL

DR. BOB GRIFFIN

CREATION
HOUSE
A STRANG COMPANY

FIRESTORMS OF REVIVAL by Dr. Bob Griffin
Published by Creation House
A Strang Company
600 Rinehart Road
Lake Mary, Florida 32746
www.creationhouse.com

Unless otherwise noted, all Scripture quotations are from the Holy Bible, New International Version. Copyright © 1973, 1978, 1984, International Bible Society. Used by permission.

Scripture quotations marked NLT are from the Holy Bible, New Living Translation, copyright © 1996. Used by permission of Tyndale House Publishers, Inc., Wheaton, IL 60189. All rights reserved.

Scripture quotations marked KJV are from the King James Version of the Bible.

Scripture quotations marked NRSV are from the New Revised Standard Version of the Bible. Copyright © 1989 by the Division of Christian Education of the National Council of the Churches of Christ in the USA. Used by permission.

Scripture quotations marked NKJV are from the New King James Version of the Bible. Copyright © 1979, 1980, 1982 by Thomas Nelson, Inc., publishers. Used by permission.

Cover design by Terry Clifton

Library of Congress Control Number: 2006929486
International Standard Book Number-10: 1-59979-064-5
International Standard Book Number-13: 978-1-59979-064-0

First Edition

06 07 08 09 10 — 987654321
Printed in the United States of America

This book is dedicated first to Connie Griffin—my wife, my best friend, and my partner in ministry. Second, it is dedicated to the city of Rockford, Illinois, and to all who are interceding with Connie and me for area-wide transformation, a sweeping revival of the church, and a great awakening in which thousands come to faith in Jesus Christ—our Savior, Lord, and soon coming King.

Acknowledgments

I GRATEFULLY ACKNOWLEDGE THE outstanding professors who mentored and inspired me at Trinity International University. Special mention goes to Dr. David Larsen, who coached me through my doctoral program. He shares not only my love for the church of Jesus Christ and the city of Rockford, Illinois, but also my passion to see a sweeping revival of the church and another great awakening in our day.

My heart is very thankful for Connie—my wife and partner in the gospel—who has displayed patient endurance through the years of my ministry and maturing (I still have a long way to go). I deeply appreciate her steadfast strength and commitment, especially in the later years as God called us out of our comfort zone and into the faith adventure of Rockford Renewal Ministries. The renewal ministry and this book would have been impossible without Connie. She read and edited this manuscript before anyone else saw it.

Finally, I want to express special thanks to Ken Holmgren, who patiently edited this manuscript with great skill, and Dinah Wallace, the copy editor. Going beyond the call of duty and excellence was the expertise of Virginia Maxwell, the production manager. I will forever be grateful to this team for coaching me through the rigorous challenges of detail and documentation in the publication of *Firestorms of Revival*.

Contents

Will you not revive us again, that your people may rejoice in you? Show us your unfailing love, O LORD, and grant us your salvation. I will listen to what God the LORD will say; he promises peace to his people, his saints—but let them not return to folly. Surely his salvation is near those who fear him, that his glory may dwell in our land. Love and faithfulness meet together; righteousness and peace kiss each other. Faithfulness springs forth from the earth, and righteousness looks down from heaven. The LORD will indeed give what is good, and our land will yield its harvest. Righteousness goes before him and prepares the way for his steps.

—Psalm 85:6–13

Introduction

I SAT IN A small cabin in Wisconsin, praying and listening to God's still, small voice. It was a day set aside to be with God, my adoptive heavenly Father. The sun was bright, but a cold, strong winter wind blew snow across the woods and the path to the door. As I asked God for a sweeping move of revival across our area, He lovingly assured me, *Be still and patient, My son. The wind of My Spirit shall blow again as at Pentecost.*

The wind howled through the woods and shook the cabin. Through the large window in front of me, I watched the trees bend in the gusts, the smaller ones nearly snapping while the larger ones stood strong against the wind's mighty power. I was thankful for the warmth from the potbellied stove in the corner of the cabin.

My heart cried, *Oh God, bring the wind of Your Holy Spirit soon. Blow across the nation and the world again as at Pentecost. Bend Your church back to passionate obedience and fiery first love. Oh, Father, do it again as Isaiah prayed,*

> Oh, that you would rend the heavens and come down, that the mountains would tremble before you! As when fire sets twigs ablaze and causes water to boil, come down to make your name known.
>
> —*Isaiah 64:1–2*

Still listening, I heard the sweet song of a bird. God spoke again, *As the wind of My Spirit blows, as My fire falls, My bride will reflect My glory. She will be refined by My fire. Beautiful songs of praise will accompany the winds of revival.*

God Has Told Us What to Do

When will the wind of the Holy Spirit blow across the land? When will the fire of Pentecost fall across America? When will beautiful songs of revival fill the air? God is ready. He is waiting for His church to prepare the way through obedience to Him.

God told us exactly what to do after He made one of His most incredible visitations in Israel's history at the dedication of Solomon's temple. After the construction of the temple was complete, the stage was set for God to fill the house. In grand fashion, Solomon offered a lengthy prayer to dedicate the new temple in 2 Chronicles 6. As he poured out his heart to God, he asked Him over and over to hear Israel's cry and forgive her when certain disasters came as a result of the people drifting into sin, idolatry, and rebellion.

Second Chronicles 7:1 says that when Solomon finished praying, God's glory fell like a firestorm from heaven and consumed the sacrifices.

> When all the people of Israel saw the fire coming down and the glorious presence of the Lord filling the Temple, they fell face down on the ground and worshiped and praised the Lord.
> —*2 Chronicles 7:3, NLT*

Two weeks of great celebration followed this phenomenal high. The temple was spectacular, and God's presence—His glory—so filled the house that the people couldn't stand. With faces to the ground, they worshiped God. Oh, how wonderful it must have been!

When Solomon returned to his palace—probably excited and exhausted—God spoke to him in the night and answered the questions and concerns he had expressed in his prayer of dedication. What would happen in dark and difficult times? Would God meet the people of Israel in times of great need? Would He answer when they cried out to Him at this great temple? Would He help them? Would He restore them?

Solomon knew that tough and terrible times would come. It was a matter of *when,* not *if.* There would be times of spiritual decay and drift. God's people would turn away from Him in sin and rebellion. It would be bad economically, spiritually, socially, and militarily. Graciously, God spoke to Solomon:

> If my people, who are called by my name, will humble themselves and pray and seek my face and turn from their wicked ways, then will I hear from heaven and will forgive their sin and will heal their land.
>
> —*2 Chronicles 7:14*

This text stands throughout history as God's instructions for His people when things turn bad. Although it is specific to Israel, its truth can be seen anytime God's people anywhere drift away from Him. When life turns dark and difficult, they begin to humble themselves, seek Him, pray, and repent. This thread is woven into the history of Israel, and it is also evident in the New Testament and post biblical history. In difficult times of apostasy and drift, in economically and socially dark times, revival comes when God's people obey His clear instructions.

BACK TO THE BASICS

The fire and winds of revival come on a highway of holiness. The church in America and the West must build this highway with passion, in hot pursuit of biblical truth and obedience. It is time to follow God's instructions—to humble ourselves, turn from our wicked ways, passionately seek His face, and turn back to Him. No amount of passionate praying for revival will matter until a highway of holiness is built. Repentance must go hand-in-hand with prayer. It is time to *turn around* and go back the way we came. This is where revival begins.

We are drifting into the sinful condition of the culture around us. According to surveys, little difference can be found between the ethics and behavior of the church today and the culture she has been called to redeem. In a recent poll, George Barna, a Christian sociologist and research expert, compared the lifestyles of Christians and non-Christians. Using 131 different measures of attitudes, behaviors, values, and beliefs, he found "no visible differences" between Christians and non-Christians in the aspects of lifestyles where Christians can have their greatest impact on the lives of non-Christians.[1]

The popular consensus is that church congregations, instead of making a redemptive impact on their surrounding neighborhoods, are irrelevant and inconsequential. Today, numerous studies confirm that the public—especially media and intellectual leaders—does not see Christianity as a dominant, social force.[2] Instead, "six out of ten Americans believe the church is irrelevant."[3]

"In the lives of the 170 million non-Christians in America (this makes our country the third largest mission field in the world), that irrelevance provokes an ever-increasing cynicism and hostility... For all its frenetic activity and supernatural posturings, the overall impact of the church on American culture is generally understood to be... just slightly above zero."[4]

We have many fine strategies and booklets to help us share the gospel, but we do not have that for which Jesus prayed: unity. The Holy Spirit will cross over into our cities on the bridge of a church that is unified in humility, repentance, and sacrificial efforts. When will we break down the religious and cultural barriers that have divided the church for years? How long will the church stand in open defiance to her Savior who prayed that she would be one? Jesus said, "If a kingdom [including God's kingdom] is divided against itself, that kingdom cannot stand. If a house is divided against itself, that house cannot stand" (Mark 3:24–25).

Although there may be many congregations in an area, there is only one church. Through unity, our cities and our nation will know the gospel: that the Father sent His Son (John 17:20–23). Hear it again. *Through the unity of the church, our cities will know that God the Father sent His Son.* Revival will not cross the bridge until unity is well under construction. God will not come until the religious patterns of encrusted Christianity have been shattered by an intentional return to basic New Testament faith, the Great Commandment (Deut. 6:5; Mark 12:30; Matt. 22:37; Luke 10:27), the Great Commission (Acts 1:8; Matt. 28:19–20), and unity.

Every Christ follower is to be a builder of the bridge of unity and the highway of holiness. Each of us must be intentional about breaking out of our comfort zones. For some, the connotation of unity is that all Christian groups are forced to be identical, to lose their historic distinctiveness. However, unity is better understood as harmony—the blending of diverse notes and melodies into a beautiful symphony of worship.

In revival, the wind of the Spirit will sweep away the debris of sin and compromise in the church. The number of those who gather for services will no longer be the measure of her success. Pecking-order pride among clergy will diminish. Religious forms and rituals, long drained of significance, will no longer be important. The church will seek God's face, desperate for His manifest presence among them.

The church will get back to basics. She will no longer sacrifice her children on the altar of Western hedonistic culture and media. Instead, she will be committed to obedience, which God requires. Obedience will release God's covenant blessings for His people (Lev. 26; Deut. 11 and 28; Josh. 1; 1 Sam. 15:22). The church will flourish. Her cities will be transformed, and she will be characterized by the redemptive mission "to act justly and to love mercy and to walk humbly with [her] God" (Mic. 6:8).

A loving passion for God and intimacy with Him are absent too often. In many congregations, culture and programs have made Christianity so nominal that it can hardly be recognized as having New Testament characteristics. It is time to return to our first love (Rev. 2:4). Are we like the church of Laodicea (Rev. 3:16), the lukewarm church that God wanted to spit out of His mouth? Could God be getting sick to His stomach?

It is time to get back to passion, to loving others sacrificially instead of judging them or criticizing them. It is time to so embody the love of Christ that people are drawn to Him through us. "Mercy triumphs over judgment" (James 2:13). It is time to speak the truth in love, not in anger or with nasty rhetoric (Eph. 4:15).

Through our love and obedience, the church will push back the principalities, powers, and the enemy encampments over our cities and nation. She will take back the ground she has lost. She will penetrate the heavenly realms to defeat satanic forces. She will make known the manifold wisdom of God to the rulers and authorities in these realms, according to God's eternal purpose, which He accomplished in Christ Jesus our Lord (Eph. 3:10). With these powers broken over our cities, and through a motivated and mobilized church, our cities will be transformed. The power of the enemy will be broken. The darkness that has infiltrated the church and held entire regions in darkness will be broken.

WHY THIS BOOK?

This book is the story of revival, the story of how revival always happens and how it will happen again. The fire will fall, revival will come, and our cities will be transformed when the church follows God's instructions. When I built fires in our wood furnace as a boy, I had to wad up newspaper first, lay the kindling on it, then add some larger pieces. We will need to build the fire—place the paper of humility in the church, lay the kindling of prayer, and add the wood of seeking God's face and repentance. God will light the match. When God's people do their part, God will do His.

Why this book? Why this passion for revival? America is rotting at her core. A billboard along the northbound lanes on route I-65 in Indiana declares, "One out of three high school students will graduate in 2005 with a sexually transmitted disease." Pornography in America has grown to be an industry of over $51 billion annually.

Judicial tyranny is raping the nation. The Constitution of the United States, our nation's ethical and moral anchor for two hundred years, is now being called a living document. In other words, it can be interpreted according to our current ethical trends. The Ten Commandments are being removed from the public square.

A very small percentage of Jesus' followers ever lead anyone to salvation. The church measures success by the cultural standards of the day, rather than the number of people who are coming to faith in Jesus Christ and growing into service for Him. In her decline, the church stands impotent against the tide of secularism and godlessness.

Desperate for revival and the transformation of our cities, I began to ask, *Is there hope? What has happened in the past when God's people have drifted into idolatry, secularism, and spiritual impotence? Is there a pattern that will help us trace God's response?* With Solomon of old, I asked, *Oh God, what will You do in these dark and difficult days of drift?*

An Old Testament scholar had affirmed my belief in 2 Chronicles 7:14 as the simple instructions for revival, and it had motivated me to begin facilitating a movement of prayer gatherings in our area. Shortly after we began these gatherings, my wife, Connie, and I were called to launch Rockford Renewal Ministries. About the same time, with passion burning in my soul, I chose to study and write on revival for my final doctoral paper.

It was a great opportunity to learn about revival. I discovered ten characteristics that could be traced throughout Scripture and post-biblical history, and I am writing to share them with you. I want to light a *firestorm* of great historic revival. First, however, I will tell you the story of our revival journey. I love to tell this story, but if you can't contain your curiosity to get into the book, jump ahead to the first chapter, and join me as I chase revival fire through time.

THE BIRTH OF CITYWIDE PRAYER

In 1994 the Evangelical Free Church of America established a National Prayer Accord. As a part of the strategy, groups of three churches in each city were encouraged to meet quarterly for combined prayer for revival in the church and for the transformation of the city. When the plan was presented to the staff of the Evangelical Free Church where Connie and I were serving in Rockford, Illinois, I volunteered to lead the effort. I called the pastor of a large Assembly of God church across the street, and he was enthusiastic about praying together. At last, two very diverse congregations were going to pray and work together. But what about a third church?

Months earlier I had met with fellow clergy, city officials, and the mayor to hear Dr. Ray Bakke, a Christian urban specialist, speak about the urban crisis in America. He had led a church in Chicago for a number of years and had written books on city transformation. After Bakke's talk, the group discussed why cities deteriorate and what needed to happen for our city to be transformed.

At the conclusion of the meeting, a pastor suggested that we pray. Rockford was in great need. Homicides were off the chart—more per capita than they were in Chicago. The local school district was under federal control, having been convicted of inequitable treatment of students from the west side of town, where the population was primarily African American and Hispanic. Businesses had been moving out of the city, and families had also been moving outside the city limits because of rising taxes needed to meet the government's requirements to reorder the school district.

When God led me to pray aloud, I began to share the pain I was feeling. Gripped with sadness for our city, I began to weep softly and could not continue to pray. My shoulders shook with sobs. An African American pastor slipped in beside me, took my hand, and prayed until I regained my composure.

At that moment, it hit me like a ton of bricks: This is what needs to happen in this city: pastors of different races and denominations pray and weep together. In that moment I whispered to God, *Our city is desperate. I am just one small person, but if there is any way You want to use me to help bring revival and restoration to this city, Oh, God, I am available.*

I had volunteered in the city council chambers, doing anything I could to help the city. I told the church staff that I would coordinate our denomination's prayer initiative. As the Assembly of God pastor and I discussed what church we could ask to join us for prayer, it grabbed me: Call the African American pastor who had taken my hand, shared my concern, and joined me in prayer.

I called him. When he checked the suggested date for the first prayer meeting, he exclaimed, "That's Brotherhood Sunday. Could we meet at our church?"

It was arranged. The two larger congregations of several thousand each—predominantly Caucasian, Pentecostal, and non-Pentecostal— gathered at Pilgrim Baptist, a predominantly African American church of several hundred. We met on the west side of the Rock River, which had divided the city from her inception. Many drove to the meeting from the east side. Others, who were afraid to drive into the west side at night, were taken in church buses.

People came from all across town, and God showed up. Pilgrim Baptist was packed, and people were turned away. The local press heard about the gathering, and a young woman from the newspaper asked for an interview after the service. The next morning, the prayer gathering had captured front-page headlines and was the lead article. A large picture showed a crowd of great diversity, African American and Caucasian folks, worshiping and praying together.

What had been organized for three congregations became citywide. A steering committee of four African American pastors and three Caucasian pastors was formed. I was asked to coordinate the effort. As time passed, the committee grew to include representatives from all who considered themselves evangelical (Orthodox) Christians: Protestant, Catholic, African American, Caucasian, and Hispanic—both male and female.

Concerts of Prayer were held quarterly (except for the summer) beginning in February, 1995. The largest crowd—about fifteen hundred people—met in a downtown theater. At the twenty-fifth citywide gathering on October 4, 2002, a crowd of over nine hundred read a litany together, crowning Jesus Lord and King over the city (see Appendix I). Saturday, November 23, accusations of arrogance, exclusive religion, and intolerance of other religions were expressed in the *Rockford Register Star*, the local newspaper. It was a great opportunity to respond with editorials that spoke biblical truth in love.[5]

After the climax of the twenty-fifth Concert of Prayer gathering, some of the leadership, especially Connie and I, felt that God was saying it was time for a change. I was deeply disturbed. We couldn't quit. Revival had not come! Twenty-five area-wide Concerts of Prayer had been a wonderful accomplishment in prayer and growing unity—but quit? Yet, God's leading was clear. Those with whom we talked all agreed. The Spirit of God had been speaking to us, and it was time to end the Concerts of Prayer.

God had a new plan. After much prayer and discussion, the leadership decided that the unified, area-wide church needed a more regular and visible expression. As a result, in January 2003, GRIPP—Greater Rockford in Prayer and Praise—was born. Meetings were scheduled across the area—north, south, east, west, and central—on the third Friday of each month. The gatherings were simplified to keep the meetings free from a parade of leaders, a tight schedule, and a formal order of service.

A large steering committee was no longer required, and Connie and I began to coordinate the events with a host pastor and congregation. Accountability was achieved through my covenant group, clergy with whom I met once a week. Monthly inter-denominational, and multiracial gatherings continue to this day, with both men and women involved in platform leadership. GRIPP continues to be intentional about diversity, but it is now simply praise, repentance, and passionate prayer for revival.

Rockford Renewal Ministries Begins

Early in the history of the prayer movement, the Concert of Prayer steering committee held a breakfast for pastors. Since I was leaving to minister in India, I could not attend. However, I produced a video that told the story of how Concerts of Prayer were born and also cast a vision for the revival of the church and the transformation of the city. At the breakfast, a pastor who led a weekly church prayer meeting of about two hundred people saw the video. His prayer group had been asking God to raise up someone full-time to facilitate revival efforts for the area-wide church. As he watched the video, God quietly said to him, *This is the one for whom you have been praying.*

When I returned from India, this young pastor made an appointment to see me. Entering my office, he introduced himself and reported what God had spoken. I was surprised, if not shocked. *Lord,* I thought, *this is strange. What does it mean? Did You speak? Who is this wild man with so much passion and energy? Why me?* I tucked this experience away and proceeded with my pastoral ministry, including the work of facilitating citywide prayer meetings.

In December 1996, Connie and I left our church positions to seek God's direction for a new chapter in our lives. Our assumption was that God would lead us to a senior pastor position, and the search process began. Two months after our resignation, a businessman in the city asked me to meet him for lunch. He knew of me through a mutual friend, and after we became acquainted, he began to share his passion for revival. He was confident that God was bringing revival to Rockford. The citywide church would need elders or leaders, he said, to facilitate God's work in the city.

Then he dropped a bomb. God had spoken to him, and he believed that Connie and I were to stay in the city to facilitate the prayer and revival efforts full time. This was the second man who had spoken about serving in the city. What was this unusual thing we were to do?

Not long after this lunch meeting God met me in an early morning "burning bush" experience. I was praying, listening, and writing. (Only one other time had God spoken to me so clearly. Years earlier He had called Connie and me to leave an exciting university ministry, raise missionary support, and travel internationally serving missionaries and national pastors.) As God spoke, I wrote. It was brief and clear. He said,

Renewal Ministries—for the healing of hearts, help for the church, and hope for the city.

My best understanding was that God wanted Connie and me to continue helping people with broken hearts and nurture them—especially leaders and pastors—to healing. He also wanted us to call the church in the city to passionate prayer for revival, according to 2 Chronicles 7:14. As the church obeyed God's instructions to seek His face in humble, repentant prayer, revival would come. With revival, the deep wounds in the city would be healed. She would be transformed.

Connie was praying that God would lead us to a senior pastor role where we could each use our gifts and experience. Neither of us wanted to stay in Rockford. We were ready to move. This strange word from God was far from the security Connie desired, and it was a significant stretch for me. Had I heard from God, or was it too much morning coffee? Connie agreed to pray about it and seek God for a clear call and confirmation. Weeks later she slipped into my study early in the morning. God had confirmed the call to her while she was praying in the night.

We still wanted to make sure. It would be foolish to begin a new faith ministry and humanly impossible without God's call and the confirmation of His people. We knew of no one who had ever done such a thing. We also knew it would draw enemy fire, especially in a city where the church was deeply divided and the enemy had well-established strongholds. In the past, we had traveled internationally under Barnabas International, ministering to pastors and missionaries. Although we had raised financial support then, it was common knowledge that support for a home ministry was very difficult to raise. (It has been!)

Had God spoken? We needed confirmation, and we decided to hold a banquet downtown at the City Club. Since we had been facilitating city-wide Concerts of Prayer for two years, we had worked with many Christians across the city, and we needed their help and support. Thus, ninety-two pastors, city leaders, and friends met together for a great meal in April 1997. Pastors from different ethnic groups gave leadership. An African

American soloist sang the popular song, "The Impossible Dream."[6]

After dinner, Connie and I shared our story and invited people to pray together at their tables. When they filled out response cards, they were very positive. An offering was taken to pay for the evening, and it exceeded expenses by fifteen hundred dollars. We asked a pastor in the city to close the evening with prayer. As he began to share his excitement, he spontaneously asked pastors to gather at the front to commission us for the new work. Connie and I knelt before them. We had heard from God.

From this beginning, Rockford Renewal Ministries was born. The following morning we engaged an attorney to prepare incorporation papers. We prayerfully created a board of directors and asked a team of friends to both cover us in prayer and also to pray for revival each day. A vision statement sprang quickly from our hearts, and our mission statement followed naturally. We would call the church in Rockford, Illinois, to prayer and repentance for revival. A fourteen-point revival strategy was developed to make the vision a reality. (See Appendix II.)

> *The Vision of Rockford Renewal Ministries* is a sweeping revival of the church of Jesus Christ in the city of Rockford, Illinois, and a great awakening across the city, accomplished by effectual, fervent prayer and personal and corporate holiness.

> *The Mission of Rockford Renewal Ministries* is to call the church of Jesus Christ across the city to repentance and to seek God with humble prayer for revival and a great awakening according to 2 Chronicles 7:14. The results shall be personal and corporate righteousness, people and congregations on fire for God and His kingdom, and dramatic social change—the transformation of the city.

I had been working on a doctoral degree at Trinity University in Deerfield, Illinois, and I needed to select the topic for my final paper shortly after we launched the ministry. I had planned to write on lay counseling—life coaching, as we called it. However, with my new passion for revival, I began to ask God, *How does revival happen? Is there a pattern in Scripture? Is there a pattern throughout church history? Are they the*

same? Help us understand these things if we are to serve Your new calling.
It didn't take me long to decide to write on revival. I needed answers, and
my doctoral committee readily approved the topic.

GOD ACCOMPLISHES HIS KINGDOM WORK

Since the birth of Rockford Renewal Ministries, Connie and I have pur-
sued its vision and mission. We have worked the simple strategy that
God gave us, and our board has stood with us month after month for
almost ten years. God has provided us with an ideal office in the heart of
the city, a beautiful home well suited for hosting city leaders and pastors,
and a new car. Let me tell you about the first two miracles now. I will tell
you about the third in chapter seven.

Long before we were called to Rockford Renewal ministries, our
youngest son, Jonathan, believed God had led him to study at Wheaton
College. Our other two children had been able to attend Taylor University tuition free when Connie and I were on staff there. We decided to
sell our nice and more-than-we-needed newer home to downsize so we
could handle our part of the college expenses; we also wanted to find a
home that would serve our need for an office.

We tried to sell our home for seven years; three times with a realtor.
Connie is a gifted artist in interior design, and everyone who saw our
home loved it. However, when we did not have success with realtors, we
tried to sell the home by ourselves. Finally, in frustration and uncertainty
about God's plan, we gave up. We told the Lord, *We quit. If You want the
house to sell, send someone to the door asking to buy it.*

Months came and went until one Friday afternoon when we noticed
people looking around in the backyard. Connie went out to ask if she
could help them, and in embarrassment, they said they didn't think we
were home. Then they asked, "Would you sell your home?" They were a
pastoral family on the way to the city, and their house purchase had fallen
through. Their realtor knew our realtor, and though our house was not
on the market at the time, our realtor knew of our interest in selling.

We responded positively, indicating that we had been waiting for
them. They asked us if we could be out in twelve days. "Sure!" We said.
We knew God was at work. The congregation to which they were coming

had apartments for their discipleship program, and the church offered us two of them as a stop gap plan: one to live in and the other for storage.

As we moved into the apartments, we realized that looking for a house was going to be a challenge of faith on several fronts. Connie wanted an old home with character, and larger rooms for hospitality. She is gifted in hospitality and cuisine, and one of our ministry strategies was to invite denominationally and racially diverse clergy and leaders into our home for dinner. I enjoyed old homes, but since we had lived in several, I knew that it would take a lot of time, money, and energy—things I didn't have to give—to fix one up. We decided to scour the older sections of town for an old home with character and large rooms—all fixed up and ready for us.

The second challenge was our schedule. We had only about thirty days to close a deal before the discipleship students would come to live in the apartments, and we were going to be away two different weeks—half of that time. Thus, we were left with our first week home to find our miracle house and close a deal. Looking and praying, we began to drive the older sections of the city.

When we first moved to Rockford, our realtor had shown us the city. As we drove down Calvin Park Boulevard, we fell in love with the neighborhood. Old classic homes graced both sides of a wide, park-like center boulevard with one-way streets on each side. It was idyllic and one of the most beautiful streets we had seen. We dreamed of living on such a street.

Now, years later, as we looked for homes for sale, you guessed it—a very nice old home was on the market on Calvin Park. As we looked at it, I knew it was the one. The rooms were nearly perfect for our ministry. The owner had worked for nearly ten years to fix it up, spending much more than he would ever get out of it. Only one problem loomed in front of us: It was more money than we wanted to spend.

The realtor called us the next morning to say the owner had just purchased another home for his growing family and was hungry to sell. He had dropped the price ten thousand dollars. We offered even less, and we had our dream home on our dream boulevard. It was about seven minutes from the office that we had found in the heart of the city. We closed on the house and moved in just as students began to return for their new term. We have added our touches and continue to be grateful for the gift and provision of God. It has been an ideal home and a wonderful place for hospitality.

The office was another story of God's amazing provision. We needed a separate office for our ministry because our work was stressful, and spiritual warfare was a daily engagement. I wasn't doing well working out of our home because I didn't know how to go home from work. Also, when I was counseling in the family room, Connie had to be there. However, she was forced to stay sequestered upstairs.

Connie wanted an office with windows and lots of light. The city was upon my heart, and I wanted an office in the heart of the city. There was, however, a challenge. We couldn't afford to pay much rent. As we began looking and asking on our faith adventure, we made some offers. However, the locations were not good, and most of the space was in the basement of an office building.

One morning I had an idea. Perhaps a downtown bank would tithe space to us—an office with windows in the heart of the city. I called a former mayor who had gone into leasing and handled bank space. He nearly laughed when I shared my idea. The banks were short on space, and any space available was being converted into apartments. Then he paused and said, "I was just walking down the street this morning and saw an empty space in front of the Luther Center, the retirement high-rise."

It didn't take long to call the Luther Center. The manager confirmed that they did have office space on the street level facing State Street and Wyman, one of the central intersections on the West Side of the city. "Does it have windows," I asked.

"Yes," she said. "They wrap around the front of the office, floor to ceiling."

When we looked at the space, we discovered that it was all they had described, but much worse. It was pie shaped, with a post in the middle and filled with garbage. Wires hung from the walls, and nicotine covered everything, even the drop ceiling and grills. After looking at the space, Connie called to ask what the monthly rent would be. Three hundred dollars a month, came the reply.

Connie couldn't believe it. "Did you say three hundred dollars a month?" We could have 1100 square feet for three hundred dollars a month in the heart of the city.

Connie has the ability to envision a completed project. Although I could never imagine moving into the space, she could see it as beautiful. In fact, months earlier, when Connie had been praying about an office, God gave her a vision. She saw beautiful landscaped gardens with water—which she knew was the location of our office. Then God showed her a warehouse full of furniture. It didn't make sense at the time, but she told me about it, and we tucked it away for future reference.

We agreed to lease the space. Weeks, then months went by, but the center was not keeping its promise to clean out the garbage, remove the old computer wires, patch the walls, and paint everything. In the meantime, people began to give funds to help us. A builder designed the inner walls to hide the pillar and provide a perfect arrangement for an entry, two large offices, a conference room, and a space in the back for a small kitchenette next to the bathroom.

About the same time, we heard about a large corporation that was making much of their executive office furniture available to non-profit organizations. We called to make an appointment and were given an address where we could meet someone who would show what they had to offer. As we walked through the door of an old warehouse and up some steps, Connie stopped dead in her tracks. There was part of the vision. We felt like children in a candy store. We selected what we needed, and they agreed to store it for us until our office was ready.

But still we waited…and waited. Finally, we took action. Thinking about the walls of Jericho, we decided to march around the building once a day for six days and seven times on the seventh day. Intercessors, including one with a shofar, joined us. We met at the front of the office and began to walk.

As we went around to the back of the building, Connie exclaimed, "There is the garden, the pathway, and water of my vision!" Sure enough, Luther Center backs up to the Rock River, and a beautifully landscaped walking path weaves its way along the river. We kept walking with greater excitement. On the seventh day, we walked around the building seven times and blew the shofar from the State Street bridge. Not long after this, we received the call that the space was ready, with new paint.

The work on the office began, and three friends completed all the framing when we were out of town one weekend. Another friend, who was raising missionary support and doing construction on the side, came in to do the drywall. About the time the drywall was ready, a contractor called and said that he heard we needed help. His people completed all the trim (which he paid for), and hung the doors. Connie and I and our youngest son, Jonathan, did all the painting.

Three significant events happened in a period of twelve hours. We heard from the Luther Center that the carpet would be laid and we could sign the lease; we received a phone call to select desks, lamps, and chairs; and we accepted an offer on our house. Six weeks later, we moved into both our office and our house the same weekend. With financial gifts and the offer of furniture from a dealer, Connie created beautiful offices. We have been given a large conference table and chairs, and copy and FAX machines. We were able to lease computers and phones. We work in the heart of the city in beautiful space with floor to ceiling windows—all for three hundred dollars a month. Amazing! God has met our needs and our dreams.

I finished my doctoral degree—another miracle of God's provision—writing on revival, while Connie and I launched the ministry. We have been able to work side by side for nine years as partners in ministry. Like many married couples, we are very different from each other; yet, we have learned to compliment and complement each other. I was given the title of President; Connie took the title, Chief Executive Officer; and we both share the jobs of secretary and janitor.

GRIPP continues. We are facilitating weekly prayer meetings across the area in strategic locations: the jail, the court, city hall, the school board, the marketplace at a corporate office, and two other locations downtown. One weekly prayer gathering is for all who want to attend. Another is by invitation only—for those we know are called and gifted intercessors.

We continue to cast the vision and call the church to unity, repentance, and prayer. I have the opportunity to speak regularly in African American, Caucasian, and Hispanic congregations. I put on a robe to minister in an Episcopalian church, and I dress casually for more informal gatherings. In most African American congregations, we are invited to sit on the platform and bring a greeting.

In addition, we have invited many pastors and their spouses to our home for dinner with no other agenda than helping them become acquainted with others of denominational and racial diversity. The evenings have ended with great joy as we have held hands around the table and prayed for each other and for our city. Significant friendships have been formed, and racial and denominational divisions have faded before our eyes.

Second Chronicles 15:7 has pushed us forward through dark and difficult times of discouragement: "But as for you, be strong and do not give up, for your work will be rewarded." We were correct in our assumptions. We have attracted enemy fire. To raise support for a local ministry has been difficult. More and more pastors and Christian leaders have grasped the critical importance of area-wide church unity, prayer, and repentance. However, their number is small when one considers that there are over 250 congregations in the city. It is not uncommon to receive blank stares when we share our vision.

The call and promises of God have encouraged us, and His Word has reminded us how He accomplishes His kingdom work.

> "Not by might nor by power, but by my Spirit," says the Lord Almighty. "What are you, O mighty mountain? Before Zerubbabel you will become level ground…Who despises the day of small things?"
>
> —*Zechariah 4:6–10*

Small Clouds on the Horizon

Our vision has not changed—revival *will* come. No one has ever known how long it will take for historic revival fire to fall, or exactly when it will happen, but we know that "The Lord is faithful to all his promises" (Ps. 145:13).

A firestorm of revival could very well sweep Rockford, jump to Chicago, and then move across the nation. We have watched God do amazing things. The downpour of rain that came as a result of Elijah's prayers began with "a cloud as small as a man's hand" (1 Kings 18:44). Elijah had told his servant to go look six different times before the small cloud appeared on the horizon. We have already seen the small clouds of God at work. Look toward the horizon with me.

The Rockford School District was convicted for inequitable treatment of minorities on the city's west side and came under federal control. The issue consumed the city, and negative rhetoric filled the local paper month after month. Taxes were increased to pay for remediation costs, and people began to move out of the city limits. Housing values declined. The school board was polarized into two warring groups. Today the board is more unified than it has been for many years. A new superintendent was hired unanimously, and his first budget was approved unanimously. The district is stabilizing financially. Best of all, the district is out from under federal control.

When the prayer movement began in 1996, there were thirty-seven homicides for the year in the county, mostly made up of the city of Rockford; more per capita than in Chicago, Illinois. In 2004 they were down to eight. In July 2005, a local newspaper reported that in the last ten years, the violent crime rate for the county had dropped 34.6 percent.[7]

The Evangelical Minister's Fellowship nearly disbanded; today it has been reborn and is strong and growing.

City-focused pastors have been called to the city and are forming a strong coalition of unity. A servant leader group is meeting each month to prepare for revival and to give leadership to it under the Holy Spirit's guidance.

Area-wide prayer gatherings have been sustained since 1994, and they continue to express great diversity.

Over one thousand people or households have agreed to be Lighthouses of Prayer, a commitment to pray for their neighbors, to look for opportunities to build relationships with them, and in time, to share the gospel with them.

Many redemptive, city-focused ministries have been birthed in the area. They are making a significant impact for the kingdom of God.

The citywide church has never been more unified. Several congregations have been partnering across ethnic and denominational lines. In 2005, Youth With A Mission's (YWAM) Impact World Tour came to the city. Forty congregations and over two thousand volunteers worked together to raise and exceed the budget, to train teams for counseling and follow-up, and to see 1,957 people declare decisions for Christ on completed commitment cards.

- In August 2005 Rockford won high honors in the National City-In-Bloom contest.

- An *Endowment for Transformation Ministries* has been birthed to support strategic faith-based ministries.

- Rockford's Heartland Community Church began in 1998 with a passion to reach the culture creatively, a new way to do church. Today they are filling five weekend services with a total average attendance of 3,800 and baptizing an average of 250 new Christ-followers each June. They have just purchased a shopping center to make room for more people and to expand their outreach. They are a church of irresistible influence.

Visiting prophetic leaders have come to the city and have said that revival is coming to the area.

The city is experiencing a growing passion for redevelopment and efforts to re-build her economy. The city's esteem among people is growing.[8]

Sports Illustrated magazine named Rockford a 50th Anniversary Sports town in the State of Illinois. Signs to this effect are at the major entry points to the city and sports figures were listed in the magazine's 50th Anniversary Edition on September 27, 2004.

Love, INC—Love in the Name of Christ—has grown from a struggling ministry to sixty-five congregations that have networked to meet special needs in the city.

As the city prepares for the construction of a new jail, God has already been preparing strategic ministry in the vicinity. Across the street to the northwest is Hope Place, the area's new state-of-the-art Rescue Mission, with a new strategic approach to recovery. The post care Reach-Out Jail Ministry is directly across the street to the north next door to a new Pregnancy Care Center, the second in the city. One block away, a new life center is providing many social services and ministries. Also in the neighborhood, Reformers Unanimous, a Christian addictions program, is redeeming many broken lives and families.

A healing room opened in Rockford in 2004.

The chairman of the county board is a Christian leader who was formerly chairman of his church board. In April 2005, the city elected a new mayor, who is a Catholic Christian, pro-life, anti-gambling, and pro-development of the city. He prays publicly in Jesus' name. The sheriff affirms faith in Jesus Christ. The new superintendent of the school district is a Catholic believer.

These are a few of the small clouds on the horizon that give evidence of God's answers to prayer. He is very much at work. Hope for a sweeping revival and the transformation of the area is as bright as the promises of God. Revival shall come.

This book is the product of my doctoral study on revival and my heart's passionate cry for it. How does revival come? How does *the fire of God fall* across a region or nation? There is a clear pattern, accompanied by consistent characteristics. I invite you to join me in tracing the footprints of God's Spirit—or shall I say, the Holy Spirit's trail of smoke and flame—across the history of revival. I want God to light revival fire in your heart.

I hear the voice of one crying...Prepare ye; prepare ye the way of the Lord...Make His paths straight. Make straight His path in the wilderness. Let His light shine in the darkness. Let Your rain fall...in this desert...I feel it in my spirit; feel it in my bones. You're going to send revival...bring it all back home. I can hear the thunder in the distance, like a train on the edge of town. I can feel the brooding of the Spirit. Revival! Revival! Revival! Revive us with Your fire![1]

—*Revival in Belfast*

1

The Rumbling in the Distance

THE CHURCH OF Jesus Christ has been drifting. Darkness seems to have been holding the light at bay, and secularism has been spreading like a virus across America. The Ten Commandments have been removed from the public square. In a much-debated controversy in 2003, Judge Roy Moore defied a court order to remove the Ten Commandments from the State Capital building in Alabama, and he no longer serves the court. Since that time, the United States Supreme Court has refused to take a strong stand to allow the Commandments to keep their place in the public square in America. The entire story is told by Judge Moore and John Perry in his book, *So Help Me God: The Ten Commandments, Judicial Tyranny, and the Battle for Religious Freedom.*

When America tossed the Ten Commandments away as ethical trash, she discarded her moral compass. The demand for homosexual couples to have equal marriage rights is capturing the minds of Americans. Promiscuous teen sex has been growing in epidemic proportions and is killing our young people.[2] American corporations, once outstanding as excellent and ethical, have fallen in disgrace before the eyes of the world. After George W. Bush was elected to four more years in the White House in 2004, many Christians were inspired with hope that some of the secular drift could be abated. Interestingly, secular pundits credited his victory to concerns for moral values.

Church leaders have been raising alarm about the decline of the church for many years. Below is a portion of a personal letter from Steve Hudson, Executive Director to Pastors and Constituents of the Evangelical Free Church of America.

> It is estimated that one third of the existing churches in America will close their doors within the next decade. Because of this

precipitous decline, many are now calling the United States a major mission field.[3]

In 2001, Robert Lewis wrote, "The white water of popular senti-ment…increasingly views the church as inconsequential, a sideshow along the interstate of the world's 'real' traffic." He reported that numer-ous studies confirmed that the public, especially media and intellectual leaders, do not see Christianity as a dominant social force. Lewis quotes Jack Dennison, the author of *City Reaching,* saying:

> Church growth specialists have placed the percentage of unhealthy congregations in the United States at between 70–80…such congregations have little, if any sense of the needs and opportunities of their community and have lost sight of their rea-son for existing.[4]

The decline of mainline congregations has been severe. The title of Britt Minshall's book, *Renaissance or Ruin,* spoke powerfully about the critical need for radical renewal.

> Lay leaders who wish to see the problems of the dying church addressed are, like their clergy partners, chastised or ignored. These "heroes of the faith" often leave the fold and join one of the more conservative fast growing churches, or far worse, abandon the church once and for all. Twenty million families have left our once great denominational churches in this manner. Yet even as I write, our leaders choose to remain in blissful ignorance and the church continues to die.[5]

Ten years have come and gone since Minshall expressed his concern, but the decline of mainline denominations has continued at a rapid pace.

Several clergy friends and I meet in a covenant group each week for mutual accountability, to share what God has been saying to us from His Word or other reading, and to pray together. Dr. Bob Kopp, a friend in this group, is the pastor of a Presbyterian USA congregation in our area. Bob, an outspoken member of the Confessing Church Movement in his denomination, is passionate about seeing the PCUSA return to her biblical orthodox constitution and historic roots. In his recently published book, *Fifteen Secrets for Life and Ministry*, Bob writes:

> Fortunately, the recent movement of mainliners from museums of spirituality to mausoleums of theological uncertainty at best, or duplicity at worst, makes little difference to the ultimate triumph of God's Kingdom. As Jesus assured, "I will build my church, and the gates of hell shall not prevail against it" (Matt 16:18). Mainliners have lost so many members over the past four decades that they're quite insignificant players on the national and world stages. Nobody seems to notice them and very few movers and shakers listen to them as they fade into lesser obscurity. My franchise, for example, has lost nearly 2 million members since 1965; though in amusing irony, more bureaucratic and para-denominational booths pop up in the exhibition halls of our annual meetings as membership plummets.[6]

Nine years before his death, Bill Bright spoke passionately about the decline of the church. He concluded, "It is asleep. Polluted with the desires and materialism of the world, she knows little about spiritual discipline and living the Spirit-filled life. She is complacent and at ease, thinking she has everything and is in need of nothing...a mirror image of the churches at Ephesus and Laodicea."[7]

Two years later, Dr. Gregory Frizzell wrote in the introduction of his book, "No words can express the urgent nature of our present need for massive revival and spiritual awakening. America is indeed poised on the very brink of catastrophic judgment."[8]

In *Desperate for His Presence,* a passionate encouragement for the transformation of cities, author Rhonda Hughey reports on estimates indicating that more than ten million born-again believers in the United States are now considered "unchurched." They are disillusioned and jaded; many are unwilling to return to the local church in its current condition."[9]

Rhonda reports on research that indicates a large portion of Americans now contend that there is no absolute moral truth. More than two out of three adults, Christians and non-Christians, say that truth is relative to the individual and circumstances. She states that relativism is being embraced by much of the church, resulting in a new level of tolerance and comfort with sin, even when it blatantly contradicts the clear teaching of God's Word.[10]

Nancy Leigh DeMoss is a passionate writer and communicator. Several years ago, her message gave rise to a Campus Crusade revival that hit during one of their annual training conferences for staff members. I was moved with her graphic description of the church in *Spirit of Revival* magazine.

> If plumbing or septic problems caused raw sewage to overflow into the hallways and aisles of your church, one thing is for sure: the problem would not be ignored. Everyone would be horrified. The health hazard would prompt immediate action. Business would not continue as usual. Services would be relocated and crews would work overtime, if necessary, until the problem was resolved.
>
> The fact is that something far more serious than raw sewage is running through the lives of countless professing Christians and most of our evangelical churches. And by and large, we are oblivious to the threat.
>
> The floodgates of unholiness—including willful, presumptuous, blatant sin—have opened up within the church. Adultery, drunkenness, abuse, profanity, outbursts of temper, divorce, pornography, immodest dress—such sins among professing believers—often members in good standing of respected local churches—are no longer rare exceptions.
>
> And then there are the more "respectable" forms of sewage that are often overlooked and tolerated among believers—things like overspending, unpaid debts, gluttony, gossip, greed, covetousness, bitterness, pride, critical spirits, backbiting, temporal values, self-centeredness, and broken relationships. Sadly, the church—the place that is intended to showcase the glory and holiness of God—has become a safe place to sin.[11]

Will the church continue to risk speaking up on biblical and moral issues, or will she step back into silence? If non-biblical laws are made the law of the land, the church could lose her tax-exempt status or incur stiff fines. She could lose her right to teach biblical morality. As in other countries hostile to Christianity, Christians could face incarceration for sharing the gospel. If revival does not come, if followers of Jesus Christ do not arise in prayer, America could continue her drift into secularism.

Consider recent history. About sixty years ago, the Supreme Court created the "separation of church and state" rule, a standard that had not existed for two hundred years. About forty years ago, prayer and Bible reading, which had been acceptable and encouraged for two hundred years, were taken from our public schools. If you drew a line from this decision, you could trace the negative results. SAT scores in American public education, both math and verbal, declined by 10 percent. Teen suicide escalated by over 400 percent. Child abuse rose 2,300 percent. Illegal drug use by youth climbed 6,000 percent. The criminal arrest of teens grew 150 percent. Divorce climbed 350 percent. Births to women ages fifteen to nineteen increased 500 percent.[12]

Thirty years ago the legalized killing of pre-born babies was made the law of the land. Since then, over 40 million babies have been killed, and indescribable genocide has occurred to generations of youth.[13] It will take passionate prayer and action to reverse this downward spiral. It will take historic revival.

Postmodernism, as I define it, is the lack of right or wrong. It has grown like ravaging cancer. It has been like the author of Judges described: "In those days Israel had no king; everyone did as he saw fit" (Judg. 17:6). Could we describe America in a similar way today?

In those days, the church was not unified and had gone adrift from her biblical moorings. It was difficult to tell her apart from the culture surrounding her. With racial tensions and divisions, with denominational differences and competition, the church was divided. The world did not know the Father sent the Son (John 17:20–23). Everyone did what he or she wanted to and called it his or her right.

As infanticide was forced on the nation, the church was quiet. As marriage unraveled under the pressure of the gay movement, the church stood silent. As laws were passed in opposition to biblical truth, she stood by uninvolved. As more and more cities became addicted to gambling revenues to boost their economies, she abstained from the discussion, and even hoped to gain benefit for herself through gambling related jobs and revenue.

It is certain that Satan, the enemy, will become more visible as the church begins to awaken and threaten her power and influence. The days and years ahead are going to be a time of conflict between the church and the secular culture. The apathy that has characterized the church has been one of the most serious signs of decline in the church and in democracy. Apart from revival and the social transformation that follows, snowballing secularization in America will pick up speed.

Great fear gripped the world as it anticipated the turn of the millennium. Would the massive computer systems that ran the world and nations shut down? Would crisis follow with looting, crime, homicides, and rioting in the streets accompanying efforts for mere survival? Christians and secularists alike stored food and water, and many people purchased generators. Some moved into remote areas to avoid the anticipated chaos. As the year 2000 approached, many felt that revival was possible—crisis was coming. Many gathered to pray. The crisis did not come. Revival did not come. Prayer declined.

Spiritual leaders believed the terrorist tragedy of September 11, 2001, would spark a nation-wide revival in America. The nation was shocked and grieving. The tall symbols of America's wealth and economic power were a pile of smoking rubble. Our trusted air travel system had been used for terror. Never had an attack hit American soil in such proportions.

As in most battlefield foxholes, there were few atheists. There was a dramatic increase in church attendance, and public prayer, which had been frequently spurned, was common, even from the lips of civic officials. There was great hope in many hearts, including mine, that this tragic crisis would spark revival.

Sad to say, however, the burst of spiritual interest faded fast. By election time in 2004, efforts and resources to deal with such terror were being criticized. The horror of 9/11 had been taken in stride by many. Although many citizens were supportive when President Bush launched the war on terror, it didn't take long for their support to turn to criticism. Within a few months, some even stooped to associate him with Hitler. A bumper sticker in our neighborhood declared, "Bush is a weapon of mass destruction." The fear of terror and the passion for prayer faded like the dust clouds that covered New York City after the attack.

The following editorial, which I submitted to our local paper, was published the day before the November elections in 2004:

THE MUSCLE OF FREEDOM

Muscles have to be used and exercised to remain strong. Freedom to vote has to be exercised or we will lose it and, of course, our freedom. In my opinion, voting for principles and values must supercede voting for a candidate or a party. The key question is: "What is their platform and what ethical standards govern their actions?"

Alexander Tyler, a Scottish history professor at The University of Edinburgh, wrote a commentary in 1787 about the fall of the Athenian Republic, 2000 years earlier. This was about the time our 13 original states adopted their new constitution. He wrote, "A democracy is always temporary in nature; it simply cannot exist as a permanent form of government...The average age of the world's greatest civilizations—from the beginning of history—has been about 200 years. During those 200 years, these nations always progressed through the following sequence: From bondage to spiritual faith; From spiritual faith to great courage; From courage to liberty; From liberty to abundance; From abundance to complacency; From complacency to apathy; From apathy to dependence; and From dependence back into bondage."

America has beaten these odds, but I am concerned. I am shocked that so few Christians vote (less than one third), especially those claiming to be biblically based. Generally, apathy prevails across most sectors of America. The press gives us the voting statistics each election and each time I am shocked by the lack of involvement. Freedom isn't free. It must be exercised wisely. We are given life, but apart from good management, exercise and a healthy diet, we lose it much sooner than necessary.

You get the point. I am urging the citizens of the greater Rockford area to vote, or we will lose the opportunity. I am urging them to vote wisely, considering carefully the platforms and or ethics of those running.[14]

Recently I heard a tragic story that came out of the Holocaust from a fellow pastor in my covenant group. A Christian church was located alongside the railroad tracks on which thousands upon thousands of Jews were being taken to the death camps. As they would pass the church, often during meetings, the people who were traveling to places of death would cry out in desperation for help from the church. What did the church do? They closed the windows and sang louder to drown out the pleading cries.

As the American culture has slipped further and further from biblical moorings, as over forty million pre-born babies have been killed, as God and biblical truth have been removed from the public sector, has the church closed the windows and turned up the volume?

CAN YOU HEAR THE RUMBLING?

Yes, it is bad—dark and difficult times are swirling around us. But wait! Listen! There's a rumbling of thunder in the distance. There is good news, too—a rebirth of hope, passionate prayer, and the beginnings of change. It is not just the "blip" on the screen from the 2004 election. God is patient, and unique and unexpected events continue to happen.

We can trace the heart of God as He listens to the growing number of His people praying and calling out for a return to obedience and biblical basics. Prayer movements have been springing up in cities across the nation and the world for at least twenty years. Slowly the church is waking up, and there are flashes of light.

Megacongregations with thousands in attendance have made massive changes and continue to grow. They are impacting the culture with God's truth. These churches are generally not associated with denominations, but are led by gifted people who plant congregations that form a bonded network and fellowship. Some groups see it as a return to apostolic leadership and a rebirth of the five-fold ministry of Ephesians 4:11–12. Others believe it is just a fresh contemporary approach, a new move of God's Spirit being birthed alongside aging and dying denominations.

Pick up a list of best-selling Christian books. Authors are saying that we are nearing the end of human history. End-Time events are taking shape. As I have heard others say, Jesus is coming soon for His bride, not a harem. It is time to passionately pray, repent, and seek God's face in humility. The church is standing in open rebellion to the unity for which Jesus prayed in John 17:20–23. She is spurning the commanded blessing of Psalm 133. She is not working out the unity in diversity and the mutuality described in Ephesians 4:1–16, not speaking the truth in love and growing up into the fullness of the stature of Christ (Eph. 4:13).

As we will see in the chapters that follow, a clear pattern of revival is revealed throughout history. When things turn dark and difficult for God's people, He tells us what to do. When we obey His clear instructions in 2 Chronicles 7:14, revival comes. It is time to obey.

Are there any signs that revival is coming, or is it just wishful thinking? The late Dr. Bill Bright, founder and president of Campus Crusade for Christ International, began a monthly newsletter, *Fasting and Prayer,* in 1994. After his personal fast of forty days, Dr. Bright began an annual conference for fasting and prayer for America. The movement grew as revival interest across the nation picked up momentum. Three thousand five hundred attended the "Fasting and Prayer" gathering in Los Angeles, California in 1995.[15] God's people were beginning to break through apathy, to begin to pray and seek God's face.

The Promise Keepers men's movement swept America about the same time. Millions of men gathered in athletic stadiums for teaching, prayer, worship, and mutual encouragement. In 1997, well over one million men gathered in the nation's capital for a solemn assembly of prayer and fasting for revival. I was there with my youngest son, Jonathan. At one time, with faces on the ground, over a million men called out to God for revival. We will never forget the experience. It marked our lives.

Promise Keepers gatherings have become smaller and more regional, but they are still significant. Men's ministries have sprung up in many congregations in the last few years, some of them as a direct result of this powerful movement. Men are holding each other accountable and are praying and studying the Bible together.

Pastor's Prayer Summits have been held across America in recent years. With deep concern for the church and pastors, Dr. Joe Aldrich, the former president of Multnomah School of the Bible, began to call pastors to prayer gatherings. The only agenda was spontaneous prayer and worship. Pastors set aside denominational differences to pray for personal revival and for revival in their cities and the nation. As they prayed, individual pastors would often come under conviction and begin to confess sins openly. A chair was usually placed in the middle of the room. A pastor who felt the need for prayer could sit in the chair, and others would gather around and pray.

The Prayer Summits were just one of many developing movements mentioned in the introduction to Ed Silvoso's book, *That None Should Perish: How to Reach Entire Cities for Christ Through Prayer Evangelism.* He wrote, "During the past ten years, prayer has begun to emerge as one of the central parts—if not the central part—of the life of the church worldwide."[16] Because of my understanding of the central role of unified prayer in historic revival, I find this encouraging.

Driving home the call of God to prayer, Silvoso mentions the work of Dr. Paul Cedar, past president of the Evangelical Free Church of America and dean of the Billy Graham School of Evangelism. "Cedar," he states, "has instilled thousands with a sense of awe in God's presence as they gather in 'solemn assemblies.' He is…challenging them…to a lifestyle of prayer."[17]

He also mentions others. David Bryant, the founder of Concerts of Prayer International, leads a movement of prayer across the nation. Neil Anderson teaches thousands to reclaim their freedom in Christ through prevailing prayer. Paul Yonggi Cho, pastor of Yoido Full Gospel Church of Seoul, Korea, the largest church in the world, challenges Christians to at least three hours of prayer a day. Omar Cabrera, the leader of an indigenous group of congregations in Argentina—with over 80,000 in attendance—pioneers all night prayer vigils for spiritual warfare. Cindy Jacobs leads Generals of Intercession, a group of militant intercessors who pray for nations all over the world.

Dr. C. Peter Wagner's series of eight books on prayer, is teaching the church to pray. Thousands have learned to pray from his writing. Silvoso says, "Dr. Wagner is being used by God to motivate, train, and mobilize the largest army of praying Christians ever mustered to storm the gates of hell in order to set captives free."[18] Silvoso concludes by saying: "All over the world there is a compelling sense of urgency to take the gospel to every person on the face of the earth now."[19]

The National Day of Prayer, established by the Continental Congress of the United States in 1775, has become a significant event with millions joining the prayer meeting by video broadcast. Though once nominal and routine, within the last seven years the estimated number of participants has escalated into the hundreds of thousands. The format of these events has been similar to David Bryant's Concerts of Prayer, which began nearly twenty years ago. Groups across America have held citywide Concerts of Prayer for revival in the church and the nation. Such has been the case in our city, Rockford, Illinois. They began in 1995 and are now meeting on the third Friday night of each month.

The enthusiasm of David Bryant is easily captured in his book, *The Hope at Hand: National and World Revival for the Twenty-First Century*. He lists a number of hopeful signs, with prayer as the central force. There is, he writes, an "unrelenting development of revival prayer throughout the Christian community."[20]

Books on revival and prayer are being published in increasing numbers. In literature on revival, prayer is the central key, and this will be reinforced in this book. Brian Edwards's book, *Revival: A People Saturated With God*, is in its fifth printing. Edwards surveys many of the revivals in history to discover common features and inspire Christians to pray. In his second chapter, "Before Revival," he claims that urgent prayer is the most significant cause of revival.

> You cannot read far into the story of a revival without discovering that not only is prayer part of the inevitable result of an outpouring of the Spirit, but from a human standpoint, it is also the single most significant cause.[21]

Edwards grabs the reader's attention when he quotes great revivalists and revival preachers. For example, he tells how Matthew Henry, the Puritan leader, commented on God's promise: "I will pour out on the house of David and the inhabitants of Jerusalem a spirit of grace and supplication" (Zech. 12:10). Henry remarked, "When God intends great mercy for His people, the first thing he does is to set them a-praying."[22] Edwards also includes a great word from John Wesley: "God does nothing but in answer to prayer."[23] He adds a statement from Arthur Pierson, who was for many years the editor of *The Missionary Review*.

> From the day of Pentecost, there has been not one great spiritual awakening in any land which has not begun in a union of prayer, though only among two or three; no such outward, upward movement has continued after such prayer meetings have declined.[24]

Jim Cymbala, a New York City pastor, tells how his experience of revival grew out of a desperation that led to a passionate commitment to prayer. In *Fresh Wind, Fresh Fire: What Happens When God's Spirit Invades the Hearts of His People*, he writes about starting a church in the inner city of New York. When he was under stress and fatigue from the difficulty of the call, God gave him the secret for growing a vital, effective ministry. Away on a fishing trip, burned out, and desperate to hear from God, he stood on the deck of a boat and cried out to God for help and understanding. Listen to God's gentle instruction to him and the response of his heart:

> "If you and your wife will lead my people to pray and call upon my name, you will never lack for something fresh to preach. I will supply all the money that's needed, both for the church and for your family, and you will never have a building large enough to contain the crowds I will send in response."
>
> I knew I had heard from God, even though I had not experienced some strange vision—nothing sensational or peculiar. God was simply focusing on the only answer to our situation—or anybody else's, for that matter. His word to me was grounded in countless promises repeated in the Scriptures; it was the very thing that had produced every revival of the Holy Spirit throughout history. It was the truth that had made Charles G. Finney, Dwight L. Moody, A. B. Simpson, and other men and women mightily used of God. It was what I already knew, but God was now drawing me out, pulling me toward an actual experience of Himself and His power. He was telling me that my hunger for him and his transforming power would be satisfied as I led my tiny congregation to call out to him in prayer.[25]

Paul Yonggi Cho has long been convinced that prayer is the key to revival. In fact, he has stood as a living demonstration of the fact. As early as 1984, when his church was growing at the rate of twelve thousand people each month, he wrote, *Prayer: the Key to Revival*. Prayer was and still is the key to the massive church growth in Korea. Yonggi Cho's congregation has been growing toward one million members, and by the time you read this, it may have surpassed that mark. It has been the largest Pentecostal church in the world for twenty years.

Intercessory Prayer: How God Can Use Your Prayers to Move Heaven and Earth, one of the most rapidly selling books on prayer in 1998, came from the pen of Dutch Sheets. In his introduction to this book, C. Peter Wagner summarized the growth of the prayer movement and said that the modern prayer movement began around 1970. It had been growing in Korea for decades, but it also began to spread worldwide. In addition to noting the exponential growth of the quantity of prayer in recent years, Wagner also pointed out that the quality of prayer is increasing:

> Flames of prayer are being lit in virtually every denomination on every continent. Pastors are giving prayer a higher priority …prayer movements and prayer ministries are proliferating, theological seminaries are introducing courses on prayer and even secular magazines have been featuring cover stories about prayer.[26]

Brush fires of the Holy Spirit's stirring have broken out on college campuses in recent years. John Avant, Malcolm McDow, and Alvin Reid tell the story in *Revival: The Story of the Current Awakening in Brownwood, Fort Worth, Wheaton, and Beyond*. Not only has revival come to college campuses, but powerful brush fires of revival have come to several congregations in America. The Airport Fellowship in Toronto, Canada, has experienced a revival that has impacted thousands across America and the world. A similar move of the Holy Spirit broke out in Pensacola, Florida. Smithton/Kansas City, Missouri experienced the same.

The stories have filled the Christian press. *Christianity Today* follows some of these movements and reported on an outbreak of revival in Modesto, California. In a city of 176,000, it was reported that 33,000 people professed Christian faith. The magazine said, "Many local Christians believe a four-day prayer summit in early 1994, involving fifty-three pastors, established the foundation for the revival."[27]

When stirrings of the Holy Spirit hit San Francisco, California, *Pray!*

magazine reported that it followed a series of prayer meetings and prayer summits. The largest summit of pastors totaled four hundred. With this foundation, the city held a Billy Graham Crusade, and 246,300 people attended. Those who made public professions of faith in Jesus Christ numbered 18,953.[28]

The stories have continued. God has been lighting brush fires. If the church across America continues to gather together in consistent passionate prayer and humble repentance, revival will sweep the nation. It has always been the same pattern. For example, *Charisma* magazine reported on a movement of the Holy Spirit among youth in the most unchurched region of the United States, a bedroom community of Seattle, Washington. Nearly eight hundred young people filled a church in the small town of Marysville week after week. The leader of this movement credited prayer as the primary cause.[29]

An entire issue of *Pray!* magazine, September/October 1998, was devoted to the unusual movements of the Holy Spirit among American youth. The cover asks, "Is This the Generation? Praying teens capture the world for Christ." The current generation of young people, committed and passionate about prayer, is potentially the generation that will lead the nation to revival.[30]

Experiencing God: Knowing and Doing the Will of God, a Bible study series written by Henry T. Blackaby and Claude V. King in 1990, swept the country several years ago. Sales reflected the church's hunger for intimacy with God. These same authors followed this study with a book entitled, *Fresh Encounter: Experiencing God in Revival and Spiritual Awakening*. Be encouraged! "From across America and around the world, an intensifying cry is being raised to God for a fresh encounter with Him in revival."[31]

Mission America was born less than twenty years ago as an outgrowth of the International Congress on Worldwide Evangelization in Lausanne, Switzerland. First held in 1974 and again in 1989, the congress produced *The Lausanne Covenant*, which was, and remains, a doctrinal statement and commitment of Christians from one hundred fifty nations of the world to unify to reach the world for Christ. The conclusion of the covenant declared, "We enter into a solemn covenant with God and with each other, to pray, to plan, and to work together for the evangelization of the whole world."[32]

To accomplish this, national and regional organizations, including Mission America in the United States, were formed in each country. In its first brochure, Mission America quoted Evangelist Billy Graham's statement, "As we approach the dawn of a new millennium, our country stands in great need of a genuine spiritual awakening."[33] Mission America created *Celebrate Jesus 2000* with a goal to pray for and to share Christ with every person in the nation by the end of the year 2000. This effort was not only massive, but reflected a growing passion for revival and for turning America back to God and His Word.

Another of Mission America's initiatives was to identify and encourage city-reachers. Before God called Connie and me to form Rockford Renewal Ministries, we had never heard of such people. However, early in our ministry, we learned that we were city-reachers and that God was raising up people like us all across America. We were invited to a meeting of city-reachers in Colorado, and with no agenda, we sat around tables and shared God's calling and what was happening in our cities. This movement has been unmatched in American history. These leaders have formed a kingdom army, passionately seeking God for spiritual awakening.

In Mission America's February/March 1998 newsletter, John Quam, then the National Facilitator for City/Community Ministries, listed ten indicators that give "a heightened sense of anticipation for unusual growth in the church." Four of them were within the church, and six were outside the church. The list included a growing spirit of prayer, a growing spirit of unity, the public witness of Christians, a search for values in the decline of the moral climate, the emergence of new technologies for communicating the gospel, and the beginning of a reduced rate of crime in America. Each part of the list was related to increased prayer and passion for revival.[34]

In spring 2004, Mel Gibson's film, *The Passion of the Christ*, burst on the American and international scene. It was the light of the gospel beamed out of the darkness of Hollywood's film industry. Who would ever have expected it to happen? Even with secular naysayers criticizing the film before its release, it broke most sales records. A deep felt need for spiritual truth and salvation was growing.[35]

God is really up to something. These are exciting days, and the results are significant. In our county, homicides have declined from thirty-seven after the prayer movement was launched in 1995 to eleven in 2000.[36] This is not the time to slack off or give up. It is the time to intensify our intercession for revival and repentance. It is the time to increase our intentional efforts for the unity of the church. Although God has every right to severely discipline America and His church, His mercy triumphs over judgment (James 2:13). We must continue to follow the instructions of 2 Chronicles 7:14.

Revival is coming. We cannot give in to what some city-reachers call "Revival Fatigue Syndrome." Connie and I feel it at times. Sometimes, we hang on financially by a thread, but we cannot quit now. Tenacity is a must—bulldog tenacity. The bulldog's nose is set back on its face. It can grab someone's leg, hold on for a long time, and still breathe. Pacing our efforts is important, but our passion must not wane at this critical juncture in history.

Listen! Can you hear the rumbling in the distance?

Here I am! I stand at the door and knock. If anyone hears my voice and opens the door, I will come in and eat with him, and he with me. To him who overcomes, I will give the right to sit with me on my throne, just as I overcame and sat down with my Father on his throne.

—Revelation 3:20–21

2

Tracking the Storms

THE FILM *TWISTER* is a nail-biter! Highly motivated, risk-taking scientists chase tornadoes because, in theory, we can know how to deal with these monsters if we understand them. However, one gets the idea that this is as much about adventure and risk as it is about science. Still, it is good science, I think. Study the storms. Create theories. Test them. What conditions generate them? How can they be managed? How can early warnings be made and disasters avoided?

Tracking the history of revival, the powerful wind and fire of the Holy Spirit, is like tracking tornadoes. How does revival come? What conditions generate it, and what is its consistent pattern? Does the move of God's Spirit in recent history follow the move of God's Spirit in the Bible? Let's track these firestorms together. It is a great adventure.

The timing of both tornadoes and revival is unpredictable. Although God's people can prepare for revival, we can't put God in a box, and we can't dictate how He will work. Like storm chasers, people in revival settings do some strange things, what we may call excesses. They are easily caught up in the power of the Spirit's storm. Revival is not like a snooze in a hammock on a warm summer afternoon.

Each revival is distinct, and yet there are similarities. If we can identify the characteristics, if we can understand what brings on the storm—the fire and wind of revival—we can get ready. If we can understand the pattern of revival, we can prepare. If we can understand why revivals fade, maybe we can keep them alive longer.

Unfortunately, many of God's people do not care about revival. However, when the dark clouds of difficulty loom overhead, when sunny comfort zones and security in life are disturbed, they may become passionate for God to intervene. If God allows the natural and spiritual consequences of their sin to multiply, more than likely, as in past history,

God's people will begin to seek Him.

Revival has a pattern. History demonstrates how revival has happened and how it will happen again. The Old Testament is a great starting place to trace the move of God. Time and again, God's people drifted into rebellion or were sucked into the cultures that surrounded them. When things became unbearable, they began to seek God, repent, and once again obey Him. Revival came, and they enjoyed the covenant blessings of God and fulfilled His exciting redemptive purpose. Psalm 106 is one of the sad summaries of Israel's up and down history. Read it and weep. Look at the church today. Weep again.

In the New Testament, after four hundred years of biblical silence, God sent His prophet, a storm chaser, John the Baptist. God's people had become encrusted with tradition and dangerously detached from His purpose. With passion and power he preached repentance. He stayed on the outskirts of the city where people flocked to hear him. Many were baptized in the Jordan River to symbolize their repentance.

Jesus, the Son of God in human flesh, came on the scene. He taught the people about the kingdom of God and told and showed them how to live. He sacrificed His life in death by yielding to the hideous Roman crucifixion. He arose from the dead, conquering Satan, death, and hell. He was caught up to the Father's right hand after promising the coming of the Holy Spirit.

As one hundred twenty followers of Jesus met in unity and prayer, the Holy Spirit burst onto the scene. Unity and prayer are the keys to revival. Talk about a historic move of God, mighty rushing winds—a storm of massive proportions—swept through Jerusalem with a roar. People were drawn to the scene, as tongues of fire fell on the head of each person in the gathering. It happened to be a high holy day, and people from all over the known world were in the city. As they gathered, they heard the Good News about Jesus the Messiah in their own language. Three thousand received Him by faith. This great account is New Testament revival, and similar moves of God's Spirit followed.

We can know how the fire falls. Twelve moves of God can be found in the Old Testament and eight in the New Testament. They follow a pattern that can also be traced through major revivals of more recent history. As we track these firestorms, we will see that pattern. The lists of revivals we will study are as follows:

OLD TESTAMENT REVIVALS

1.   Jacob: Gen. 35:1–15
2.   Moses: Exod. 32–33
3.   Samuel: 1 Sam. 7:1–13
4.   Elijah: 1 Kings 18
5.   Joash: 2 Kings 11–12; 2 Chron. 23–24
6.   Hezekiah: 2 Kings 18:4–7; 2 Chron. 29–31
7.   Josiah: 2 Kings 22–23; 2 Chron. 34–35
8.   Asa: 2 Chron. 15:1–15
9.   Jehoshaphat: 2 Chron. 17:6–9, 20:1–37
10. Zerubbabel, Haggai, and Zechariah: Ezra 5–6
11. Ezra and Nehemiah: Neh. 8:9, 12:44–47
12. Jonah in Nineveh: Jon. 1–4

NEW TESTAMENT REVIVALS

1.   Awakening under John the Baptist: Matt. 3:1–12
2.   The revival at Pentecost: Acts 2:1–4, 14–47
3.   The revival in the church: Acts 4:23–37
4.   The revival that grew out of fear: Acts 5:1–16
5.   The revival that grew out of persecution: Acts 7:54–8:25
6.   The revival with Cornelius and the gentiles: Acts 10:23–48
7.   The Pisidian Antioch revival: Acts 13:44–52
8.   The revival at Ephesus: Acts 19:1–20

POST-BIBLICAL REVIVALS

1.   The first Great Awakening: 1726–1756
2.   The second Great Awakening: 1776–1810
3.   The New York City Prayer Meeting Revival: 1857–1858
4.   The Welsh Revival of 1904
5.   The Azusa Street Revival: 1906–1909

Before we look further at revival, we need to define it. Revival is certainly not a week of special meetings with an outstanding speaker. From my study and for the purposes of this book, I define revival as follows:

> Revival is a spontaneous spiritual awakening by God the Holy Spirit among His people. It comes in answer to their humble prayers as they passionately seek His face and repent of their sins. The awakening results in deepened intimacy with God, passion for Him, holy living, evangelism, and citywide or area-wide transformation expressed through social reform.

Ten themes have characterized the firestorms of biblical and post-biblical history. In all my reading and research, I have found no exceptions, only variation of these themes.

1. Revival occurred in times of personal or national crisis and great spiritual need, and in times of deep moral darkness and spiritual decline among God's people, Israel, or His church.

2. Revival began in the heart(s) of one or more consecrated servants of God, who became the agent(s) God used to lead His people back to faith and obedience in Him.

3. Prayer was central to revival. Leaders called out to God in prayer, passionately seeking His face in repentance and in the confession of personal and national sins. In many instances, they led God's people to do the same.

4. Revival rested upon the powerful proclamation—preaching and teaching—of the law of God and His Word. Many revivals were the result of a return to Scripture.

5. Revival in the Old Testament reflected the work of God the Father to awaken His people, Israel, to a restored relationship with Him, to obey Him and serve His redemptive purpose. Revival in the New Testament and post-biblical history reflected the work of the Holy Spirit in miracles and the equipping of people for ministry. It resulted in the spread of the gospel and the growth of the church.

6.   Revival was marked by a return to the worship of God.

7.   Revival led to the destruction of idols and ungodly preoccupations and also to separation from personal and corporate sin.

8.   Revival brought a return to the offering of blood sacrifices in the Old Testament and a concentration on the death, resurrection, and return of Jesus Christ—celebrated in the Lord's Supper—in the New Testament.

9.   Revival resulted in an experience of exuberant joy and gladness among God's people.

10.   Revival was followed by a period of blessing and area-wide transformation that produced social reform.

This is how revival fire falls. We have much more to see and learn as we chase God's firestorms. However, it is clear that the story of Israel's history and the church of Jesus Christ is the story of drift, a condition that sets up the first characteristic of revival. Because of God's mercy, grace, and love, He calls His people back to Himself time and again. Most often, they are suffering the terrible consequences of their sins when He sends someone to call them back to obedience and intimacy with Him.

God will not allow His redemptive purpose, which He has assigned to His people, to be thwarted for long. What is His call? It follows His words to the church in Laodicea:

> Here I am! I stand at the door and knock. If anyone hears my voice and opens the door, I will come in and eat with him, and he with me. To him who overcomes, I will give the right to sit with me on my throne, just as I overcame and sat down with my Father on his throne.
>
> —*Revelation 3:20–21*

This is the doorknob to revival. Obedience to God's instructions in 2 Chronicles 7:14 swings the door open. It is time for America to open the door, to follow God's Word, and to enter in.

God's plan was never to allow us to be passive bystanders, but to give us a strategic and fulfilling part to play, to be an important part of His great redemption plan. It has never changed.

—Dr. Bob Griffin

3

Tracing the Storm Pattern

I N 2004 SEVERAL severe tropical storms hit the coast of Florida like consecutive punches from a hard-hitting boxer. In some areas, people were just getting on their feet, dealing with loss and assessing the damage, when another storm hit. Were the storms a shift in the weather patterns? Did the jet stream change?

At the end of 2004 a violent earthquake in the Indian Ocean spawned one of history's most damaging tsunamis, causing damage into the billions of dollars and taking the lives of over 300,000 people. On the January 6, 2005 CBS evening news, a special report asked about the role of God in the quake and the resulting killer waves.[1] Was He behind this natural disaster? Was it a freak of nature? There was no conclusive answer, only a range of opinions from theologically diverse perspectives. Scientists were asked if there was any way to predict and track such phenomena. Were patterns available? The scientists who were interviewed reported that small efforts were in place, but those who were watching for tsunamis were caught by surprise.

We can count on some weather patterns. The order of seasons is spring, summer, fall, and winter. Summer can be unusually hot and humid where I live, and yet it may be mild. In some years, mountainous areas do not have enough snow to support winter sports, while in other years there is too much to manage. Highly paid meteorologists try to forecast weather patterns. Although we often joke about the weather forecasters, especially when they really miscalculate, we still base many decisions on their predictions.

What is the pattern of revival? What conditions spawn a mighty rushing Pentecostal wind of the Spirit? What is the pattern of restoration? Before we examine the ten characteristics of God's firestorms of revival, it is important to look at some theological meteorology. There are seasons of spiritual drought and great storms of revival. As we seek to know God and His ways, we learn of His heart for redemption and revival. God is sovereign, and yet He allows man considerable freedom, even to change the course of history. In dark and difficult times, revival comes when God's people do what He tells them.

The Bible records a great cry for revival in Psalm 85:6. "Will you not revive us again, that your people may rejoice in you?" Notice the word *again*. As I will show, God answers the prayers of His people for revival when they follow His instructions.

Another passionate call for revival comes from the prophet Isaiah. Out of desperation he prays,

> Oh, that you would rend the heavens and come down, that the mountains would tremble before you! As when *fire sets twigs ablaze and causes water to boil*, come down to make your name known.
>
> —*Isaiah 64:1–2, emphasis added*

The prophet was desperate for a firestorm in his day. God had intervened in the past and had answered the desperate prayers of His people when they humbly called out to Him. Isaiah pleaded, "Do it again!" He was writing at a time when God's people were in trouble. Dark and difficult days were at hand. Would God answer as He had in the past? How long would God be patient with the pattern—great blessing; drift; disaster; repentance; blessing. Again and again, apostasy was a dark thread woven through redemptive history.

The cry of Isaiah is our cry here in America. Dark and difficult conditions and the stirrings of prayer and repentance are evident in many areas of the nation. What can we anticipate from God? Although we hear reports of thousands coming to faith in Jesus Christ across the world, the North American continent is an exception. The church in America stands impotent against the pervasive move of secularism, humanism, and non-biblical morality.

Rather than pressing in to the Great Commission—to go into the world as witnesses in the power of the Holy Spirit (Matt. 28:19–20; Acts 1:8)—the church often appears to be isolated in its own world of media, music, bookstores, magazines, and even language. The church has become isolated from society, hidden behind her culture, traditions, and denominational walls. It is no wonder that her growth is flat-lined and in many cases, in serious decline. As reported to me by a pastor who serves the Presbyterian Church USA, his mainline denomination is losing one member every thirteen minutes. The church is half of what it was in 1965.

The Great Commandment—to love God with all you are and all you have and love those around you as you love yourself (Matt. 22:37–39; John 13:34)—is hard to find as the motivating assignment and vision in many congregations. Outspoken Christians are labeled radical; some fairly and some not. Some are angry as they speak out. They forget that God is love and that the mark of the Christian is love. We must speak truth clearly and lovingly, for love is to be the oil that lubricates the truth.

Our nation lacks a God-honoring social order, and the church is ineffective in its diffusion of the light of the gospel. Rhonda Hughey's excellent book, *Desperate for His Presence,* raises a critical question: Is God present or absent in the church today? Hughey skillfully takes her readers through the Bible to create a list of things that come between God and His people. They are idolatry, immorality, ambition, independence, a spirit of unbelief, harlotry, self-righteousness, and a religious spirit. Religion is the counterfeit of real biblical faith.[2]

The implication is that these maladies are behind the powerlessness of the church today. After identifying these robbers of God's presence, Hughey concludes,

> When the presence of Jesus is not manifest in the church in a tangible way and we continue in our programs, we are inviting the religious spirit to set up her throne in our congregations and ministries. This spirit is more than happy to become a substitute for Jesus; in fact, it has been the goal of the enemy all along. Eventually, as the church grows more and more compromised and disconnected from Jesus and from her ministry in the world, two things happen: true believers will leave the empty institutionalized church in pursuit of life and intimacy with Jesus, and others will remain, determined to shape and mold it after their own image.[3]

Hughey believes, and I agree, that the western church has become a subculture rather than a counter-culture. A subculture reflects the value system and worldview of the culture and cannot be an agent of change. By definition, it has become part of the culture. We must ask the question: What is the church today? Is it a biblical culture of New Testament Christianity—a kingdom culture? Or is it the culture of the world around her—humanistic and self-centered?

I believe the answer is clear. Kingdom culture reflects unity among believers, humility, meekness, holiness, contentment, God-centeredness, serving and giving, living by faith, generosity, sacrificial living, and even suffering for the sake of God's kingdom. Hughey says, "The church has become a well-trained institution, and the reality is that we are capable of functioning without the manifest presence of God. That is alarming."[4]

George Barna is a premiere Christian statistician and research analyst. He summarized his research on the church at the end of 2001 in an online report.

> It is a bit troubling to see pastors feel they're doing a great job when the research reveals that few congregants have a biblical worldview, half the people they minister to are not spiritually secure or developed, kids are fleeing from the church in record number, most of the people who attend worship services admit they did not connect with God, the divorce rate among Christians is no different than that of non-Christians, only 2% of the pastors themselves can identify God's vision for their ministry they are trying to lead, and the average congregant spends more time watching television in one day than he spends in all spiritual pursuits combined for an entire week.[5]

The church has a problem when she measures herself by herself rather than by New Testament Christianity, her effectiveness in fulfilling the Great Commandment and the Great Commission, the unity required by John 17:20–23 and Ephesians 4:1–16, or her impact on the culture. For example, how about measuring success of the Great Commission by asking: How many people are coming to Christ, embracing God's great love, and growing in their faith each year?

Another evaluation point is to ask how closely God's people reflect Jesus. The church will never see her cities transformed until her people are transformed into the likeness of Jesus and are characterized by the beatitudes and the fruit of the Holy Spirit. As Hughey says,

The issue isn't about having enough Christians to do kingdom business; rather, the issue is finding Christians who have pressed through the fire and now look, talk, and smell like Jesus.[6]

It is time to join Solomon in prayer.

> When your people…have been defeated by an enemy because they have sinned against you and when they turn back and confess your name, praying and making supplication before you in this temple, then hear from heaven and forgive the sin of your people Israel and bring them back to the land you gave to them and their fathers. When the heavens are shut up and there is no rain because your people have sinned against you, and when they pray toward this place and confess your name and turn from their sin because you have afflicted them, then hear from heaven and forgive the sin of your servants, your people Israel…When famine or plague comes to the land, or blight or mildew, locusts or grasshoppers, or when enemies besiege them in any of their cities, whatever disaster or disease may come…Forgive, and deal with each man according to all he does.
>
> —*2 Chronicles 6:24–30*

God responds to this prayer by saying, "I will." He always fulfills His Word. However, when God had finally had enough of Israel's rebellion and disobedience, He sentenced her to captivity. Obviously, there was a point of no return. Yet biblical history shows that the mercy and grace of God is consistent to revive and restore His people.

WHAT IS REVIVAL?

So, what is revival? Revive what? Isn't it to make alive something that is dying? Isn't it to take something back to its original purpose? What was God's ordained purpose for His people? They were made to glorify God by knowing Him, and in the fullness of His Spirit, to declare His praise to the ends of the earth.[7]

When God created us, He gave us dominion over the creation:

> Let us make man in our image, in our likeness, and let them rule over the fish of the sea and the birds of the air, over the livestock, over all the earth, and over all the creatures that move along the ground. So God created man in his own image, in the image of God he created him; male and female he created them. God blessed them and said to them, "Be fruitful and increase in number; fill the earth and subdue it. Rule over the fish of the sea and the birds of the air and over every living creature that moves on the ground."
>
> —*Genesis 1:26–28*

Psalm 8:3–8 gave us a similar mandate:

> When I consider your heavens, the work of your fingers, the moon and the stars, which you have set in place, what is man that you are mindful of him, the son of man that you care for him? You made him a little lower than the heavenly beings and crowned him with glory and honor. You made him ruler over the works of your hands [this indicates that we were to manage what God created]; you put everything under his feet: all flocks and herds, and the beasts of the field, the birds of the air, and the fish of the sea, all that swim the paths of the seas.

Genesis 3 presents the tragic story of our Fall through Adam and Eve, the breaking of our intimate fellowship with God. Forced to leave the Garden of Eden, Adam and Eve struggled, not only with their own sin, but also with the result of it. They lived in a fallen world under the curses shaped by their sin. The Fall also introduced the tragic news that there would be a struggle between people and Satan. This enmity plays out across human history and in the heart of every person.

However, God revealed His gracious care for people by clothing Adam and Eve before they were removed from the Garden (Gen. 3:21). He also promised a redeemer in Genesis 3:15: "And I will put enmity between you and the woman, and between your offspring and hers; he will crush your head, and you will strike his heel." Jesus fulfilled this promise in His death and resurrection. He defeated Satan, sin, death, and hell, and He opened the gates for mankind to be restored to their Creator.

It has always been God's plan to give us a strategic and fulfilling part in His great redemption plan. For years I have enjoyed telling people that one of the greatest privileges I have—the most exciting reason I have to live—is to be a part of what God is doing in the world.

The Israelites were called to this purpose through Abraham when God established a covenant in which they were to be agents of God's redemptive purpose. Sad to say, the history of God's chosen people was a tragic roller-coaster ride, up and down. They drifted in and out of their relationship with God and their service for Him. Their acts of repentance were followed by the restoration of God's presence, His blessings, and His covenant promises. Through restoration, they returned to redemptive service, and God's plan marched on with new force. Then they drifted again, and suffered spiritual, social, and economic decline.

God's covenants with Israel found its ultimate fulfillment in the coming of Jesus, Israel's Messiah. The eternal Son of God who came in human flesh was the Savior, the Son of David. He lived among the people of Israel and identified Himself as "I AM," the self-existent One, God incarnate. Demonstrating His deity with phenomenal signs, wonders, and miracles, He proclaimed the Good News of God's kingdom and modeled it by the way He lived.

Toward the end of His three short years of ministry, the religious and political tide turned against Jesus. He was brutally tortured and crucified on a Roman cross, and a large boulder sealed the entry to the borrowed tomb in which He was buried. But the grave couldn't hold Him, and death died in His magnificent resurrection. Restoration to God, eternal life, and salvation were the gifts He provided for all who would believe in Him and accept His death as the sacrifice for their sin.

After Jesus' return to the right hand of the Father, the church was born. In obedience to His instructions, the early Christ-followers met to wait in the upper room and came together in unity and prayer. Just as He promised, they were clothed with power from on high. As they prayed, the Holy Spirit came; a mighty rushing wind and tongues of fire rested on their heads. He came to live in each person who would receive Him as Savior, to give them power and gifts for serving His kingdom purpose. All His followers became the redemptive agents of His kingdom through the church. With Jesus as their head, they became the second incarnation—His body, living and active on Earth.

The ancient pattern of drift so tragically seen in the history of Israel has been repeated in the church and in the lives of Christians. There have been periods of great spiritual vitality, obedience, and intimacy between God and His people. In these times, the church has flourished under God's covenant blessings—physically, spiritually, socially, and economically.

As the church fulfilled the Great Commission and the Great Commandment, the gospel spread; cities were transformed. Then she drifted away from God and from serving Him. Subtly and slowly, she, like Israel, was sucked into the culture around her again and again. Physical, social, spiritual, and economic decline followed, according to the curses forewarned in Deuteronomy 28.

We are in the dark part of this cycle. Today the church in America is marginalized. At the same time, stirrings of prayer are growing across the land. There is a rebirth of hope that the church may be waking up from sinful slumber. God's people are recognizing the impotence of the church and are beginning to pray, repent, and seek His face. Is it too late? Is the severe judgment, the withdrawal of God's blessing and protection, at hand? Although I believe it may get worse before it gets better, I also believe that revival is coming. The momentum of prayer and repentance is growing.

The word commonly translated *revived* or *revival* in the Old Testament is the Hebrew word *chayah* (*khaw-yaw*). Its primary root meaning is "to live." *Strong's Concordance* includes the definitions "quicken, recover, repair, restore (to life), revive." The familiar prayer for revival in Psalm 85:6 is all about this: "Will you not revive us again, that your people may rejoice in you?" Here is a snapshot of revival. God is the source. When His people call on Him, rejoicing follows.

Habakkuk uses the word *revive* in a similar prayer. In Habakkuk 3:2, he says, "Lord, I have heard of your fame; I stand in awe of your deeds, O Lord. Renew them in our day." The King James Version translates the word *renew* as "revive."

The Old Testament records the story of redemption through Israel's history and community life and in her relationship with God. Revival in the Old Testament brought Israel back to God and to her redemptive calling and purpose. When she fell away from Him and her covenant relationship and purpose, He disciplined her and judgment fell. Spiritual, economic, moral, and social decline resulted, and it was time for revival. According to the promise of 2 Chronicles 7:14, when God's people followed His instructions, He heard from heaven, forgave their sin, and healed their land.

The story climaxes, of course, in the New Testament, with the coming of Israel's Messiah, Jesus Christ the Son of David. He is the eternal Son of God who came in human flesh. The Old Testament sacrifices were a picture of the perfect Lamb of God who would, one day, come to pay for the sins of Israel and the whole world. Through this sacrificial system, trusting God's provision of redemption by faith, Israel looked forward to the Messiah's coming.

In contrast, the church has looked back at the death and resurrection of the Messiah, Jesus Christ, the Lamb of God, slain before the world. Both Israel and the church were to proclaim God's redemption, live in intimacy with Him, and serve His purpose as summarized by the Great Commandment and Great Commission.

How sad it is to see history repeat itself, to realize that the church has not learned from the history of God's people in the Old Testament. Why don't we *get it*? The Bible itself tells us the importance of being instructed by the Old Testament. Second Timothy 3:16 says, "All Scripture is God-breathed and is useful for teaching, rebuking, correcting and training in righteousness." Paul tells us in Romans 15:4 and 1 Corinthians 10:11 that the things written in Old Testament times were provided to teach us today so that we, through Scripture, might have hope. Thankfully, the character of God—His mercy, justice, and love—has not changed for us.

ISRAEL'S MISSION

Join me in looking at Israel's mission. Her faith was rooted in her concept of God as someone utterly unique and unlike the gods of the surrounding nations. As Creator, He demonstrated His power, design, and purpose. He stands alone in omnipotence and is above and beyond everything He brought into being. Creation reveals His wisdom in its perfection and intention. It accounts for the origin of man and the universe, including nature and the animal world. Mankind is created in the image and likeness of God, and that physical creation was the prelude to God's redemption. Creation established God as the author of life and the controller of destiny.[8]

To Israel, God was self-existent, the *I AM*. He created, called, and enlisted humanity into service, controlled the forces affecting life, and maintained a living and vital relationship with the people He created. God was a person, and the proof of His existence was in His activity. He made plans and carried them out. He met with Moses and spoke to him. He entered into covenants with Israel. He was described as King, Father, Shepherd, Judge, and Lord.

God possessed and exercised will. He initiated, planned, demanded, judged, and expressed pleasure and displeasure. He was the Lord over nature and could order and reorder it to accomplish His plan. Jehovah was Lord of history, and He shaped history. Nations were used to accomplish His will. History was not an arbitrary series of events directed by man or other gods. It was the story of God's plan rooted in His choice of Israel to be His redeemed people. Israel was on a mission.

The people of Israel agreed to God's plan. They chose Him as Lord and committed themselves to serve Him. Through the Abrahamic covenant God called Israel to Himself. In the Mosaic covenant she became a royal priesthood. God was eternal in contrast to the gods of surrounding nations. He alone was God, and He alone was to be their only God.

Tragically, the gods of surrounding nations became one of the greatest sources of drift and defection for God's people. Just as Satan in the form of a serpent deceived Adam and Eve in the Garden of Eden and perpetrated the great historic Fall, the same demonic powers drew Israel into sin again and again through the worship of false gods and idols. It obviously wasn't just the draw of impersonal, wood, stone, and expensively decorated objects of gold, silver, and precious stones; it was the demonic powers associated with them.

Israel's history can be summarized as creation, covenant, and eschatology. God creates everything—people and history. Israel's relationship with God is shaped by His covenants with her. Her history moves toward a climax at the end of time and will be complete only when God's plan of redemption is finished and His divine community is in heaven with Him.

History is more to Israel than a record of what happened. It contains a view of God and His purpose in creation and life.

Revival in the Old Testament, therefore, was critical to the accomplishment of God's divine plan of redemption. Much was at stake when Israel drifted from God and neglected her calling and relationship with Him. The people of Israel had a strategic, eternal purpose, an eternal God-given identity, and a unique destiny. They agreed to it. God kept His part of His covenants with His people, but they didn't.

The special role of Israel and her relationship with God was not just about privilege. It was also about grace. When God renewed and enriched His covenant with Israel through Moses, He reminded His people that He did not choose them because they were larger or stronger than other nations. Instead, it was because He had made a covenant with Abraham to make her a great nation. Each new generation was chosen because of that promise.

The Abrahamic covenant wasn't replaced; God added to it. Under Moses, God's covenant was to be based on grace and faithfulness. Israel would be His chosen people, but there would be a condition:

> Now if you obey me fully and keep my covenant, then out of all nations you will be my treasured possession. Although the whole earth is mine, you will be for me a kingdom of priests and a holy nation. These are the words you are to speak to the Israelites.
>
> —*Exodus 19:5–6*

Obedience would keep their covenant relationship strong and God's blessings flowing. But watch out! Israel's historic problem would be disobedience and drifting from God. Because of disobedience, God would release His covenant curses listed in Deuteronomy 28. Through grace, God would one day give additional help and strength to His people by writing His law in their hearts through His Spirit. Sad to say, however, God's people would still vacillate in their love and commitment. Redemptive history would be an exciting, yet sad story. Praise God, it is a story of His mercy and grace.

As the people of Israel progressed from patriarchy to a kingdom, their responsibilities grew. The law mediated by Moses differed from the codes of law common to life in the Fertile Crescent. God's will had to be lived out not only between man and God, but now, in relationship with each other and with the people living around them. A moral code was developed, and obligations were made mandatory in the community of faith. Israel was a unique nation, a chosen, redemptive community, living among other nations. Her calling was to demonstrate who God was. If she obeyed, she would fulfill God's purpose for her.

God promised Abraham that all the nations of the earth would be blessed through Israel. She was a missionary nation long before Jesus and Paul in the New Testament. The people of Israel were God's redemptive agents to the nations. Isaiah the prophet wrote:

> This is what the LORD says: "In the time of my favor I will answer you, and in the day of salvation I will help you; I will keep you and will make you to be a covenant for the people, to restore the land and to reassign its desolate inheritances, to say to the captives, 'Come out,' and to those in darkness, 'Be free!' They will feed beside the roads and find pasture on every barren hill."
> —*Isaiah 49:8–9*

This was the same call God gave the church in the Great Commission (Matt. 28:19–20; Acts 1:8). God's missionary heart, which is to be expressed through His people, has never changed. It was even clear in His covenant with Moses. Israel was called to be a royal priesthood. Later, Isaiah proclaimed in Isaiah 2:2–5 that the nations would come to God's people and request to be taken to the mountain of God.

The people of Israel were called the servants of the Lord (Lev. 25:42, 55; Isa. 54:17), a picture of the time when Jesus the Messiah—the Servant King—would come. Redemption was foreshadowed through their sacred life of sacrifices, festivals, and temple services. They were to demonstrate the nature of God and His redemptive purpose through their community of faith.

In the New Testament (Gal. 3:15–16) Paul the Apostle wrote that the promise was made to Abraham and to his seed, Jesus Christ. Jesus perfectly fulfilled God's plan and purpose for Israel. He was a descendant of the nation, but so much more. He was the nation personified, its perfect expression. Servanthood and service were perfected in Him, and the priesthood reached perfection in Him, the Great High Priest. He was the

Son of Man, the Messiah of Israel sent from God the Father. God's revelation reached its apex in Jesus. God was glorified in Him, and history found its ultimate meaning, the redemption of fallen people.

Solomon's great prayer of dedication at the temple rehearsed Israel's mission. It said that foreigners who did not belong to Israel were to hear of God's great name and come from a distance to pray to Him. Solomon instructed,

> As for the foreigner who does not belong to your people Israel but has come from a distant land because of your name—for men will hear of your great name and your mighty hand and your outstretched arm—when he comes and prays toward this temple, then hear from heaven, your dwelling place, and do whatever the foreigner asks of you, so that all the peoples of the earth may know your name and fear you, as do your own people Israel, and may know that this house I have built bears your Name.
>
> —*1 Kings 8:41–43*

King David's song of thanksgiving to God in 1 Chronicles 16 exhorts us to "proclaim [the Lord's] salvation day after day" and "Declare his glory among the nations, his marvelous deeds among all peoples" (1 Chron. 16:23–24). He invites all the families of the nations to "Ascribe to the LORD...glory and strength...the glory due his name" (1 Chron. 16:28–29).

Psalm 67 requests the blessing of God so His ways would be "known on earth," and His salvation "among all nations" (vs. 2). It continues, "May the peoples praise you, O God; may all the peoples praise you. May the nations be glad and sing for joy, for you rule the peoples justly and guide the nations of the earth." Finally, verse seven says, "God will bless us, and all the ends of the earth will fear him."

In Psalm 96, we read an invitation for all peoples, all nations, to praise the Lord, to declare His glory. It declares that the gods of the nations are idols, unlike the God of Israel, the maker of the heavens. Families of nations are invited to ascribe glory and strength to the Lord. In verse ten, the worshipers are invited to say among the nations, "The LORD reigns...he will judge the peoples with equity." And in verse thirteen, God "comes to...judge the world in righteousness and the peoples in his truth."

Psalm 105:1 declares, "make known among the nations what [God] has done." Also, Psalm 117:1 urges: "Praise the LORD, all you nations."

Isaiah the prophet refers to the coming Messiah as the branch of Jesse who will "stand as a banner for the peoples; the nations will rally to him" (Isa. 11:10–11). In Isaiah 12:4–5, Israel is instructed to "make known among the nations what he has done." God declares, "I will also make you a light for the Gentiles, that you may bring my salvation to the ends of the earth" (Isa. 49:6). In Isaiah 51:4 God says, "my justice will become a light to the nations."

God's Word through Isaiah continues. Isaiah 52:9–10 says that because the Lord has redeemed Jerusalem, He will "lay bare his holy arm in the sight of all the nations, and all the ends of the earth will see the salvation of our God." In Isaiah 56:3–8, we read an invitation for foreigners to come to God's holy mountain where their sacrifices will be accepted. It says that God's house will "be called a house of prayer for all nations" (Isa. 56:7). In Isaiah 66:18, God promises to gather all nations to come and see His glory.

Jeremiah was called to be a prophet to the nations in Jeremiah 1:5. He proclaimed that if Israel would return to God, put away her idols, and live in "a truthful, just and righteous way…the nations [would] be blessed by him and in him they [would] glory" (Jer. 4:2). Although Jeremiah prophesied judgment and disaster for Israel, it also says that when she was restored, "the nations [would] come from the ends of the earth and say, 'Our fathers possessed nothing but false gods, worthless idols that did them no good'" (Jer. 16:19). As a result, they would know that God was the Lord (verse 21).

God has always kept His promises. The fulfillment of His promise to Abraham is described in Zechariah 2:11: "Many nations will be joined with the LORD in that day and will become my people." Zechariah 9:10 adds that Zion's King "will proclaim peace to the nations. His rule will extend from sea to sea and from the River to the ends of the earth."

Israel's missionary role is clear, and one more text reinforces it. Malachi 1:6–14 gives a tragic description of Israel's apostasy in bringing blemished sacrifices that did not demonstrate the holiness and greatness of God. The people showed contempt for God's name and did not honor Him or their mission. Verse fourteen says:

"Cursed is the cheat who has an acceptable male in his flock and vows to give it, but then sacrifices a blemished animal to the Lord. For I am a great king," says the LORD Almighty, "and my name is to be feared among the nations."

In the midst of this darkness, however, God declares, "My name will be great among the nations, from the rising to the setting of the sun" (Mal. 1:11).

The great redemptive plan of God, which was given in the Abrahamic covenant, is a grand symphony that is played through both the Old and New Testaments. Paul the Apostle rehearses the music in Galatians 3:6–9:

Consider Abraham: "He believed God, and it was credited to him as righteousness." Understand, then, that those who believe are children of Abraham. The Scripture foresaw that God would justify Gentiles by faith, and announced the gospel in advance to Abraham: "All nations will be blessed through you." So those who have faith are blessed along with Abraham, the man of faith.

We must also mention the Davidic covenant. In 2 Samuel 7:9, God promised to make David's name great. In fulfillment of this, the coming King was known as the Son of David. Second Samuel 7:10–11 also says that God's people would have a safe homeland, where they would have the freedom to pursue their divine mission. Through this covenant God also promised to give David's descendants his throne forever (2 Sam. 7:16). This covenant established a relationship like that of a father and a son. God disciplines His people, but He does not disqualify them, as in the case of King Saul. Nothing can stop God's redemptive mission.

I once sat under the teaching of the late George Ladd, a theologian and professor of theology at Fuller Seminary and one of the church's most informed students of the kingdom of God. Ladd wrote that Israel had been the possessor of the kingdom of God. Until the time of the coming of Christ in human flesh, God's redemptive activity in history was channeled through them as a nation. The residual blessings of God on Earth were poured out on Israel and channeled through them. Gentiles could share these blessings only by entering into relationship with Israel.

However, the time came for God to show His redemptive activity in a new and wonderful way. The kingdom of God visited men in the Person of His Son and brought them a fuller measure of the blessings of His divine plan. Israel rejected both the kingdom and Jesus, the Bearer of the kingdom. Therefore, God's kingdom in its new form was taken away from Israel and given to all who receive Jesus as Christ and Savior. This new people was the church—"a chosen people, a royal priesthood, a holy nation" (1 Pet 2:9).[9]

THE CHURCH'S PRIMARY PURPOSE

If we want a complete view of revival and its pattern throughout history—a theology of revival—it is necessary to consider more than just the accounts of revival. We need to understand more about how God works in response to His people and the dark threads of "drift-itis" that is so pervasive throughout their history. Why does God continue to pursue them? Francis Thompson, an English poet, calls God "The Hound of Heaven." This is the old, old story—a gracious story of Jesus' love.[10]

The dark thread that runs through redemptive history also runs through the heart of every person. It is the thread of our fallen nature, the evil in the heart of every person, that we inherited from Adam and Eve. It is in the human DNA. Allow me to rewind and review the big picture again. God created Satan and people with an element of free will. We were created to be free moral agents, not robots. We were created in God's image, but His image was seriously flawed by our fall.

Satan had enough choice to be destroyed by his own pride. He has shouted through time: "I will be like the most high." He was driven out of the presence of God to earth (Ezek. 28:17). As the god of this world, he has pushed pride ever since. And tragically, God's people have been attracted to it. Satan became the embodiment of evil, all that is opposed to God, His holiness, righteousness, goodness, and love. Satan became the personification and perpetuator of evil.

Other angels, some of high rank, fell with him and are identified in Ephesians 6:12 as "principalities...powers...the rulers of the darkness of this world...spiritual wickedness in high places" (KJV). They have served Satan's evil opposition and his promotion of hideous sin, both overt and subtle. They have served their boss night and day, seeking to draw people into bondage and away from God's truth and freedom. Satan has been out to devour those created in God's image (1 Pet. 5:8). However, God's truth has empowered Christ's followers to discern the enemy's deceitful ways and has set them free (John 8:32).

When Satan tempted Adam and Eve to use their free will to sin against God, they chose to break the pristine intimacy they enjoyed with Him in the perfect environment of the Garden of Eden. We inherited the problem and went down with them. In perfect justice, holiness, and righteousness, God had to expel Adam and Eve from the garden. Not only did mankind fall, but nature did as well. We inherited not only a sinful nature, but also a sin-cursed Earth.

What if our sin and the curse of the earth were the end of the human story? I can't imagine it! The good news is that God set out to accomplish the redemption of those He created, to restore them to loving intimacy with Himself. He established gracious covenants between Himself and His chosen people, Israel. As the first agents of God's redemptive love and mercy, their sacrificial system was a picture of His plan to restore broken humanity unto Himself. Their worship looked forward to the coming of the One who would be the ultimate sacrifice for their sin, the perfect Lamb of God—their Messiah and Redeemer, Jesus.

The great story of redemption rolls through time, reaching its apex in the life, death, and resurrection of Jesus Christ. It is the gospel, the Good News. Without the shedding of blood there is not, and never has been, remission for man's sin (Heb. 9:22). Jesus is the Lamb of God slain before the foundation of the world (Rev. 5:12; 13:8), once for all (Heb. 9:26). He is the payment for the penalty of sin, and we must personally accept His payment for us.

Jesus bridged the gap that sin brought between God and His creation. He reestablished relationship between God and man. By embracing His provision of salvation, the redeemed followers of Jesus join the great army of kingdom agents who serve God's eternal purpose in the world. Read again, the great story in a nutshell:

> For God so loved the world that he gave his one and only Son, that whoever believes in him shall not perish but have eternal life. For God did not send his Son into the world to condemn the world,

but to save the world through him. Whoever believes in him is not condemned, but whoever does not believe stands condemned already because he has not believed in the name of God's one and only Son.

—John 3:16–18

For it is by grace you have been saved, through faith—and this not from yourselves, it is the gift of God—not by works, so that no one can boast. For we are God's workmanship, created in Christ Jesus to do good works, which God prepared in advance for us to do.

—Ephesians 2:8–10

One's response of repentance and personal faith in Jesus Christ provides forgiveness for the sin that separates everyone from Him (Eph. 2:8–9; Rom. 10:9–12). It also reestablishes a personal relationship with God through Christ (John 1:12). All generations, being fallen and sinful, need this salvation (Rom. 3:23; 6:23).

However, the Good News doesn't end there. Receiving Christ as Savior and Lord has a wonderful bonus. The Holy Spirit of God comes to indwell people who trust in Christ as Savior. His presence creates a new spiritual nature and bestows wonderful spiritual gifts (Eph. 4:7–13; 1 Cor. 12:4–11; Rom. 12:3–8). The Greek root word *charis* is translated "grace."[11] We are able to grace others through the gifting of the Spirit. With these tools, every redeemed person is called to serve God's redemptive purpose until they leave this world though death or until Jesus returns for them. They are His Bride, the church (Matt 28:16–20; Acts 1:1–11).

It was different in the Old Testament. The Holy Spirit was only given to people on special assignment from God. Think about it. With the Holy Spirit living in each Christian, why has the tragic pattern of sin repeated itself over and over again? It seems that we could have done much better. It has been a sad, old story because the dark thread of man's inherited sinful nature has woven its way through every human heart.

Jesus was born miraculously of a virgin. His brief earthly life demonstrated how to live in fellowship with God the Father. His teaching prepared us to know and serve Him. He set the stage for the birth of the church, God's new redemptive community. The Holy Spirit came to live in each one of us. Couldn't we have lived more consistently in loving intimacy with God and service for His kingdom? After all, we were to be God's redemptive agents, filled and fueled by the Holy Spirit. Jesus was supposed to come alive again through us, the church, making us the second incarnation.

It has been heartbreaking to trace our drift. *Oh, God, send Your Spirit in a massive firestorm before it is too late; before Your judgment falls again.* We must remember our redemptive mission, our primary purpose, which is summed up in the Great Commandment (Mark 12:29–31) and the Great Commission (Matt 28:19–20; Acts 1:8). We are created for loving intimacy with God and for serving Him. Our ultimate identity and security can only be found in Him.

One of the best-written philosophies of life comes from the apostle Paul.

> But whatever was to my profit I now consider loss for the sake of Christ. What is more, I consider everything a loss compared to the surpassing greatness of *knowing Christ Jesus my Lord* ... I press on to *take hold of that for which Christ Jesus took hold of me.*
> —*Philippians 3:7–12, Author's emphasis*

Paul understood that knowing Christ and capturing God's purpose for his life was his highest good and ultimate fulfillment. Notice so you don't get discouraged, that in the same text Paul hadn't arrived or become perfect. However, he pressed on. This is maturity, he says, or "perfect," as it is translated in the King James Version.

Throughout history, the need for revival has been centered in our basic purpose to know God, to enjoy Him, and to serve Him. When men and women created for this purpose have embraced it through salvation (John 1:12, 3:16; Eph. 2:8–9), the subtleties of apathy begins to encroach upon God's people. Fanned by the god of this world, this encroachment increases ever so gradually, even when the grace and love of God is fresh and exciting. Spiritual decline lurks in the shadows, even when loving and serving Christ is the top priority.

Without a solid anchor of intimacy with God and obedience to His truth, God's people throughout history begin to drift in secular currents stirred by Satan. It seems that God's people are not able to handle His lavish love, good gifts, and covenant blessings. With apathy and self-absorption, they slip away from intense love for God, worship, and service, and fall into disobedience and even apostasy. Bad times follow, and life unravels. As they seek God with humility, prayer, repentance, obedience, holiness, and righteousness, they return to a place of restoration, abundance, strong witness, loving intimacy with God, and a transformational impact on society. This cycle repeats itself over and over.

God is the ultimate Father, and He knows how to balance love and discipline. His "Mercy triumphs over judgment" (James 2:13). God loves and guides His children graciously throughout history and disciplines them so restoration will come. It is all about revival—firestorms of the Holy Spirit. God in mercy and grace returns His people to their designed purpose and greatest fulfillment. In the worst situations, God graciously, yet severely, judges or disciplines His people. The crucial issue is not just their relationship with Him or His reason for creating them, but the redemption of the world.

WHO INITIATES REVIVAL?

As we consider the theology of revival, we must ask an age-old question: Does revival come as a result of our obedience to 2 Chronicles 7:14, or does God initiate it? The answer is a mystical *yes!* The text is conditional: if—then. God will not respond unless we repent and seek His face. On the other hand, given our human bent to sin, it seems that we would never take the initiative.

God gave Israel the Promised Land. It was a gift, but she had to form an army and fight for it. She had to wage aggressive battle at the cost of sacrifice and loss. We are called to serve God, to evangelize, but it is God who draws people to salvation (John 6:44–65; 12:32). We know that apart from God, we can do nothing (John 15:5). God Himself empowers and directs our service and accomplishes His purpose through us.

Dr. David Larsen, the chair of my doctoral committee, blends our responsibility with God's sovereignty, God's activity and initiative, and ours. He quotes Isaiah 64:1: "Oh, that you would rend the heavens and come down, that the mountains would tremble before you!" Then he writes,

Among the issues widely discussed in relation to revival, one stands above all others: From where does revival come? We long to see and experience that supernatural visitation which Scripture and history excite us to seek. To listen to Jonathan Edwards the answer seems clear: God does it! To read Charles Finney the answer seems clear: It is up to us! The Scriptures make it clear both that there are spiritual laws governing revival and that if we conform to the rules we shall experience the desire of our hearts. Each viewpoint conveys needed truth. All of us must recognize that revival lies within the sovereignty of God. God must do it! This truth preserves us from despair and an overwhelming burden when things are dry. God sees all and knows all, and hope for revival depends upon Him. But that is only one aspect of the reality. Just as we must maintain the tension between divine sovereignty and human responsibility, between the threeness and the oneness of God, between the divine and the human natures of our Lord in the hypostatic union, so we must maintain both God's divine initiative and the significance of our response to Him. Second Chronicles 7:14 does say, "If my people...." There are conditions for revival.... Even the most ardent Calvinist preaches that prayer is necessary preparation for revival. We must affirm both divine sovereignty and human responsibility in revival.[12]

Stephen Olford agrees. "The longing for revival must be schooled by the way revival happens," he says. He takes us to the message of John the Baptist, "Prepare the way for the Lord" (Luke 3:4). "So many of us," he writes, "are obstructions to Christ." He agrees with G. Campbell Morgan, whom he calls "the prince of expositors," and adds, "We cannot organize revival, but we can set our sails to catch the wind from heaven when God chooses to blow upon His people once again."[13]

In *Rain From Heaven*, Arthur Wallis writes, "Revival can never be explained in terms of activity or organization, personality or preaching...it is essentially a manifestation of God...We cannot explain or understand Him in His holiness and sovereignty, and for that reason we cannot really completely understand revival. The wind blows where it wills. Though we do not understand its vagaries we may still 'trim the sail' and work with it. To move with God in the day of His power means understanding and conforming to those principles by which He has chosen to work."[14]

Revival comes in God's time when His people have fulfilled certain conditions. Blackaby and King put it simply, quoting the words of Malachi 3:7, "Return to me, and I will return to you." They continue, "The essence of revival is returning to the Lord. This can happen quickly or it can take place over a period of time."[15]

God's promises are, for the most part, conditioned on obedience as in 2 Chronicles 7:14, *If you will…then I will.* We cannot force God to do anything. Yet, in His sovereignty, God has set forth the requirements for revival.

Thomas Ashbridge says, "Revival is the work of God and of Him alone; but His people provide the essential conditions. The more who are ready, the more quickly revival will come, and the more wide-sweeping its operations and results will be. Reduce it to actual, heart-searching reality; revival depends upon me and you. Am I now in that condition of heart and attitude toward God that He can work revival through me?"[16]

God's part and our part are both necessary for revival! If we do our part, God will do His. If the church drifts too far beyond God's limits, He will discipline her and revive her. He will use people to accomplish it. There certainly is a creative tension between our part and God's. If we move too far in the direction of God's sovereignty, we could easily become apathetic. If we go too far in the direction of our responsibility, we could easily become crushed by it.

THE DOCTRINE OF REVIVAL

A common body of belief has accompanied historic revival, and it helps to have scholars like J. Edwin Orr lay it out for us. He gives us a formal statement that has shaped the move of God in revival during the eighteenth and nineteenth centuries. Basically consisting of the doctrines of the Reformation, it actually re-emphasizes basic New Testament teaching, according to Orr. It was the original doctrinal statement of the Evangelical Alliance, established in 1846 as a unified fellowship of biblically orthodox Christians for the purpose of strengthening global mission movements and networks. Here is the statement.

I.   The divine Inspiration, Authority, and sufficiency of the Holy Scriptures, and the right and duty of Private Judgment in the interpretation thereof;

II.   The Unity of the Godhead, and the Trinity of Persons therein;

III.   The utter Depravity of Human Nature, in consequence of the Fall;

IV.   The Incarnation of the son of God, His work of atonement for sinners of mankind, and His mediatorial Intercession and Reign;

V.   The Justification of the sinner by Faith alone;

VI.   The work of the Holy Spirit in the Conversion and Sanctification of the sinner;

VII.   The Resurrection of the Body, the Judgment of the world by the Lord Jesus Christ, the Eternal Blessedness of the Righteous, and the Eternal Punishment of the Wicked.

According to the history of post-biblical revival, there was no departure from these statements. "It was so widely adopted," says Orr, "that it led to a practice of fraternal fellowship having the force of a major doctrine."

> All things considered, the nineteenth-century Awakening represented no great discovery or rediscovery of doctrine. Its theology was largely that of the New Testament stated in the language of the reformers and the Revivalists of an earlier century. The real contribution of the Awakening was its application of these doctrines in the evangelization of the great mass of unchurched at home and the heathen abroad.[17]

Earl Cairns writes in *An Endless Line of Splendor: Revivals and Their Leaders from the Great Awakening to the Present* and states that all revivalists, whether Calvinists or Armenians, affirmed the sovereignty of God as Creator or Redeemer. "They emphasized God's holiness and justice, before which sinful man must quake as the Israelites did before Sinai." No revival leader had difficulty with the idea that all men are sinners. They believed everyone *was* guilty of original and actual sin and sinners by birth and choice. Redemption was provided by Christ's death on the cross. "God had made salvation for the sinner possible in the virgin-born Christ, who was true man as well as true God. Revivalists preached the law so that men might be convicted of sin...Faith would bring justification before God and regeneration, the New Birth that all the revivalists proclaimed." Character would be transformed, and the sinner "would become more like his Saviour."[18]

Theological differences like those between Wesley and Whitfield over election and sanctification, and between Finney and Nettleton, all great revival leaders, did not stop them from agreeing on the main doctrines of biblical faith. They disagreed in love and went on preaching salvation.[19]

Cairns says that a Niagara conference in 1878 led to the development of a fourteen-point doctrinal platform in 1890. Called *Five Points*, this doctrinal paper was published in 1895 and established scriptural standards on inerrancy of the Bible, the virgin birth, the deity of Christ, substitutionary atonement, the resurrection of Christ, and His bodily return to Earth. In 1917, after years of writing and theological effort, a document called *The Fundamentals* was published in a four-volume edition. It was published again in 1958 by Charles Feinberg in a two-volume edition. One hundred articles codified the basic doctrines that revival preachers had been proclaiming since 1726. It was "scholarly, rational, and ecumenical in authorship."[20]

God has been at work redeeming His people since the fall of humanity. Those who embrace the knowledge of God and His redemption are engaged in the ministry of fulfilling His redemptive purpose. The tragic and persistent drift of God's people makes revival necessary, and He gives instructions for this in 2 Chronicles 7:14. God's forgiveness of sins and the healing of the land are conditioned on obedience to this text.

Revival is a partnership between the sovereign work of God and the responsibility of His people. The theology of revival is the basic orthodoxy expressed by the Evangelical Alliance and summarized by the authors I have cited above.

SPARKS THAT IGNITE

When I was much younger, camping was a special treat. It usually had to do with fishing, and I was usually skunked—no fish! After a brief effort at fishing without success, I would go to catch little crabs or climb rocks. Campfires were the greatest. We cooked fish—not mine—over an open fire. One of my memories was a serious caution about the campfire. "Be careful around the campfire and be careful to watch that sparks do not hit the tent. They can burn the tent and all our stuff, or even worse, ignite dry brush and begin a forest fire."

What does God use to light new fire in His people, to ignite the dry brush of the apathetic church? Revival is like a forest fire, a *firestorm* of the Holy Spirit. Three sparks—pain, proclamation, and prayer—seem to be particularly hot and are frequently used by God. All three are equally involved in the birth of revival, and they are central to the ten characteristics of revival. I am including separate chapters on prayer and the proclamation of the Word. Pain, the first characteristic, is more circumstantial and does not require a separate chapter.

Pain

Difficult circumstances form the backdrop of 2 Chronicles 7:14. Israel's history shows that they began to call out to God at the low state of their spiritual condition. When life was falling apart and circumstances were dark, they began to look for answers in the law of God. The same kind of setting has drawn the church back to prayer and the Word of God.

God's judgment is often behind the pain. His people may experience His covenant curses as the direct activity of God or as a natural result of their unhealthy choices. As I consider America's social and spiritual deterioration and the impotence of the church, I often wonder, how close we are to receiving severe judgment.

Prayer

Prayer has always been central to revival. R. A. Torrey wrote, "There have been revivals without much preaching, but there has never been a mighty revival without mighty prayer."[21] I agree with Torrey. Prayer has been the most consistent spark that ignites revival. Charles Spurgeon said, "If we are importunate in prayer, it must happen again…Preaching is beginning at the wrong end. Instead thereof, we ought to hold meetings of prayer."[22]

In his book, *Eight Keys to Revival,* Lewis Drummond says that leaders have stressed prayer or intercession almost to a fault. He continues:

> But still we do not pray, or at least we do not pray very much...But if we will pray, if we will get before God personally, if we will develop prayer groups, if church leaders will organize a vital prayer ministry...then God will surely show us His plan...a vital means of producing spiritual awakening. God is far more ready to give than we are to receive.[23]

Brian Edwards writes powerfully but simply:

> Historically the church has prayed its way to the outpouring of God's Holy Spirit....You cannot read far into the story of a revival without discovering that not only is prayer part of the inevitable result of an outpouring of the Spirit, but, from a human stand-point, it is also the single most significant cause. Those whom God uses in revival are men and women of prayer. That is their great priority. And this is true of a community also. If we really want God in revival, we must ask for it. Praying for revival is not enough: we must long for it, and long for it intensely.[24]

In her book, *Flames of Revival,* Elana Lynse sees the cycles of revival as cycles of prayer. For example, her study has led her to believe that the Moravian Prayer Vigil of 1727 can be credited with the Frelinghuysen revival in New Jersey, the ministry of Jonathan Edwards in 1734, and the ministries of Wesley and Whitfield in 1739. She identifies fifty years of Concerts of Prayer beginning in 1792 and concludes that they produced the frontier revival of the 1800s, the formation of missionary societies, the ministry of Charles Finney, and the beginning of the YMCA in 1840.

Lynse links the New York City Prayer Meeting revival of 1857 and 1858 to the ministry of Spurgeon, the beginning of the Salvation Army, D. L. Moody's ministry, the beginnings of the China Inland Mission, and an era of great lay ministry expansion. She identifies prayer as central to "the year of the Holy Spirit" and marks 1905 as its beginning. A world-wide awakening was sparked by prayer as well as the birth of the Pente-costal movement.

Finally, Lynse points to 1914 as the beginning of a significant prayer cycle that resulted in rally evangelism and the ministries of evangelists, such as Billy Sunday and Billy Graham. This extended even to the birth of the Jesus movement, the counter cultural revival in the 1960s and 1970s.[25]

As a result of his research, Stephen Olford wrote in his book, *Heart-Cry for Revival*, "I came to the conclusion that the two outstanding conditions for revival are unity and prayer."[26] James Burns, the editor of *The Laws of Revival*, says:

> Even as spiritual life is receding there begins to gather a power and volume to return to God. Growing dissatisfaction grows with decline...Gradually, the number of people praying increases ...more urgent and more confident...[It] is not the cause of a revival, but the human preparation for one. By prayer we prepare the soil.[27]

Prayer is how God gets His work done. It stands as the apex of 2 Chronicles 7:14 and, yes, every revival. As J. Hudson Taylor wrote, "The spirit of prayer is, in essence, the spirit of revival."[28]

Proclamation

Proclamation—the powerful preaching and teaching of the Word of God—is the third spark that God has used to fire revival. The truth of God sets people free; those in the church and also nonbelievers (John 8:32). It is alive and powerful, sharper than a double-edged sword. It skillfully penetrates as fine as a laser to divide even the soul and spirit and the joints and marrow of a person. It judges the thoughts and attitudes of a person's spirit. Everything is laid open before it; nothing is exempt from exposure (Heb. 4:12–13).

Great revivals are known for great preaching and teaching from people such as Isaiah, Jeremiah, John the Baptist, Peter, Paul, Barnabas, Charles Finney, George Whitfield, D. L. Moody, Jonathan Edwards, Phoebe Palmer, and Asahel Nettleton. However, strong, consistent preaching and teaching are missing in many congregations today. Sermonettes, or simple life lessons, capture much of the speaking or teaching time.

It is one thing to be intentional about evangelistic preaching at the main services of local congregations. However, if there is not a central place for careful teaching and discipleship, congregations soon consist of immature, childish followers of Christ. Sermonettes produce Christianettes. The church is to *gather* for strategic biblical preaching and teaching and then *go out* to reach the world and transform her cities and nations.

The proclamation of the Word of God and a commitment to the centrality of prayer are missing from the average Christian congregation. Without them, the church stands impotent against the culture of secularism, materialism, and sensuality. Apart from a rebirth of these essential characteristics of revival, pain will certainly follow. *Oh, God, stoke the fire. Let the sparks fly!*

That is why the Israelites are running from their enemies in defeat. For now Israel has been set apart for destruction. I will not remain with you any longer unless you destroy the things among you that were set apart for destruction. Get up! Command the people to purify themselves in preparation for tomorrow. For this is what the Lord, the God of Israel, says: Hidden among you, O Israel, are things set apart for the Lord. You will never defeat your enemies until you remove these things.

—*Joshua 7:12–13,* NLT

4

Old Testament Firestorms

I
T IS A great honor and encouragement to be chosen for a special purpose or position. For example, I recall the excitement of being chosen first chair trumpet in high school. I remember the honor of being selected for a much desired university ministry, and on several occasions, being over other candidates for pastoral positions. I didn't know the other candidates, and it wasn't about competition. However, I felt honored and desired. And I remember the thrill when Connie said yes to my proposal of marriage. Out of all the other possibilities, she chose me.

In a much more important and historically significant sense, the nation of Israel was chosen to be God's special betrothed, the great nation through whom Jesus the Messiah would come. As I have already shown, the people of Israel were God's redemptive agents throughout Old Testament history. In His perfect time, He sent Jesus—a Jew, from the line of David—to redeem the world. He was the eternal Son of God who came to us in human flesh through God's people, the Jews. Unfortunately, the glory faded many times in Israel's history and relationship to God and His calling.

It is a stormy history: the story of Israel's call, her promises made to God, and her repeated drift toward other lovers. She is finally declared a prostitute people (Ezek. 16:15; Hos. 4:10–11; 5:4). With this brief backdrop, let us look at revivals in the Old Testament. We will examine the up and down pattern of Israel's relationship with God; from the glorious manifestation of His presence to ignominious low periods of apostasy.

Arthur Wallis, who wrote *Rain from Heaven*, describes Israel's pattern of drift.

> Decline and decay, inherent in human nature, are not confined to the physical and moral realm, but appear in the spiritual also.

> We see it in the history of Israel. We see it in New Testament times. We see it in the subsequent history of the church. God has seen fit to counteract this ever-present tendency by seizing the initiative, and working at times in unusual power. In this way ground has been recovered from the enemy, and the spiritual equilibrium restored.[1]

The story of Old Testament revival begins in Genesis 35:1–15. This is where Jacob returns to Bethel, which means "house of God."[2] God had first met him there in Genesis 28:10–22 and promised that all the nations of the earth would be blessed through him. Now, as Jacob prepares to go to Bethel again, he acts on God's instructions for his household to get rid of their foreign gods and to purify themselves (v. 2). After he returns home from worshiping God at Bethel, God changes his name to Israel, which means "struggles with God" (v. 10).[3] God confirms to him the covenant promises He had made to Abraham (Gen. 17:1–8).

Fast forward to the Book of Deuteronomy, which means "repetition of the law." Skim some of the early history with me to set the stage for Israel's up and down struggle with God. In Deuteronomy Moses gives careful instructions for God's people as he prepares to transfer the leadership of Israel to Joshua. Beginning in Deuteronomy 1:5, Moses delivers his farewell address and carefully reviews Israel's covenant with God. There, in the territory of Moab, where the Jordan River flows into the Dead Sea, the people reaffirm it.

Woven into the Book of Deuteronomy is a clear presentation of the love of God for His people and, in their better moments, their love for Him. Moses calls God's people to a radical commitment of worship and obedience. If they obey and live out their love relationship and calling with Him, He will bless them abundantly in every area of life. If they disobey, they can expect just the opposite, the covenant curses in Deuteronomy 28.

In chapter thirty-one, Moses prepares Israel for difficult times. As they move into the Promised Land, in partnership with God, He will deliver the nations and the land into their hands. Moses tells them to be strong and courageous (v. 6), not terrified or afraid. God goes with them, and He will not leave or forsake them. Sadly, God warns Moses of the pattern that will repeat itself throughout Israel's history:

> These people will soon prostitute themselves to the foreign gods of the land they are entering. They will forsake me and break the covenant I made with them....I know what they are disposed to do, even before I bring them into the land I promised them on oath.
>
> —*Deuteronomy 31:16, 21*

In Deuteronomy 32 and 33, Moses blesses each of the twelve tribes before he dies.

Another great leader, Joshua, steps into position. The book that bears his name tells how the nomadic Israelites conquered the Promised Land. The first major battle is a great victory for Israel and her leader, as the people take the great walled city of Jericho with an unusual military strategy from God. With amazing creativity, God demonstrates that He is in charge.

From this high point, Israel, confident of victory at Ai, sends a small army to take the city. It is here that the nation learns or relearns a powerful lesson; sin does not pay. Snubbing his nose at God's instructions and covenant, Achan had become enamored with some spoils from the victory at Jericho and had hidden them in his tent. As a result, Israel loses what should have been an easy battle at Ai. Thirty-six die.

Recognizing that something was very wrong, that perhaps God had not kept His promise of victory, Joshua tears his clothes and falls face down before the Lord. The elders of Israel follow suit. How does God respond?

> Stand up! What are you doing down on your face? Israel has sinned...That is why the Israelites cannot stand against their enemies...I will not be with you any more unless you destroy whatever among you is devoted to destruction...You cannot stand against your enemies until you remove it.
>
> —*Joshua 7:10–13*

Hit the pause button. What does this say to the declining church in America? Could it be that she is powerless against the encroachment of secularism and sensuality because she has become devoted to that which brings destruction? Is it possible that Satan and his hierarchies of evil have the legal right to defeat God's people? I fear that a lot of secular goodies—sin that needs to be exposed—are hidden in the homes of God's people, and in the church.

Repentance is long overdue. It is time to listen to God's clear instructions in 2 Chronicles 7:14 and His letters to the churches in Revelation 2 and 3. We are not standing strong against the culture and the enemies of God's kingdom, and we won't until we remove the sin and disobedience that pervades the church today.

Back in the Book of Joshua, with a lesson well learned, Joshua and the nation move across the promised territories. With God going before them, they experience great victory and growing prosperity. In chapters 23 and 24, Joshua, like Moses before him, bids God's people farewell with reminders of His faithfulness and the covenant they have established with Him.

Again there is a warning, "If you forsake the LORD and serve foreign gods, he will turn and bring disaster on you and make an end of you, after he has been good to you" (Josh. 24:20). This is the same thing God told Jacob when he returned to Bethel. The people of Israel held on to foreign gods, but the people responded, "We will serve the LORD."

I wish good news followed the life and leadership of Joshua, but it didn't. The next book, Judges, tells the sad story about centuries of Israel's unfaithfulness to the Lord. Her apostasy, with her surrender to the allurements of Canaan, provoked God's discipline. Under the difficult circumstances that followed His discipline, the people made urgent appeals to Him for help. As they repented and returned to God in revival, God raised up leaders—judges—who in God's power and wisdom threw off Israel's enemies and restored the land to peace and prosperity.

Only the grace and mercy of God spared Israel from being totally wiped out and absorbed into the surrounding nations. A sad commentary summarized Israel's condition. "In those days Israel had no king; everyone did as he saw fit" (Judges 17:6; 21:25).

The Book of Judges highlights the pattern of revival in the Old Testament. Israel went through an up and down cycle six times. The first cycle set the pattern with Othniel (Judges 3:7–11), and five more followed. They began with this tragic commentary: "The Israelites did evil in the eyes of the LORD" (Judges 2:11) and by God's grace conclude with, "the land had peace" (Judges 3:11). The cycle can be summarized as apostasy, oppression, distress, deliverance, and blessing. Unfortunately, the history of Israel's kings followed a similar cycle.

HOW DOES REVIVAL COME?

By the time King Solomon took the throne, he understood Israel's pattern of *decline.* After he completed the temple and was giving his prayer of dedication (2 Chron. 5–7), he asked God what would happen in bad times. What would God do? After two weeks of celebration, with the beautiful temple in place, the glory of God filling the house, and the people on their faces in worship, would the cycle of drift and restoration finally be broken? Wise Solomon somehow knew that life for Israel would not always be as glorious and exciting as this high point of their history and relationship with God.

After the festivities, Solomon returned to his home, probably elated with the events surrounding the dedication, and yet weary. It was then that God spoke to him in the night and answered his questions about bad times that would come.

> If my people, who are called by my name, will humble themselves and pray and seek my face and turn from their wicked ways, then will I hear from heaven and will forgive their sin and will heal their land.
>
> *—2 Chronicles 7:14*

In God's preface to this in verse thirteen, He did not say "*If* things get bad," but "*when*" (NIV). Terrible times were to be expected; times of sin, drift, economic failure, and the judgment and discipline of God. This was God's instruction for what to do when things got bad. It was a wake-up call for His people when life was unraveling and they realized that the covenant curses were operating because of disobedience. It was a blaring alarm that would shatter painful spiritual stupor and direct them when they recognized that they had pulled up anchor from the Rock of Ages and were in dangerous drift. This verse was written for all God's people for all time. The past cycle would be a continuing pattern.

Of the many volumes written on revival, only a few authors concentrate on the Old Testament. One such author is Dr. Walter Kaiser, one of the most highly regarded orthodox (evangelical), Old Testament schol-ars, and the president of Gordon-Conwell Theological Seminary. I was amazed by his grasp of the Old Testament and his textual dexterity and ability to quote and explain it from the Hebrew language when I took a doctoral course he taught.

In his book, *Quest for Renewal: Personal Revival in the Old Testament*, Kaiser defines revival and then establishes the need for it. He moves immediately to what God told King Solomon when He appeared to him at night. "Almost everyone," he writes, "will agree that the greatest text on the subject [of revival] is 2 Chronicles 7:14."[4]

IS 2 CHRONICLES 7:14 ONLY FOR ISRAEL?

Some say that 2 Chronicles 7:14 is only for Israel. They tell the church, "Don't go to 2 Chronicles 7:14! If you want revival in the church, find your instructions in the New Testament." It is true that the New Testament calls us to obedience and back to our first love, and Revelation chapters 2 and 3 provide good examples. Yet, excellent scholarship has built a strong case that God's words to Solomon and Israel are for all God's people through-out all time. Yes, it is specific to Israel. It is what she must do in her dark and sinful times. And it is what the church must do if she wants to see a firestorm of the Holy Spirit sweep across the nation.

In the text, God addresses "my people." This is our first clue that God's instructions go beyond Israel. It is for God's people throughout all time, all who are called by His name. It is a progressive pattern. They must humble themselves, pray, seek God's face (having to do with pas-sion, spiritual hunger, intensity, and deep desire), and repent (turn from their wicked ways). God will answer by forgiving their sin and healing their land; He will transform their cities and nation. These are the revival instructions for God's people throughout all history.

Kaiser explains it well:

> First of all, the phrase "If my people" is immediately glossed, or explained, by the little exegetical, or appositional, clause "who are called by my name," a clause so distinctive to both Testa-ments that its meaning could never be confused or mistaken. What God or man named, he owned and protected, whether

that included cities (2 Sam. 12:28; Jer. 25:29; Dan. 9:18–19), the temple (1 Kings 8:43, Jer. 7:10–11,14,30, 32:34, 34:15), or men and women (Isa. 4:1; Jer. 14:9, 15:16). Thus when Israel walked by faith, Moses promised that "all peoples of the earth will see that you are called by the name of the LORD" (Deut. 28:10). In the same way, James noted how God did "visit the Gentiles, to take out of them a people for his name" (Acts 15:14, KJV). Most convincing of all is the appearance of the phrase in Joel 2:32, "all who call on the name of the LORD will be saved." Those who did not believe were "like those who [were] not called by my name" (Isa. 63:19) The fact that Peter used this expression on the day of Pentecost to inaugurate the age of the Spirit, the New Covenant, and the church is not altogether accidental. Therefore, although this promise was originally given to Israel, it is also most assuredly intended for us.[5]

The same principle is used in applying the New Covenant to the church. Kaiser said that the New Covenant was first addressed to the house of Israel and to the house of Judah (Jer. 31:31). However, he added, we are ministers of the New Covenant (2 Cor. 3:6) and drink the blood of the New Covenant in the Lord's Supper (Matt. 26:28; 1 Cor. 11:25).

The climactic fulfillment of the New Covenant will not come until the Deliverer comes to Zion and he banishes ungodliness from Jacob in that day of the restoration of Israel to her Lord and her land (Rom. 11:25–27).[6]

Kaiser's final argument came from two New Testament scriptures. Romans 15:4 taught, "Everything that was written in the past was written to teach us, so that through endurance and the encouragement of the Scriptures we might have hope." Also, 1 Corinthians 10:11 added: "These things happened to them as examples and were written down as warnings for us, on whom the fulfillment of the ages has come."

The Old Testament scholar explained that 2 Chronicles 7:14 formed the outline for the Book of 2 Chronicles and set the agenda for the material selected from the lives of five key Davidic kings of Judah. One of the four steps given in 2 Chronicles 7:14 was strategic for each king. Kaiser said that the pattern formed an *inclusio* with the first and last king sharing the same step. An *inclusio* in the Hebrew Bible was a literary device that created a frame by placing similar material at the beginning and the end of a section, word, phrase, or even a larger portion of the text. (For a complete definition and explanation, see www.wikipedia.org/wiki/inclusio.) Nearly half of 2 Chronicles was dedicated to the leadership of these five kings and the revivals they led.

1.   "Humble yourselves": Rehoboam in chapters 11–12
2.   "Seek my face": Asa in chapters 14–16
3.   "Pray": Jehoshaphat in chapters 17–20
4.   "Turn from your wicked way": Hezekiah in chapters 29–32
5.   "Humble yourselves": Josiah in chapters 34–35[7]

As he concluded his discussion of 2 Chronicles 7:14, Kaiser addressed the need for revival in the church. He wrote:

> Therefore, today's believers must begin by following God's program for revival as set forth in 2 Chronicles 7:14, or our land will lie fallow and overgrown. If we follow the instructions of this revival text, the floodgates of heaven will open, and both we and our culture will be the surprised recipients of the blessing of God. When will revival come? No finer answer can be given than our paradigmatic verse from 2 Chronicles 7:14, which laid out the program for each of the revivals that span almost half of the chapters of that great book…[While] we affirm that the work is most decidedly and uniquely the special prerogative of our Lord…we must prepare for that revival by following the four verbs…humility …prayer…spiritual hunger (seeking God's face)…confession and repentance.[8]

THE CHARACTERISTICS OF OLD TESTAMENT REVIVAL

Several authors identify features, keys, or characteristics of revival in the Old Testament. Kaiser lists ten *features* from the ten Old Testament revivals that he identifies. The revivals are listed in Table 1 on page 87. The features are:

1. Get rid of idols.
2. Confess sin.
3. Serve the Lord alone.
4. Let God be God.
5. Seek the Lord.
6. Pray to the Lord.
7. Turn back to the Lord.
8. Humble yourself before the Lord.
9. Renew the work of God.
10. Rejoice in the Lord.[9]

Lewis Drummond, the president of Southeastern Baptist Theological Seminary and the Billy Graham Professor of Evangelism and Church Growth at Beason Divinity School, has also written about revival. In his book, *Eight Keys to Biblical Revival,* he states that 2 Chronicles 7:14 gives us the keys that unlock revival. Compare Drummond's *keys* to the *features* on Kaiser's list.

1. Seek God.
2. Humble yourself.
3. Seek His face; God reveals Himself as hope (2 Chron. 29–32).
4. Turn from your wicked ways; God reveals Himself as holy (Exod. 32–34).
5. Forgiveness of sins; God reveals Himself as grace (Jon. 1–4).
6. God will hear from heaven; He reveals Himself as power (Acts 1–2).
7. God will heal our land; He reveals Himself as love (1 Sam. 4–7).
8. God reveals Himself as available when we pray (2 Chron. 6–7).[10]

Compare the nine *characteristics* of Old Testament revivals listed in Wilbur M. Smith's revival classic, *The Glorious Revival Under King Hezekiah.*

1. Each revival occurred in a time of deep moral darkness and national depression.

2.   Each revival began in the heart of one consecrated servant of God, who became the energizing power behind the revival, the agent God used to quicken and lead the nation back to faith in and obedience to God.

3.   Each revival rested upon the Word of God, and most of the revivals were the result of a return to the Word of God and the preaching and proclamation of the law of God with power.

4.   All the revivals were marked by a return to the worship of Jehovah.

5.   Each revival, except the last two, witnessed the destruction of idols. These exceptions—the revival under Zerubbabel with Haggai and Zechariah in Ezra 5–6 and the revival under Nehemiah with Ezra in Nehemiah 8:9 and 12:44–47—occurred after the exile, when no idols were found in Judah.

6.   Separation from sin was noted in each revival, with the exception of the revival under Asa. However, we can assume that it was also true then because of the context of the revival and the behavior of God's people.

7.   Every revival included a return to the offering of blood sacrifices.

8.   Almost all the revivals resulted in an experience of exuberant joy and gladness among the people of God. The only two where this was not recorded were the revival in the house of Jacob, and the revival during the reign of Josiah (where it can be assumed from the context and the behavior of God's people).

9.   Each revival was followed by a period of great prosperity.[11]

Smith identifies twelve revivals in his book. They are listed in Table 1 below.[12]

TABLE 1

LISTS OF OLD TESTAMENT REVIVALS	
Wilbur M. Smith	**Walter C. Kaiser**
1. Jacob—Gen. 35:1–15	1. Jacob—Gen. 35:1–15
2. Asa—2 Chron. 15:1–15	**10. (2. Moses—Exod. 32–33)**
3. Jehoash—2 Kings 11–12 2 Chron. 23–24	**11. (3. Sam.—1 Sam. 7:1–13)**
	12. (4. Elijah—1 Kings 18)
4. Hezekiah—2 Kings 18:4–7 Chron. 29–31	5. Asa—2 Chron. 14–16
	6. Jehoshaphat—2 Chron. 20
5. Josiah—2 Kings 22–23 2 Chron. 34–35	7. Hezekiah—2 Chron. 30:1–9
	8. Josiah—2 Chron. 34–35
6. Zerubbabel, Haggai Zechariah—Ezra 5–6	9. Zerubbabel—Hag. 1; Zech. 1:1–6
7. Nehemiah, Ezra—Neh. 8:9; 12:44–47	10. Nehemiah—Neh. 8
8. Jonah in Nineveh	
9. Jehoshaphat—2 Chron. 17:6–9	
(Revivals are added to Smith's list to total twelve.)	

Humility, prayer, spiritual hunger (seeking God's face), and confession and repentance, the four steps of revival in 2 Chronicles 7:14, are woven throughout the above characteristics and the revivals that are identified. Take note! Write it down! If you want revival, follow the instructions! Revival comes in obedience to 2 Chronicles 7:14.

Revival begins in difficult, dark days, times of moral decline, national depression, and despair. If God's people follow the instructions, great results follow. Smith calls it "exuberant joy." Leaders are necessary. Prayer is central. History demonstrates that the church has prayed its way to the outpouring of God's Holy Spirit. If the church of Jesus Christ wants to see historic revival sweep through her cities and nations with a mighty, rushing wind and the *firestorm* of Pentecost, she can be sure of what it will take.

Brian Edwards adds important characteristics of revival in his book, *Revival! A People Saturated With God.* While he agrees that the role of prayer is central, he explains that prayer, repentance, worship, and evangelization are heightened and intensified in revival.[13]

He also concludes from his study that two significant things could be missed. First, revival is *spontaneous* and *unpredictable.* (Note that I have included the description *spontaneous* in my definition of revival in chapter 2.) Revival comes suddenly at a time of God's choosing. God moves in revival when His people set the stage by seeking Him in prayer, but the timing is up to Him. Second, Edwards says that God's people become generous and redemptive as demonstrated in 2 Chronicles 31:4–5.

Out of dark and difficult times, as God's people humble themselves, repent, and seek Him desperately, God affirms His willingness to heal and restore His people.

> But Zion said, "The LORD has forsaken me, the Lord has forgotten me. Can a mother forget the baby at her breast and have no compassion on the child she has borne? Though she may forget, I will not forget you! See, I have engraved you on the palms of my hands; your walls are ever before me."
>
> —*Isaiah 49:14–16*

Although some authors emphasize different characteristics of revival, the characteristics emerge very clearly in their writings. Any list of characteristics must include prayer, for I believe it is the primary catalyst that begins the move of God in revival. That is why I have included a chapter on prayer in this book. Revival depends on passionate prayer and repentance—a significant spark that lights revival flame.

Elana Lynse, whom I quoted earlier, identifies the role of prayer in the Old Testament. Prayer, she said, is at the core of 2 Chronicles 7:14. It was central in releasing great renewal leaders like Moses (Exod. 2:23–25) and Samuel (1 Sam. 1:1–20). It was at the heart of Nehemiah's leadership and ministry, and the result of his prayer (Neh. 1:6–11). It was a movement of God that produced the rebuilding of the wall of Jerusalem and ultimately a new nation in the Book of Nehemiah.

Lynse did not stop with these leaders. She explained that the intercessory prayer of other great leaders in Israel's history must include Abraham (Gen. 18:16–33), Moses (Deut. 9:25–29), Solomon (2 Chron. 6:12–42), Asa (2 Chron. 14:11), Hezekiah (2 Kings 19:14–19), Daniel (Dan. 9:1–19), and Ezra (Ezra 9:1–15).[14]

Read through 2 Chronicles, but wear your seat belt. It is an up and down ride of obedience and blessing, a fall into sin and disaster, and then revival. As the author rehearses the history of the kings, one thrills with the stories of those who are deeply committed to God and to serving His kingdom. The nation enjoyed the covenant blessings of God, and they prospered in every way as they lived in obedience to Him. Then came a godless king who led the nation into sin and the disaster of God's covenant curses.

Solomon began well, but then he went down. Asa was a great king, but he, like others, drifted into sin in the end. Hezekiah stood out among the kings like a diamond that reflected the glory of God. Toward the end of his reign he became proud, but he repented and was honored in death. So went the story of Old Testament revival.

Oh, that God's people today would drop much of the church schedule and begin to pray and seek God's face—His presence! How did exiled Nehemiah respond when he heard about the tragic conditions of his homeland? "When I heard these words I sat down and wept, and mourned for days; fasting and praying before the God of heaven" (Neh. 1:4, NRS). Wallis affirmed, "Revivals have always flowed out of praying, but not of the cold, formal, and tearless variety."[15]

Before we look at the New Testament and post-biblical revivals, a preliminary list of revival characteristics gleaned from Old Testament *firestorms* follows.

1. Revival occurred in times of personal or national crisis and great spiritual need; in times of deep moral darkness and spiritual decline among God's people, Israel, or His church.

2. Revival began in the heart of a servant of God who became the agent God used to lead His people back to faith in Him and obedience to Him.

3. Prayer was central to revival. Leaders called out to God in prayer, passionately seeking His face in repentance and in the confession of personal and national sins.

4. Revival rested upon the proclamation of God's law and Israel's return to their covenant commitments.

5. Revival in the Old Testament reflected the work of God the Father to awaken His people, Israel, to a restored relationship with Him, to obey Him and serve His purpose.

6. Revival was marked by a return to the worship of God.

7. Revival led to the destruction of idols and ungodly preoccupation's and also to separation from personal and corporate sin.

8. Revival brought a return to the offering of blood sacrifices in the Old Testament.

9. Revival resulted in an experience of exuberant joy and gladness among God's people.

10. Revival was followed by a period of prosperity and social reform, Israel's covenant blessings.

Looking at revival in the New Testament and at five selected post-biblical revivals will help us refine these characteristics. It will also add consistency and affirm that there is a definite pattern of revival throughout all of history.

There is a threshold over which revival and transformation comes. The Lord has come in answer to prayer. The result has been the salvation of many and church growth... There are no cases of transformation that have happened by sheer programming, numbers of people involved, or human effort.[1]

—George Otis

5

New Testament Firestorms

W HAT'S MORE EXCITING than reading the story of Jesus' life? If you want to know what God is like, read about Jesus, for He was God in human flesh. But don't stop there. It is also exciting to read about the first century church and see how she turned her world upside down. The life, death, and resurrection of Jesus, the apex of human history, brings radical change to the lives of people.

The Old Testament is the story of God preparing for His coming. Israel is the agent for accomplishing God's redemptive purpose and preparing the way. After Pentecost, the church picked up God's redemptive mission. Unfortunately, the pattern of drift in the Old Testament was repeated throughout the history of the church.

It is more challenging to trace the pattern of revival in the New Testament because the storms are different. However, they are revival nevertheless. The entire book is a firestorm—the spread of the gospel and the growth of the church—that burned its way across the pages of the Book of Acts.

What can compare with the firestorm of Pentecost (Acts 2) and the fire of God falling on the gentiles in Acts 10? What can compare with the power of God falling on Saul as he walked along the road, on a mission to destroy followers of Jesus? Knocked to the ground gasping, he cried, "Who are You, Lord?" This brilliant man, the persecutor of Christ-followers, in time wrote most of the New Testament. God grabbed his attention, his heart, and his brilliant mind.

Let's look at revival in the New Testament. Can we isolate revivals from the birth of the church and the spread of the gospel? Malcolm McDow and Alvin L. Reid answered this in their book, *Fire Fall: How God Has Shaped History Through Revivals*. I like their title. Is there anything more like fire fall or firestorms than the work of the Holy Spirit?

The New Testament is the biblical account of one long spiritual awakening that had many revivals within the revival. Just as the First Great Awakening (1726–70) and the Second Great Awakening (1787–1843) in America were long revivals with many crests, the New Testament renewal, which was the first awakening in history that followed this pattern, experienced many revivals.

The revival started in 26 AD with John the Baptist in the Jordan region; intensified under Jesus; crested at Pentecost; spread to Samaria, Damascus, Cornelius' house, Antioch, Cyprus, Pisidia, Philippi, Thessalonica, Ephesus, and other places; and ended with John the Apostle on the island of Patmos. During those seventy years the ministries of John the Baptist, Jesus, and the advent of the Holy Spirit at Pentecost transpired. The church was birthed and expanded from the upper room to the outer borders of the Roman Empire, and even beyond. The authorship of the twenty-seven books of the New Testament and many other accomplishments occurred. Indeed, this renewal established the pattern for all subsequent biblical awakenings and is a magnificent example of the true meaning of revival.

Jesus came in "the fullness of time" (Gal. 4:4, NRSV). Before His coming, God was at work preparing the world for His royal arrival. As a vital part of the preparation, God united the Mediterranean world under one Roman government and prepared the Jewish nation with a Messianic hope. The New Testament revival occurred within the Roman world, Hellenistic culture, and a Jewish context.[2]

The Church

The church was birthed in a firestorm of the Holy Spirit at Pentecost. Oh, how amazing it must have been in the upper room! Flames of fire rested on the heads of those gathered in unity and prayer. The roar of a mighty "violent wind" (Acts 2:2) drew a crowd, just as people run to see a burning building. That day people heard about Jesus in their own language from those who could not naturally speak it. Thousands came to faith and left the city to carry the fire to the known world.

When the church was born, God's people were clothed with the power of the Holy Spirit. Just as Jesus, the incarnation, walked this earth in human flesh, He also walked it through His church, the body of Christ. The church was Jesus on Earth again in human flesh, the second incarnation. In unity, she loved as Jesus loved and taught what He taught. He was alive again on Earth.

Tragically, the church has fit this exciting description only at high points of renewal. Only when revival has pulsated through her veins has she looked like the early church. Otherwise, in disunity and disobedience, she has presented a crippled Christ, the body nearly severed from the head. The real Jesus has not been very visible. Love has not been her distinctive mark. Troubled by sin and the same old drift into the surrounding culture, she has followed the pattern of the Old Testament and mirrored God's people, Israel.

The church has gone from vibrancy—new wine in new wineskins—to encrusted institutionalism, a form of godliness without the power of God and the fresh wind of the Holy Spirit blowing through her. She had a great beginning, but syncretism and universalism have watered down her dynamic faith to a tasteless brew of anything but living water.

Since Pentecost, the followers of Jesus have had a distinct advantage over God's people in the Old Testament. There, the Holy Spirit was given to individuals to accomplish specific callings or assignments. From Pentecost forward, the Holy Spirit came to reside in each believer. He gave spiritual gifts that are necessary for making His followers all God designed them to be. Through community, Jesus was to be alive again on Earth, with all the individual gifts blended together to form the body of Christ.

Christ gave the church the Great Commandment, to love God with all her heart, soul, mind, and strength, just as Jesus loved the Father when He was here. This was always the top priority: to know Him, to seek His presence, and intimacy with Him. And, it appears to have been the greatest downfall, especially in the western church. Jesus' intimacy with the Father set the pattern for us. In choosing priorities for serving the Father, Jesus showed us what to do; He discerned what the Father was doing and joined Him (John 5:19).

Perhaps the second greatest downfall of the church has been that we have tended to do it our way or to follow patterns that are attractive to our culture. The church was to be the epitome of Jesus' love; the members of the body of Christ were to love everyone around them as they love themselves (Matt. 22:37–40). She was to be God in human flesh, living out His love and truth. The Great Commission in Matthew 28:19–20 and Acts 1:8, have always summarized the church's assignment to be God's redemptive agent in the world until Jesus returns. She has always had the assignment to be an instrument of loving transformation wherever she has been planted.

Like Israel in the Old Testament, the church is to bring glory to God through her worship and service. She is to accomplish His kingdom purpose to evangelize the world. In Acts 4:12 Peter gave a clear, strong witness as he stood before the authorities: "Salvation is found in no one else, for there is no other name under heaven given to men by which we must be saved." Acts 4:33 testifies: "With great power the apostles continued to testify to the resurrection of the Lord Jesus, and much grace was upon them all."

In the pristine days of the church, the gospel spread rapidly. Peter's preaching rang clear with the central message of salvation through Jesus the Messiah. The church was alive and functioning in great power. Acts 2:38–47 has provided a snapshot of powerful early preaching and the response of people. Listen to Peter. Note the results.

> Repent and be baptized, every one of you, in the name of Jesus Christ for the forgiveness of your sins. And you will receive the gift of the Holy Spirit. The promise is for you and your children and for all who are far off—for all whom the Lord our God will call. With many other words he warned them; and he pleaded with them, "Save yourselves from this corrupt generation." Those who accepted his message were baptized, and about three thousand were added to their number that day. They devoted themselves to the apostles' teaching and to fellowship, to the breaking of bread and to prayer. Everyone was filled with awe, and many wonders and miraculous signs were done by the apostles. All the believers were together and had everything in common. Selling their possessions and goods, they gave to anyone as he had need. Every day they continued to meet together in the temple courts. They broke bread in their homes and ate together with glad and sincere hearts, praising God and enjoying the favor of all the people. And the Lord added to their number daily those who were being saved.

The church has been most dynamic and alive when she has been passionately sharing the gospel and fulfilling the Great Commission. I saw this firsthand when I served as campus pastor at a Christian university. When students were actively engaged in evangelism, locally or overseas, they demonstrated a much more vital faith and growing intimacy with Christ. Having observed the church across the nation for many years, I see the same thing. The congregations that have been passionate about reaching people in their cities and beyond with the gospel have been the most spiritually dynamic, alive, and growing, just like the church in the first century.

Lyle Shaller, who is passionate about the church and her growth, has found that 70 percent of churches in America are in "survival mode"; 25 to 27 percent are in "growth mode," and 3 to 5 percent are in "kingdom building mode." Churches in survival mode ask, "How can we stop losing members and keep our doors open?" They are shrinking. Congregations in growth mode ask, "What programs and techniques can we implement that will attract new members?" They are growing. God's people who are in kingdom building mode ask, "How can we serve people and lead them to Christ?" They are exploding in members and ministry.[3]

REVIVAL IN THE NEW TESTAMENT

Revival is the same in both the Old and New Testaments. It is a spontaneous spiritual awakening by God the Holy Spirit among His people. It comes in answer to their humble prayers, as they passionately seek God's face and repent of their sins. The awakening results in deepened intimacy with God, passion for Him, holy living, evangelism, and social reform. Cities and nations are transformed.

The difficulty of understanding revival in the New Testament has been with its spontaneity. Did the church, as she spread out over the Roman Empire, ever fall asleep spiritually? Were there times when she needed revival? The New Testament does not give long historical accounts describing the details of revival. Yet, Blackaby and King have written the following:

> New Testament churches also departed from a right relationship with God. In Revelation 2–3 we read the words of the resurrected Christ as he calls different churches to repent and return to him.[4]

At what point did this happen? In Ephesus, the church left her first love and was called to repent, to do the works they did at the beginning. In Pergamum, some followed the teaching of Balaam, as Israel did in the Old Testament. This included sexual immorality and eating food sacrificed to idols. Others adopted the doctrine of the Nicolaitans of whom Christ disapproved. The church at Sardis was literally described as dead, but she thought she was still spiritually alive. The Laodiceans were lukewarm. All these churches were called to repent or face God's judgment.

God does not change. He was the same in the Old Testament as He was in the New. He disciplines those whom He loves (Heb 12:5–11). In the Old Testament His judgment was severe at times. He sent plagues, used surrounding nations to discipline His people, and reduced the productivity of Israel's land and flocks. The purity of the New Testament church was about to be contaminated when Ananias and Sapphira tried to fake their giving in Acts 5:1–11. They died, and "Great fear seized the whole church and all who heard about these events" (vs. 11). Acts 5:12–16 says that great signs and wonders continued; unity was strong, and many were added to the church.

Although few authors have attempted to list New Testament revivals, most writers have seen Pentecost as the greatest move of the Holy Spirit in history. Some have wondered if it was revival or just spiritual birth and growth. It certainly was the birth of the church. Most would say that the disciples had placed their faith in Jesus as their Savior or Messiah before His death and resurrection. Was Pentecost then a revival? With the four hundred silent years between the Old and New Testament, I have preferred to see it as a rolling work of the Holy Spirit in the gospels and forward.

How do others view Pentecost? Arthur Wallis uses Pentecost as the pattern of revival throughout all of redemptive history, biblical and post-biblical. In his book, *Rain From Heaven,* he reaches back to the prophet Habakkuk's prayer and vision in chapter three. Putting it simply, he says, "God came." He sees this in Isaiah's prayer for God's fire to fall from heaven in Isaiah 64:1–2. Revival is what happened at Pentecost and what happened in answer to Isaiah's prayer.

Many other Old Testament prophets living in dark days found a ray of hope in the expectation of such a visitation. When we turn to the New Testament, such times are seen to be directly related to the pouring out of the Holy Spirit. As the birthday of the church, Pentecost was unique, but as a specimen outpouring of the Spirit, it was only unique in being the first…We should not be surprised to find subsequent examples of this kind of visitation in the Acts record, notably that which took place in Caesarea, which Luke describes as a pouring out of the gift of the Holy Spirit (Acts 10:45). Similarly, Paul, who did not experience the outpouring at Pentecost or at Caesarea, uses the same expression when he reminds Titus of their own experience: "The Holy Spirit, whom He poured out on us generously" (Titus 3:6, NIV).[5]

Other authors have identified New Testament revivals. Stephen Olford included a list in his book, *Heart-Cry for Revival.* In chapter two, "The Way of Revival," he wrote that the revival under John the Baptist (Matt. 3:1–12) described how revival in the New Testament happened. John called people to repentance, and his ministry of baptism provided a tangible sign of repentance. It was preparation for the coming of Jesus' public ministry (Luke 3:1–6).

Great preacher that he was, Olford described in sermonic style the quality of Christian faith that has prepared the way for Jesus Christ to be known. This faith was expressed through the lives of believers, and he urged prayer, personal holiness, and love. He taught the importance of replacing defeat and disbelief with faith, humility, and separation from friendship with the world.

Olford included Pentecost (Acts 1:13–2:41) in his list of New Testament revivals. Following the pattern of preparation for the disciples in the upper room, he outlined how believers could be prepared for a visitation of the Holy Spirit. He called for unity among believers, unity in prayer, and prayer with expectancy, anchored in God's promise to move by the power of His Spirit.[6]

What kept the wake of revival spreading to thousands? It was the practice of being saturated with the person and ministry of Jesus. Acts 4:13 captures it when it says the Jewish religious leaders recognized that Peter and John had been with Jesus. "Jesus," Olford wrote, "was the subject of their confession, the strength of their conviction, but also the substance of their communion. Their ministry was accompanied by miraculous events and by the fullness of the Holy Spirit."[7]

E. D. Head, the former president and professor of evangelism at Southwestern Baptist Seminary, lists the following New Testament revivals.

1. A revival in the streets: Matt. 21:1–17
2. A personal work revival: John 1:35–51
3. A woman's revival: John 4:28–42
4. A revival in a graveyard: John 11:30–45
5. A revival in a church: Acts 4:23–37
6. A revival in a carriage: Acts 8:26–40
7. An unlawful revival: Acts 10:23–48
8. A Sabbath Day revival: Acts 13:44–52
9. A revival by the riverside: Acts 16:9–15
10. A revival in a jail: Acts 16:23–34
11. A revival in Rome: Acts 28:30–31; Phil 1:12–14[8]

Head's list and helpful outlines could be used for a great teaching series, but some of the revivals do not fit the definition. For example, it is questionable to say that Jesus' triumphal entry into Jerusalem qualifies as a spiritual awakening. Yes, as Matthew 21:10 says, "the whole city was stirred." And there were miracles, the significant fulfillment of prophecy, and the cleansing of the temple.

However, even though the crowds laid down clothing and branches as though to welcome a triumphant king, the text does not support the belief that the people were sincerely placing their faith in Jesus as Messiah. They wanted a king to overthrow Rome. When Jesus didn't step up to their expectations, they soon began to shout, "crucify Him." Other accounts on Head's list of revivals—such as the calling of John, Andrew, and Philip in John 1:35–51—do not fit the definition of revival either.

However, a spontaneous move of God with a broad impact is found in Acts 10:23–48, the story of Peter's visit to a gentile's home. It wasn't kosher to do this; it was unclean. As Peter obeyed God and broke out of his religious box, "the Holy Spirit came on all who heard the message" (vs. 44). The gospel had come to the gentiles.

In Acts 13:44–52, the account of Paul and Barnabas's ministry in Pisidian, Antioch describes what must have been a spontaneous visitation of the Spirit. "The whole city gathered" (vs. 44), and "the word of the Lord spread through the whole region... The disciples were filled with joy and with the Holy Spirit" (vs. 49–52).

The following list fits the definition I have given for revival in both the Old Testament and the New.

1. Awakening under John the Baptist: Matt. 3:1–12
2. The revival at Pentecost: Acts 2:1–4, 14–47
3. The revival in the church: Acts 4:23–37
4. The revival that grew out of fear: Acts 5:1–16
5. The revival that grew out of persecution: Acts 7:54–8:25
6. The revival with Cornelius and the gentiles: Acts 10:23–48
7. The Pisidian Antioch revival: Acts 13:44
8. The revival at Ephesus: Acts 19:1–20

When you add the calls to repentance in Revelation 2 and 3, an overview of New Testament revival takes shape. In both the Old and New Testaments, the characteristics of revival emerge, as listed earlier on page 90.

This, to the best of my understanding, is biblical revival. When revival comes, it will have these characteristics. How can we set the stage for biblical revival? It is already set. We are at the first characteristic. It is exciting to see the second and third characteristics: individuals and ministries are leading a growing prayer movement across the nation. It could very well be that God's purifying judgement will fall and that the fire of the Holy Spirit will be poured out at the same time as God's people fall on their faces before Him.

In the last ten years, God has called many city-reachers to serve their cities full time. One friend and fellow city-reacher has tried to identify these. He has concluded that there is not a city of any significant size in America that does not have someone who could be identified as a city-reacher. They have been calling the church to unity, prayer, and repentance. Some have focused on unifying congregations to meet the social needs of cities. Others, like Connie and I, have been cheering for this approach and participating, but our passion has been to call the church to unified prayer and repentance.

OBSTACLES TO TRANSFORMATION

George Otis, Jr., the producer of the *Transformation Videos,* was interviewed by Mission America on a conference call, February 8, 2005. Otis has traveled the world and documented amazing moves of God in revival and area-wide transformation. His videos are a must-see for anyone who is seeking God for revival. During the interview, Otis said:

> There is a threshold over which revival and transformation comes. The Lord has come in answer to prayer. The result has been the salvation of many and church growth....There are no cases of transformation that have happened by sheer programming, numbers of people involved, or human effort. It happens by divine intervention. It comes in answer to prayer as in the prayer Jesus taught us, "Thy Kingdom come; Thy will be done on earth as it is in heaven." It is the Emmanuel Principle—God with us. God comes. Weeping and praying in sack cloth...returns God to His people, as in the Old Testament.[8]

Otis said that transformation is not occurring anywhere in the western world, and he listed what he believed were the biggest obstacles:

1. We need to see a change in the way we do church in the West. It is obvious that we are falling short.

2. Where transformation has been scrutinized there is a common thread or simple formula: abandonment with expectation. In each community where transformation occurred, Christians wanted the presence of God to invade their area or church so much that they were willing to do anything to prepare the way for the Lord, and they believed He would come or respond (2 Chron. 7:14; Isa. 58).

As the phone interview continued, Otis said that most churches never experience abandonment. Instead, it is more like business as usual. We must come to a place of desperate hunger, willing to give up everything with great expectation of what God will do. America is marked by unbelief that God will come. If you ask some Christians, they can tell you how revival comes—through humility, unity, worship, and prayer—but they do not act on it. We need to pray, *God, stimulate in me a deep hunger for the things that will attract Your presence.*

A leader who was participating in the interview asked, "What is the role of theology?" Otis replied that there is a stream of theology, not major or widespread, that sees prayer and passion for revival as presumptuous. This perspective causes faith to dissipate or reduces it to a hope that somehow God in His sovereignty will choose to come in His way, in His time, and on His agenda.

Another listener asked about the significance of leadership. George responded, "Huge." He observed a curious thing:

> The best leaders are found at the back of the line; ones God chooses. God reads hearts, not lips (1 Cor. 1:20–31). They may not have degrees or compelling gifts. It is like the Hebrides revival of 1949. Two ninety-year old women, house bound, mostly blind, began to pray for hours each day.

Many people fast and pray, he said, but they are unwilling to conform to basic obedience…how we treat others, unity of the church, justice, and the like (Isa. 58). Sadly, he added,

> There is a growing passion for God's presence, but it is lacking in pastoral leaders. They are distracted by external and internal pressures and distracted by the American culture that has seeped into the church making pastors busy and compartmentalized.

Otis concluded with the tragic fact that the flower of revival usually falls off within thirty-six months of the time it began to bloom. Why? Revival brings about prosperity. Then we plateau and throttle back. It is drift. To sustain revival, we have to continue to do what birthed it. We also have to give away the blessings in kingdom transforming ministry. We must stimulate an appetite for revival. We must train people in the principles of revival, and we must serve in local venues to do the things that attract the presence of God.

After an hour-long conference call, I hung up the phone in tears. I was excited to have confirmation about how revival comes, but my heart was breaking with frustration because hedges still divide the church. She is locked up in cultural, racial, and denominational obligations that keep her nominal, unable to make a significant impact for Christ. We need a breakthrough!

The church today is like the rural English countryside, divided by nice hedges that keep us separate. We want God only within the hedges we have built. There are exceptions. Some American churches have decided to suspend all they are doing to seek God for revelation and direction, to prepare the way of the Lord. No matter what congregations choose to do, they must become desperate for God's presence to return to basic, New Testament Christianity.[9]

Are the characteristics of revival in the Old and New Testaments the same as in the major revivals of post-biblical history? Was George Otis, Jr. singing an age-old song? This is the subject of the next chapter, "Great Storms of Our Time, Part 1." The stories of these amazing moves of the Holy Spirit raise new hopes that massive revival, the Third Great Awakening, could be just around the corner.

What is the condition of your city? How many homeless roam the streets? Who cares for them? What is the condition of the public schools in your town? Do civic leaders promote gambling, secularism, corruption, and the abortion industry? Is there any sense of stewardship before God in their leadership?

—Dr. Bob Griffin

6

Great Storms of History: Characteristics 1–3

A S WE SEE the secularization of America and the limited impact of the church, nothing is more encouraging than stories of great revivals. Hope is born, longing begins to stir, and passion for more of God is ignited. Perhaps America will once again be aflame with the fire of the Holy Spirit and moved by His mighty rushing wind. Waiting for this is a little like giving birth: labor pains, pushing, straining, and praying. Long before labor and birthing, there is excitement, preparation, and anticipation.

Another picture helps me. Sometimes waiting for revival is like the heavy and exhausting vigil at the bedside of a close friend or family member who is fighting for life. Time passes, and the loved one's health seems to get worse with little hope of recovery. Every effort is made to turn the tide, but nothing seems to make a difference. Then, miracle of miracles—suddenly, or within a few brief days—strength returns, and health and vitality is restored. The celebration is great, and the story is told over and over with excitement, thanksgiving, and praise to God. New life and health are like spring after a cold, harsh winter. Light breaks through dark and dire circumstances.

In the history of revival, we first observe that spiritual and social life decline to the place where God's people fear the death of the church, the severe judgment of God, and the crumbling of a once proud, strong society and culture. Some are feeling this way about America, and comparison may be made to the Roman Empire, which declined from strength and greatness to non-existence.[1]

As we look at European nations through which great moves of God once swept, we find that the church is nearly non-existent. Wales, for example, is in great spiritual need today. In much of Europe, Christians form 1 or 2 percent of the population. The church that once produced great theology, and even historic reformation, lies near death and certainly has little impact. When I was traveling in Europe in the mid-1990s, I observed beautiful church buildings that had become mosques.[2]

The need for revival screams out of the darkness. It is engraved on my soul from the days I traveled in Europe and evangelized with college students. Many of the European nations are pagan, secular, and ruled by dark, spiritual powers. Once strong, proud, and important, they are rich in history but unimpressive and weak on the international horizon. They stand as monuments of past greatness, but have fallen far from the days of revival and the vibrant Christianity that followed.

I am among many who fear that this describes America's future, apart from a great move of God. The national church seems impotent to push back the invading darkness. America has become untethered from the strong moorings and ethics of the Ten Commandments. Some oppose the practice of placing the phrase *In God We Trust* on our coins, and biblical marriage is under attack. Families continue to unravel. The percentage of stable nuclear families, with a husband and wife who keep their vows for life, is a small minority. The gay agenda continues its attempts to win the day and redefine marriage.

The infanticide of pre-born children is over forty million, and the hideous procedure of partial birth abortion is affirmed as a right. I have heard others say in pastoral groups that a few so-called ethicists in the secular world are even saying that a newborn has no right to life after birth if the mother does not want the child. Pornography in America has grown into an industry of fifty-one billion dollars a year. According to Microsoft Worldwide, it is fifty-seven billion (see www.blazinggrace .org/pornstatistics.htm). Sin funding, such as gambling, is becoming an addiction to people and governments, a financial dependency that is rarely broken. It is time for the church—the redemptive agent in the culture—to arise from her sleep and begin to repent, pray, and return to her biblical moorings and mission.

Chuck Colson, in *Breakpoint*, December 30, 2004, highlights the tragic loss of religious freedom in America.

Pastor Richard Parker was ready to deliver the customary invocation prayer at the Warren County, Virginia, Board of Supervisors meeting. Just before he was to speak, the county attorney alerted him that he could say "Lord" or "God," but not Jesus. Pastor Parker rightly walked out, explaining that as a Christian pastor, he would not pray if he had to "exit Jesus." Literally hundreds of violations of religious freedom in the United States have been documented by a Texas-based group, the Liberty Legal Institute. On October 20, 2004, it presented the Senate Judiciary Subcommittee on the Constitution, Civil Rights and Property, a fifty-one-page report titled "Examples of Religious Hostility in the Public Square."

A Houston teacher trashed two students' Bibles, then marched them to the principal's office and threatened to report their parents to Child Protective Services for allowing them to bring Bibles to school. A ninth-grader got a zero on her research project because she chose Jesus as the topic; worse, her teacher refused to let her submit a substitute project. A St. Louis public school student was "caught" praying over his lunch. As punishment, he was lifted from his seat, reprimanded in front of classmates, and ordered never to pray in school again.

At a New Jersey Veteran's cemetery, an honor guard member was fired for telling a deceased veteran's family, "God bless you and this family." A Minnesota state employee was banned from parking in the state parking lot, because his car had sticker saying, "God is a loving and caring God" and "God defines marriage as a union between a man and a woman."

McKinney, Texas, "has no problem with people meeting in their homes for football watch parties, birthday parties, or even commercial gatherings to sell Tupperware." But when a few couples gathered in a pastor's home, they were told, "The city prohibits a church meeting in a home unless the home sits on at least two acres." And on it goes, for fifty-one well-documented pages.[3]

As we recognize the critical nature of our spiritual and social maladies, we must remember that it is never too late for revival. We can receive great hope by studying five of the great revivals of post-biblical history. From the accounts of these high points on the mountain range of revival history, we can discern if they had the same characteristics as the moves of God recorded in Scripture. Did they affirm 2 Chronicles 7:14 as the pattern of revival? If they did, the church today can be confident that her obedience to God's Word will again result in another outpouring of the Holy Spirit.

By understanding revival characteristics that have been consistent throughout time, the church can set the stage for another great historic move of God, perhaps the last one before Jesus returns for His Bride. As God raises up prayer leaders and humble passionate preachers who call God's people to holiness, God will not compromise His promises in Scripture. As the church falls before God in humble repentance and prayer and seeks His face and presence, she can count on revival. History proves that God is faithful to do what He has said He will do. With this assurance, we will take a brief overview of five great firestorms of our time. (See Psalm 145:13.)

FIVE FIRESTORMS OF REVIVAL

The First Great Awakening (1726–1756) flamed up first in Europe and then spread to the American Colonies. Puritanism had declined and faded away after the monarchy of England was restored in 1660. Godlessness, crime, and immorality followed, and deism—a form of godliness that was without power and very short on truth—arose and militated against Christian faith. A passionless brand of Christianity was prominent and defenseless.

The roots of revival came from Pietism, which was led by Philip Spener and August Francke. They birthed the Moravian movement in 1457, and Count Nikolaus Ludwig Von Zinzendorf—a central figure in the movement—sparked the flames of revival through a prayer gathering that began in his home in 1724 and lasted for one hundred years, twenty-four hours a day. John Wesley had contact with the Moravians in 1738 and came to personal faith in Christ shortly thereafter. He became one of the greatest revivalists of history. Cairns told the story of the First Great Awakening this way.

> The American Awakening occurred from 1726 to 1741 in the middle colonies among the Reformed and Presbyterian groups, in the New England Congregational churches, and in the South among the Baptists. In England, Wales, and Scotland, the Awakening was predominantly Calvinistic. In England, the awakened Christians

formed a Methodist group which later broke into Moravians, Calvinistic Methodists under Lady Huntingdon, and Arminian Methodists under the Wesleys. Multiplied thousands of Christians were renewed and sinners brought to salvation. Faith in Christ was made practical in loving service to man.[4]

George Whitfield emerged from the First Awakening as one of the most famous preachers and revivalists of history. Unity of doctrine, itinerant preaching, spontaneity in prayer and preaching, and the strong involvement of everyday people were characteristic of the revival. The breadth of its impact on the Western World was amazing.

The Second Great Awakening (1776–1810) was, like the First Great Awakening, transatlantic. It was Protestant and Anglo-Saxon and included a Scandinavian slice under a revivalist by the name of Hans Hauge. Similar to the backdrop of the preceding revival, conditions were terrible. In the church, doctrinal division and politics produced a very dull spiritual edge. Rationalism was the curse of the day and had taken over colleges, which interestingly were a common setting for the move of God's Spirit. God was gracious to bring His light into the dark places.

The most common setting for the revival was the camp meeting. Charles Finney was one of the great preacher-leaders, as well as the Methodist circuit riders, Devereux Jarratt, Peter Cartwright, and Isaac Backus. In a foreshadowing of the current prayer movement, Backus began concerts of prayer in New England. The revival profoundly touched Methodists, Presbyterians, and Baptists.

Lay preachers were prominent as they had been in the First Great Awakening, and they became the promoters of social reform. Thousands came to Christ. Could it be that the next great awakening across the United States will not come out of the religious establishment? Some have said it will be birthed among youth, while others believe it will spring up in the marketplace.

The New York City Prayer Meeting Revival (1857–1858) was birthed in prayer meetings through the ministry of Jeremiah Lanphier in New York City and Phoebe and Walter Palmer in Canada. When Lanphier called people to a noontime prayer meeting in the city, times were tough spiritually, socially, and financially. Crime was pervasive, and banks were closing. Again, the church was impotent. Prayer was predominant in the revival, and preaching, although it was important, played a secondary role. One million came to Christ, one million came back into the church, and reports indicate that one million came to faith in Christ when the revival spread to Europe. Society was dramatically impacted.

The Welsh Revival of 1904 was, like the preceding revivals of post-biblical history, born out of great social and spiritual need. In her book, *Cure of All Ills*, Mary Stewart Relfe reported that Wales topped the world in need. It was "drunken and profane due to its poor struggling mining economy. The church was largely ignored and the few believers distraught."[5] Evan Roberts was the most predominant leader in the revival, but others played important roles, too. They included Rosina Davies, who was converted through the Salvation Army, and Jessie Penn-Lewis, who set up the Welsh Keswick movement. Seth Joshua also stood out as a key leader.

Cairns has summarized the results of the Welsh Revival:

> Prayer, praise in ecstatic singing, and testimony of lay converts with much emotion was emphasized. Roberts was an exhorter rather than expositor…The 1904 awakening was more subjective and often mystical in its expression of God's love, loyalty to Christ, and the cross, the need for the Holy Spirit, and a love for souls. It did…have practical results in the short run. Confession of sin brought restitution of property and money. Gambling and the consumption of liquor dropped in many places. Swearing in the mines ended; the pit ponies even had to learn to respond to a new vocabulary of gentle words to replace the cursing of former days.[6]

The Azusa Street Revival (1906–1909) launched the Pentecostal movement and denominations across America and the world. Vinson Synan has reported:

> Central to the Azusa event was a teacher, Charles Parham; a preacher, William J. Seymour; a city, Los Angeles; a journalist, Frank Bartleman; and a building, the Azusa Street Mission.[7]

Bartleman wrote an eyewitness account, *Azusa Street: The Roots of Modern-Day Pentecost*, and Synan introduced this book in 1980. He stated, "Within a short time, the Azusa Street Pentecost became a world-wide move of the Holy Spirit." Synan also wrote that one million persons per year had accepted the premises of the Los Angeles Pentecost. In 1975, Synan reported that ten thousand Pentecostal Catholics met in Rome. Also, in 1978, two thousand Anglicans or Episcopalians met in Canterbury Cathedral in London for a similar meeting.[8]

Richard M. Riss reports that the results of the revival were nearly as great as the Protestant Reformation.

> The early Pentecostal Revival came as one of the greatest revivals of the modern period, perhaps almost as important in its effects as the Protestant Reformation of the sixteenth century…It brought into existence hundreds of ecclesiastical bodies and denominations worldwide, many of which quickly became some of the fastest growing religious organizations in the world.[9]

By 1980 fifty million people claimed to be Pentecostal, and many Charismatics were salted through more traditional denominations. Today this widening stream of Christianity includes some of the largest and fastest-growing congregations (Paul Yonggi Cho's church in Seoul, Korea, is the largest) and denominations in the world. In mission circles, Pentecostals are known for having the greatest impact for the gospel around the world. More recent movements of the Holy Spirit—such as Pensacola, Florida, the Airport Fellowship in Toronto, Canada, Smithton, Missouri, and the fourteen-year movement of revival across Argentina—are Pentecostal or charismatic in nature.

REVIVAL'S TEN CHARACTERISTICS IN THE FIRESTORMS OF OUR TIME

Can we identify the characteristics of Old and New Testament revivals in these firestorms of our time? I believe the answer is a confident yes! As we look at each characteristic in these five great revivals, we will find ourselves reviewing what God has also done in His Word. Our hunger will grow for a powerful move of God in our day. *Do it again, Lord! Come*

Holy Spirit! May your fire fall again as at Pentecost.

As we have noted, the instructions for revival, given in 2 Chronicles 7:14, came in answer to Solomon's prayer just after he dedicated the temple in 2 Chronicles 6. He had asked God to hear Israel's cry for help when they suffered difficult circumstances—defeat by an enemy, no rain in their agrarian world, famine, plagues, blight or mildew, locusts or grasshoppers, disaster, and disease—because of sin.

God's answer was clear. If they would humble themselves, pray, seek His face, repent, and turn from their sinful ways, He would hear from heaven and forgive them. He would heal their land and even bring them back to it if it had been taken away. When God answered Solomon, He used the language of the king's prayer. Needless to say, this is the climate in which the firestorms of revival begin to heat up today.

CHARACTERISTIC 1
DARK AND DIFFICULT TIMES:
STORMS APPEAR ON THE RADAR

> Revival occurred in times of personal or national crisis and great spiritual need, in times of deep moral darkness and spiritual decline among God's people, Israel, or His church.

We rarely hear a radio or TV news report without a weather forecast. Why do we care about the weather report? It helps with our planning: Can we travel? What shall we wear? Should we avoid excessive heat or a dangerous storm? Meteorologists often point to the Doppler radar to show the beginning of a pattern, "We'll keep an eye on this for you," they promise.

Revival radar, prior to every great firestorm of history shows dark clouds of economic, spiritual, and social decline. It is ominous, but it is out of these circumstances that longings for much better times begin to grow. What is happening to us? Why are we so much like the culture, sucked into a secular way of thinking and living? Why does God seem so far away? Why are things so bad? Why is sin so blatant?

Why do we fail to make an impact? Why aren't we pushing back the encroachment of Satan? Why is the church losing? When did competition and empire building sneak in and steal our obedience to Jesus' critically important prayer in John 17:20–23? Why don't our cities know that the Father sent the Son as a result of our unity as Christians? Why are we not obeying the command for unity in Ephesians 4:1–16 and Psalm 133? The pattern is consistent. It is the first characteristic of revival.

The First Great Awakening

Authors McDow and Reid have described the conditions before the First Great Awakening. They explained that there was great spiritual decline and liberalism, and higher criticism and theological liberalism had emerged from the Enlightenment. Spiritual life had been squeezed out of Christian schools and the church.[10] Darkness has often been the greatest just before the dawn, as it was just before the First Great Awakening.

McDow and Reid reported that Deism was growing in popularity, and Christianity became encrusted with powerless tradition. Pastors were some of the most ritualistic and enslaved by tradition, dry in faith like a terrible drought, "more concerned with political unity than spiritual fervency." The result was "a twin problem, which brought the need of awakening to the forefront: deviant orthodoxy (a departure from historic Christian belief) and dead orthodoxy (correct belief devoid of corresponding Christian behavior)."[11]

The wealthy were addicted to a lifestyle of behavior that would have eventually produced as much chaos as the French Revolution. "The worst vices prevailed, and were by many considered marks of good breeding; if any one condemned them, he was set down as a fool, and jeered at for his pains." Most rural laborers had no formal education, and "it is scarcely surprising that they were very widely sunk in depravity and animalism."[12] The consumption of alcohol in England rose from five and one half million gallons in a population of six million in 1735 to eleven million gallons in 1751. Signs advertised the problem on pubs: "Drunk for one penny, dead; drunk for two pence and straw for nothing."[13]

Crime was out of control, and as in today's American cities, to go out at night was to risk serious mugging. An attorney, by the appropriate name of Blackstone, reported that after hearing every clergyman of any note in London, not one sermon "had more Christianity in it than the works of Cisero."[14] Johnson quotes Archbishop Secker as saying, "An open and professed disregard to religion has become, through a variety of unhappy causes, the distinguishing character of the present age."[15]

The American Colonies were not much different than Europe. People had courageously gone west for freedom but it had turned into license. According to Warren A. Candler, "The French and Indian wars had fed all the fiercest passions of human nature…and relaxed all moral convictions and restraints. Every form of vice prevailed as never before in their history."[16]

The Second Great Awakening

Unfortunately, things were bad again before the Second Great Awakening. The source was different, however, because spiritual decline and apostasy had grown out of a more intellectual climate. Doctrinal division and politics had soured the results of the First Great Awakening. A flood of rationalistic literature came from France and Great Britain, which Dr. Timothy Dwight described as "the dregs of infidelity vomited on us…the whole mass of pollution emptied on this country."

The effect on U.S. colleges was incredible. Students embraced rationalism and called themselves by the names of famous skeptics and infidels. Even Bible colleges became centers of skepticism; Christian students became such a minority that on some campuses they felt compelled to meet secretly.[17]

The French had helped the colonists fight for freedom, but they also brought "much of the spiritual and moral refuse of the Enlightenment to the New World. Skepticism, Deism, even atheism, came through the writings of Voltaire, Rousseau, and David Hume" and were promoted by people such as Thomas Paine, Ethan Allen, and others who opposed biblical Christianity.[18]

The French and Indian Wars (1754–1763) and the Revolutionary War (1776–1783) distracted many from the fiery faith of the First Great Awakening. It was like an unsuspected curve ball. Many clergy left their congregations to report for military duty. Worship was neglected. The impact of the Enlightenment, the war efforts, and the drift from the church, produced tragic results. McDow and Reid state, "promiscuity, profanity, gambling, and drunkenness increased."[19]

Warren Candler calls the days before the Second Great Awakening, a time "of great religious declension." He adds, "When it began, the state of both the nation and the churches was gloomy by reason of faith decayed and hearts grown cold. Iniquity abounded and skepticism prevailed on all sides." Reflecting on the negative impact of the Enlightenment, he quotes a bishop who remarked, "I can truly say that…in every educated young man in Virginia whom I met I expected to find a skeptic, if not an avowed unbeliever."[20]

Have you ever been to a congregational meeting where church business is conducted and problems are defined? Consider the rise of secularism in America, as it was described in the following entry from a General Assembly meeting of the Presbyterian church in 1798.

> Formidable innovations and convulsions in Europe threaten destruction to morals and religion…We perceive with pain and fearful apprehension a general dereliction of religious principles and practice among our fellow-citizens, a visible and prevailing impiety and contempt for the laws and institutions of religion, and an abounding infidelity, which, in many instances, tends to atheism itself. The profligacy and corruption of the public morals have advanced with a progress proportionate to our declension in religion. Profaneness, pride, luxury, injustice, intemperance, lewdness, and every species of debauchery and loose indulgence greatly abound.[21]

Many would say that the denomination's secretary, using the much more formal old English, could have been taking the minutes of a congregational meeting in our times. Many colleges and universities sneer at anything biblical or Christian. Religion is OK, tolerance is nearly worshiped, and spirituality detached from biblical truth is trendy. Universalism in main line denominations, the trend of hanging out at bars after work, the party scene—promoted by sitcoms and the media—and the disgust of the secular and liberal press with anything Christian, are very similar to what Candler has reported.

The New York City Prayer Meeting Revival

Before the Prayer Meeting Revival in New York City, it was same old song, second verse, a whole lot louder and a whole lot worse! J. Edwin Orr wrote, "Religious life in the United States of America was in decline." There were many reasons for decline, political and social as well as religious. He believed that the conflict over slavery diverted attention from spiritual pursuits to this wrenching concern.

Also, the church had been attacked by a widespread teaching that Christ was going to return in 1843 or 1844. When it didn't happen as William Miller and others said it would, there was a general loss of faith in spiritual things, and public confidence was shaken. Orr said that some responded by becoming bitter infidels while others embraced a cynical materialism. Churches were ridiculed and church growth could not keep pace with the decline in attendance.[22]

Prosperity affected Christianity negatively. The accumulation of wealth was a national priority. Warren Candler wrote, "As gains grew, godliness declined. Men forgot God in pursuit of gold."[23]

The passion for the accumulation of available and inexpensive land on the frontier complicated the situation. (Perhaps the same could be said of the explosion of technology today.) Opportunities for land were abundant for those who could take a little risk. They joined many who caught the excitement of moving to the new edge of opportunity as the frontier stretched west. It all fell apart with a financial crash, the third in American history. Panic followed prosperity. Banks failed, factories were shut down, and at one time, thirty thousand men were unemployed in New York City alone. Hunger and despair characterized the city.[24]

America and the church have been plagued by the same pattern in recent decades. It was also a pattern throughout Israel's history. *God's people have not been able to handle His covenant blessing of abundant prosperity and blessing* (Deut. 28:11). Rather than turning God's gifts into generosity—"in all things at all times, having all that you need, [so you can] abound in every good work" (2 Cor. 9:8)—God's people have spent it on their pleasures (James 4:3). Somehow the age-old truth, "You cannot serve both God and Money" (Luke 16:13) has not been understood and applied.

The Bible has made it clear. "Keep your lives free from the love of money and be content with what you have" (Heb. 13:5–6). First Timothy 6:10 warns, "For the love of money is a root of all kinds of evil. Some people, eager for money, have wandered from the faith and pierced themselves with many griefs."

So what was happening in America before passionate prayer began to grow in New York City? The issue of slavery was growing into a national crisis in the 1840s and 1850s and gave birth to the Civil War. The Missouri Compromise of 1850, the Fugitive Slave Law, the Kansas-Nebraska Act, abolitionist agitation, and the march of slavery in the South and West became the birth pangs.

But it wasn't just slavery that troubled the nation. Heavy Irish and German immigration in the same period introduced the European idea of how to live on Sunday: after a morning service it was just like every other day in the week. The Economic Panic of 1857 reached a crisis level on October 14 and made people more aware of the impotence of the material goods and toys. Corruption during the Grant administration put a sour taste in the mouths of many and a call began to arise for morality.[25]

The Welsh Revival of 1904

The Welsh Revival of 1904 followed the same pattern of spiritual, moral, and societal decline. Great revival had swept Wales in 1859, and some reports indicated that as many as one hundred thousand people came to faith in Christ.[26] Unfortunately, by 1904, the country was in great decline again. Henry Johnson included a quote from Evan Roberts's journal as he told the story of the Welsh revival, "For a long, long time I was much troubled in my soul and my heart by thinking over the failure of Christianity. Oh! It seemed a failure; and I prayed and prayed."[27]

An article by Dean David Howell, written just before he died in 1902, was one of the tools God used to call the nation to prayer. In his article, Howell described the conditions of the day. Preaching he said was "able, scholarly, interesting, and instructive...but little unction and anointing." Biblical concepts like conviction, conversion, repentance, adoption, sin, became foreign ideas. He concluded, "The principal need of my country and dear nation at present is still spiritual revival through a special outpouring of the Holy Spirit."[28]

A Chicago newspaper characterized the national spirit of Wales as "dull depression and gloomy doubt." The report stated that the time was ripe for a great religious revival. The efforts of many, it reported, were unable to "stem the flood of evil or stop the growth of pleasure-seeking and mammon worship. A generation had risen that had not seen the arm of God working as it had done in 1859 in Ireland."[29] Wales was in bad spiritual and social shape.

The Azusa Street Revival

Close on the heels of the 1904 Welsh revival, the Azusa Street Revival began in 1906. In his introduction to John Bartleman's eyewitness account of the revival, Vinson Synan described Los Angeles, California before the revival. It was "a city of some 228,000, which was growing at a rate of fifteen percent a year...[Many strange] religions and a multiplicity of denominations occupied the religious attentions of the city." Los Angeles was a melting pot with large numbers of Hispanics, Chinese, Russians, Greeks, Japanese, Koreans, and Anglo-Americans.[30]

Expressing the need for revival, one of Bartleman's journal entries stated, "The Holiness people are loaded down to the water's edge with a spirit of prejudice and pharisaism...sectarian prejudice, a party spirit, and pessimism."[31] In an entry dated July 1905, he wrote, "The present warlike attitude and distress...makes us wonder if the judgment to follow may not even plunge us into the tribulation." Another journal entry said, "Unbelief of every form has come in upon us like a flood. But lo, our God comes also."[32]

Relfe described the spiritual and social scene in America around the turn of the century, just prior to revival.

> Spiritual decadence pervaded society in the late 1890s. Corruption, immorality, drunkenness, cults, gambling, and agnosticism rose in proportion to the church's ineptness. By the turn of the century, the glory had departed, the saints had defected, the salt had lost its savor, the world had lost its light, and deep moral darkness prevailed.[33]

She quoted a statement from a publication called, *The Western Christian Advocate*, printed in 1902.

> Again, there is the outcry of a public aghast at a seeming "tidal-wave of immorality" breaking over the land. On every hand political corruption is rife. Divorce and lax marriage relations, fornication, and adultery scandalize us. In great cities, like New York and Chicago, murders, suicides, and "hold-ups" crowd on each other's heels. The newspapers every morning are a record of a carnival of crime.[34]

Relfe quoted from an article written in 1904 in the Christian Harvester: "Revival is needed. Revival is possible. Revival will set back the strong tide of sin and corruption that is sweeping away the life of the nation."[35]

McDow and Reid wrote that reconstruction, the spread of the nation westward, industrialization, technical advances like the automobile, telephone, and electric light, as well as immigration and urbanization, seriously affected the nation. "Spiritual life ebbed, although there were some bright spots." On the horizon were emerging "trends that would strangle the spiritual life of the nation." Some of these trends were the rise of higher criticism, the promotion of a social gospel, and the incipient decay of conviction brought on by liberalism.[36] The stage was set again for a move of God.

What's the condition of your city? How many homeless roam the streets, and who cares for them? What is the condition of the public schools in your town? Do civic leaders promote gambling, secularism, corruption, and the abortion industry? Do they express any sense of stewardship before God in their leadership? How bad, dark, and difficult do you suppose it will become before God's judgment falls or He turns His back on America? Have you personally begun to pray and seek God in humility and repentance?

The first characteristic of revival revealed in the Scripture and the setting of 2 Chronicles 7:14 lines up in all five major post-biblical revivals. We in America are living in a world marked by spiritual decline and decadence, and revival can spring out of our dark and difficult times. A prayer movement is growing, but it does not appear that it has captured the heart of the church yet. How bad does it have to become before the national church wakes up and begins to passionately call upon God in large numbers?

What will it take to change our apathetic *business as usual* attitudes and break us out of the encrusted boxes of culture and religion that have grown over time? Is the church fiddling—just like Nero did in Rome— while our cities are burning with chaos, social need, and spiritual darkness? Could it be that Jesus' words in Mark 7:9—"You have a fine way of setting aside the commands of God in order to observe your own traditions"—apply today? Do the Great Commandment and the Great Commission characterize the national church?

It is time to seek God's face and to become desperate for His presence among us. Even now, the church may be awakening in prayer and repentance. The backdrop is in place for a great turn of events in the drama of revival. God calls and equips consecrated servants to pray and lead His people to repentance. This is the second characteristic of revival.

CHARACTERISTIC 2
LEADERSHIP: SERVANTS OF GOD STEP OUT OF THE CROWD

> Revival began in the heart(s) of one or more consecrated servants of God, who became the agent(s) God used to lead His people back to faith in Him and obedience to Him.

We hold monthly prayer gatherings in our city, and in almost every case, we ask people to pray in small groups. Without many exceptions, someone in each group begins to emerge as a leader. Perhaps they don't like chaos or confusion or even a sense that no one is in charge. In a similar way, God's ordained leaders begin to step out of the difficult times of characteristic number one to give leadership, particularly to call God's people to prayer. Often they are not wise, influential, or noble according to human standards, but foolish, weak, lowly, and despised (1 Cor. 1:26–29).

The leaders of revival are some of the most well-known heroes of modern faith. Many writers and many volumes capture their stories, and yet much more can be told. Think about the volumes it would take to tell the personal story of each one—their birth, God's shaping in their lives, their spiritual birth, God's calling, His unique equipping, their effectiveness, and God's unusual anointing. Because of the prayers, preaching, and leadership of these giants of faith, thousands come to faith in Christ. Cities and nations are transformed.

The First Great Awakening

The First Great Awakening had many leaders who called God's people to prayer and repentance and lit the match of revival. In the British Isles, the well-known Wesley brothers—John and Charles—along with George Whitfield ignited the move of God's Spirit. In Wales, Howell Harris and others were God's influential instruments. God's agents in the American Colonies included Jonathan Edwards and lesser-known leaders like Gilbert and William Tennent, Bellamy, Griswold, Wheelick, Robinson, and Blair. In 1740, the great revival preacher, George Whitfield came to America, and his preaching had great impact in the colonies as it did in Europe.

These men were the most visible and notable, but others were more localized or behind the scenes. They all set the stage for the movement of God. Earle Cairns believed that the leaders of Pietism laid a solid foundation for revival in Germany. As we have noted earlier in this chapter, Spener and Franckell—leaders of Pietism—along with Zinzendorf of the Moravians, were products of Pietism.

In the British Isles, primarily Wales, Jones, Harris, and Rowland were the key leaders. Cambuslang and Kilsyth were leaders in Scotland. Revival leaders in England included Arminian Perfectionists like the Wesleys, and Calvinists like Whitfield and Lady Huntingdon. Influential clergy were Venn, Walker, Berridge, Grimshaw, Romaine and Fletcher.

In the American Colonies, Presbyterians Morris and Davies in the South, and Frelinghuysen and the Tennents in the middle Colonies, were great leaders. Stearns, a Baptist, and Presbyterians, Morris and Davies, were great revival leaders. In New England, Jonathan Edwards, a Congregationalist, and Backus, a Baptist, gave leadership to the move of God's Spirit.[37]

Humanity had raced forward at unprecedented speed with the Reformation and Renaissance. The Enlightenment followed, and many no longer considered the earth to be the center of the universe. Rationalism, Deism, and Empiricism had a significant impact on western society. Although it wasn't so much a sprint toward heresy and rebellion against God and the Scripture, it stole the church's wonder and awe of God and her sense of His majesty. Spirituality took a nosedive, not of radical and sudden rejection of faith in the Bible, but "because of the drip, drip, drip of [the] culture, pushing the conviction of a transcendent God further to the periphery."[38]

The Puritan movement took a strong stand against this drift. The leaders of the movement included Laurence Humphrey, President of Magdalen College, Oxford, Thomas Cartwright, a professor of theology at

Cambridge, Thomas Wilcox, a London pastor, William Travers, a Cambridge professor, and John Bunyan, the author of *Pilgrim's Progress*. Many others stood strong against the drift in the Church of England, and their leadership shaped the early stages of revival.

The Second Great Awakening

Evangelical Protestant churches, on the defensive against Deism and rational religion through the Revolutionary era, recovered their confidence during the Second Great Awakening and were the primary revival force in the country. During the later stages of the Awakening, hundreds of thousands of new converts became full members of Protestant churches, many of them convinced that the kingdom of God was at hand.[39] Camp meetings, college revivals, and great interest in foreign missions were characteristics of this second great move of God.

Who stepped out of the crowd to pray, to preach and to call the church back to God? Outstanding people of God—called, anointed, and passionate for revival—led the Second Great Awakening. The best-known leader of the revival was Charles Finney, but there were others. At the turn of the century, itinerant preachers such as Asahel Nettleton were like harvesters who moved across fields of ripe grain and reaped great crops of new believers. Many professing Christians returned to their biblical "first love" and a renewed Christian faith.

On the college scene, students at Hampden-Sydney College in Virginia led the movement. Daniel Baker, a Hampden-Sydney student, spoke at Yale and "became the impetus of revival," spreading the flame. At Yale, Timothy Dwight, the grandson of Jonathan Edwards, became president. His preaching and teaching were a powerful force in turning the students to Christ from "deplorable" behavior and secularism.[40]

The Hay Stack Revival at Williams College in Massachusetts was well known as part of the Second Great Awakening. Student Samuel Mills led a bi-weekly prayer meeting where revival broke out. At prayer time one rainy day, students found shelter under a large haystack. This was the day that Mills proposed a mission to India, a vision that was later fulfilled when Adoniram Judson, Samuel Mott, Luther Rice, Gordon Hall, and Samuel Newell went to India as missionaries.[41]

John Erskine of Scotland was another great leader who lived during the First Great Awakening. His writing launched a Concert of Prayer movement and with it, fanned the revival that swept across England. Jonathan Edward's treatise, A Humble Attempt to Promote Explicit Agreement and Visible Union of God's People in Extraordinary Prayer for the Revival of Religion and the Advancement of Christ's Kingdom, written in 1747 after the crest of the First Great Awakening, provided fuel for the Second Great Awakening.[42] It was sent to two Baptist leaders, John Ryland and Andrew Fuller. Baptists Isaac Backus and Stephen Gano, and as many as twenty other pastors in New England, distributed a circular letter in 1794 calling for prayer for an awakening. All denominations supported the call and revival fires were fanned.

Francis Asbury was used to spark revival in camp meetings in Kentucky. On the American frontier, James McGready was one of the primary leaders, along with Lyman Beecher, James Caughey, and Jacob Knapp. Charles Finney's (1792–1847) ministry took place toward the end of the Second Great Awakening.[43]

The New York City Prayer Meeting Revival

Some believe that the Prayer Meeting Revival in New York City was an extension of the Second Great Awakening. Jeremiah Lanphier (sometimes spelled *Lamphier*) was the best-known leader. Having retired from business at age forty-eight, he felt called to do mission work in the inner city of New York, where he began distributing gospel tracts. Passionate about revival, and a man of prayer, he published and distributed handbills calling for a noontime prayer meeting. Conditions in the city and nation were terrible. Banks were closing, thousands were out of work and crime ravaged New York and many other cities. The church was weak against the pervasive strength of the darkness.

Lanphier was no stranger to revival. He came to faith in Christ at the Broadway Tabernacle under the preaching of Charles Finney, who led revival toward the end of the Second Great Awakening. In this setting, a passion for prayer and revival was birthed in Lanphier's soul. He had lived in difficult times. He had seen people begin to call out to God in prayer, and he knew its power. Only three people came to his first prayer meeting—and late at that. The following week there were six. Soon it became a daily event and within six months, one thousand were meeting for prayer at noon in New York.

The meetings grew into the thousands, according to the *New York*

Times. A reported ten thousand came to Christ in New York City alone. The movement spread to Texas, and then to the Ohio valley. One hundred thousand had come to Christ by May 1858. In Boston, Chicago, Pittsburgh, Cincinnati, and other cities across the country, prayer meetings were drawing thousands to Christ. "The Methodists and Baptists in the South gained a total of about two hundred thousand and one hundred thousand respectively in a three-year period."[44]

R. A. Torrey reported that prayer meetings were soon held every hour of the day and night in New York City, not only in churches but also in theaters and other public places. Horace Greeley, the newspaper giant, sent a reporter to check out what was happening. Although he could only visit twelve meetings, he counted 6,100 people. Relfe wrote, "Tens of thousands of New Yorkers were praying around the clock, seven days a week. The fire spread from New York to Philadelphia, and to other cities, and then swept the entire country." One million were drawn to Christ in the church and about the same number outside the church.[45]

Phoebe Palmer, one of the first prominent female preachers in America, was one of the most influential leaders. Relfe believed that Palmer's fervent prayers and ministry laid a significant part of the foundation and wrote, "For years she had been cloistered away in her prayer closet."[46] Phoebe Palmer was as influential in America as Catherine Booth was in England. Both women were great intercessors, used mightily by God. Relfe wrote,

> In the decade of the 1850s, Phoebe's physician-husband, Dr. Walter Palmer, decided to retire from his medical practice and accompany her as an evangelistic team. By the close of 1857, these anointed meetings had so impacted the churches in the eastern states that in December, the Presbyterians called for a Convention on Prayer and Revival in New York, and much of it was spent on their knees. Baptists and Methodists in New York set aside a day a week to pray in their churches for revival. By New Year's Day 1858, pastors all over the East were preaching on prayer, revival, and holiness with a social conscience.[47]

In Ontario, Canada, in October 1857, twenty-one came to Christ as Savior the first night of Palmer's meetings. Soon forty people were coming to faith every day. One hundred came to Christ on the last day of the meetings. The camp meetings at which the Palmers preached saw five to six thousand in attendance. Newspaper reports stated that revival was spreading across Canada.

Following on the heels of the prayer meeting movement, revival spread to the Confederate Army with estimates of conversions as high as one hundred fifty thousand. Revival flames were fanned through letters from home, Bible distribution, and godly officers and chaplains. This period was blessed with great itinerant preachers, including the best known, D. L. Moody. Children were not excluded from this revival. Under the ministries of Sam Jones and Edward Hammond, many children came to Christ.[48]

The Welsh Revival of 1904

The key leader of the Welsh Revival of 1904 was Evan Roberts, a miner's son, whom God called much like He called Samuel in the Old Testament. In the spring of 1904 Roberts was awakened many times during the night with a sense of God's presence. God was calling him to preach. In a meeting in September 1904, history records that Seth Roberts, a contemporary of Evan Roberts, was crying out to God, "Lord, bend us." Evan Roberts picked up on this passionate cry, and his plea became, "Lord, bend me." Roberts did not complete his education. He left school to go home to Loughor, and began to meet with young people. It was among the youth that revival broke out and began to spread as Roberts traveled and spoke. By the end of 1905, one hundred thousand were converted.[49]

Roberts was not the only key leader. Another one was Rosina Daves, who came to faith in Christ through the ministry of the Salvation Army. Many conversions were recorded in her meetings, including 250 in 1905. Seth Joshua, a Welsh Presbyterian, converted in 1872, was another influential revival preacher. Other leaders included Jessie Penn-Lewis and J. J. Welsh, who led Welsh Keswick conferences. The Keswick movement has been credited for stopping the rapid spiritual decline of the time. In one Keswick meeting, a young Welsh girl stood to her feet to declare, "If no one else will, then I must say that I do love the Lord Jesus Christ with all my heart." It was this simple testimony that sparked revival in the group.[50]

Dean David Howell, another significant leader, wrote an article that spread across the nation. In it he described the appalling conditions he

observed in the church and called for "a spiritual revival through a special outpouring of the Holy Spirit." W. S. Jones, the pastor of a Welsh
Baptist congregation in Scranton, Pennsylvania, experienced a personal
transformation in his own life and returned to Wales with a passion to
see revival among clergy.[51]

Leadership is God's way of shaping and reshaping His people. They rise
out of the pre-revival soil like spring crocuses pushing through the snow
and ice of winter. They call God's people to prayer and repentance. The
bloom of hope is birthed and dreams begin to take shape for a mighty
move of God to revive the church and to reform society.

The Azusa Street Revival

The Azusa Street Revival, like the other four revivals, can be credited
to chosen people, called and empowered by God to lead the church back
to her *first love* and biblical mission. Richard Riss writes about the larger
story of the Pentecostal movement that was birthed at Azusa Street.

> The early Pentecostal Revival came as one of the greatest reviv-
> als of the modern period, perhaps almost as important in its
> effects as the Protestant Reformation of the sixteenth centu-
> ry...It brought into existence hundreds of ecclesiastical bodies
> and denominations worldwide, many of which quickly became
> some of the fastest growing religious organizations in the world.
> The Pentecostal Revival started at Azusa Street in Los Angeles in
> a dilapidated building that once served as a Methodist church.
> Continuous meetings were held...every day for a period of three
> years...becoming known throughout the world as the focal point
> of the Pentecostal outpouring of God's Spirit.[52]

William J. Seymour, an African-American Holiness preacher, was the
leader God used to spark the Azusa Street Revival. He was a disciple
of Charles Parham, whose ministry was known for the baptism of the
Holy Spirit, authenticated by speaking in tongues. There had been several
localized revival movements in Parham's ministry. Seymour caught the
fire, and the mantle from his mentor fell across his shoulders. He had fire
in his bones.

The Azusa Street movement began in cottage prayer meetings led by
Seymour. It was in the home of Richard and Ruth Asberry "that the Spirit

of God fell on April 9, 1906, after many months of concerted prayer."[53] *It was a firestorm!*

Prior to the outpouring, Frank Bartleman, a young holiness preacher and emerging writer, had distributed tracts and preached on the streets of Los Angeles and in holiness missions. He had a deep passion not only for revival, but also to meet the needs of the poor. Bartleman was one of many who had heard F. B. Meyer tell about the Welsh revival when he came to Los Angeles on April 8, 1904. Meyer had met with Evan Roberts, the spark plug of the Welsh outpouring and carried the revival torch from Wales by often describing the events of what happened there. The stories burned like fire within Bartleman, who longed for a similar move of God in America, especially in Los Angeles.[54]

Bartleman and Seymour were the key leaders of the Azusa Street Revival, with F. B. Meyer carrying the spark from Wales. It was obvious, again, that out of dark and difficult times, God raises up leaders to pray, to call the church to prayer, and to preach conviction that sparks repentance across the church.

CHARACTERISTIC 3
PRAYER: IGNITING THE FIRE; FANNING THE FLAMES

> Prayer was central to revival. Leaders called out to God in prayer, passionately seeking His face in repentance and in the confession of personal and national sins. In many instances, they led God's people to do the same.

Nothing is more central to revival than passionate prayer. In fact, there has never been a revival without it. Brian Edwards says it well:

> You cannot read far into the story of a revival without discovering that not only is prayer part of the inevitable result of an outpouring of the spirit, but from a human standpoint, it is also the single most significant cause.[55]

It is time for God's people to pray; *really* pray. Jesus said, "My house will be called a house of *prayer* for all nations," not the "den of robbers" it had become (Mark 11:17, author's emphasis). Is the church across America a house of prayer? What would Jesus say about today's church?

Many things characterize the church, from contemporary worship to a vast diversity of programs for a variety of needs. I can think of only a few major congregations that have a reputation for making prayer central. The Brooklyn Tabernacle in New York City is one of these. The House of Prayer in Kansas City, as I understand it, doesn't claim to be a church. However, its twenty-four hours a day, seven days a week, harp and bowl services (Rev. 5) seem to show us something of what Jesus had in mind for His community of faith.

I believe that prayer is not only how revival comes, but it is also how God gets His work done. It is no wonder that prayer is at the pinnacle of 2 Chronicles 7:14. It is also no surprise that the enemy comes to steal this strategic weapon and to encumber the church with its traditions and cultural activities. Encrusted ecclesiology hinders the life and flow of the Holy Spirit and keeps the church bound to her old wineskins.

Matthew Henry wrote, "When God intends great mercy [for His people]...the first thing he does is to set them a-prayin'." John Wesley said, "God does nothing but in answer to prayer." Arthur Pierson captured the importance of prayer in one sentence. "There has been not one great spiritual awakening in any land which has not begun in a union of prayer."[56]

The First Great Awakening

Prayer was as central to the post-biblical revivals as it was for those throughout Scripture. The roots of the First Great Awakening were planted in Germany through the amazing life and ministry of Count Nikolaus Ludwig Van Zinzendorf. A Moravian, he established a community of believers called the *Herrnhut (The Lord's Watch)* in 1724. Prayer became central to the life of that community and was the staying force. It is difficult to imagine the duration and passion of the Moravian prayer meetings, as the community prayed for 100 years, 24 hours a day! It was reported, "In this, even children wept with power before God."[57]

John Wesley met a group of Moravians on a ship when he was coming to America. Would you have believed it? Wesley had little assurance of his salvation and was impressed with the faith and assurance of the Moravians during periods of danger at sea. Obviously they had an Anchor in the storm. It was an unlikely encounter, except in answer to prayer and

God's sovereign shaping of circumstances. However, it began Wesley's passionate search for what was missing in his own relationship with God. He wanted the kind of faith that gave confidence in difficult situations.

In prayer and through the study of Luther's *Preface to Romans*, Wesley came to the assurance of salvation through faith in Christ as his Savior. In his unique style, he described it this way. "I did trust Christ, Christ alone for salvation; and an assurance was given me that He had taken away my sins, even mine, and saved me from the law of sin and death."[58]

John Wesley became one of the greatest revival preachers of history and certainly God's instrument of revival in the First Great Awakening. Who could have guessed that this would happen because of the impact of godly Moravians on a ship in the middle of the ocean? The influence of these prayer warriors was immense, touching not only John Wesley, but also his friends in the Holy Club at Oxford University. Among them was George Whitfield.

Listen to the exciting account of the *Holy Club* as told by Wesley Duewel.

> In the early 1730s the Wesley brothers gathered several student friends into John's room at Lincoln College, Oxford University, to earnestly seek to be holy. Membership ran ten to fifteen, and never more than twenty-five.
>
> On New Year's Day, 1739, John and Charles Wesley, George Whitfield, and four other members of the Holy Club, plus about sixty other like-minded people, held a love-feast in London at Fetter's Lane. "About three in the morning, as we were continuing instant in prayer, the power of God came mightily upon us, inasmuch that many cried out for exceeding joy, and many fell to the ground (overcome by the power of God). As soon as we recovered a little from that awe and amazement at the presence of His Majesty, we broke out with one voice, 'We praise Thee, O God; we acknowledge thee to be the Lord.'" This event has been called the Methodist Pentecost.
>
> Five nights later, eight of these "Methodists" prayed and discussed 'till the early morning hours and left with "the conviction that God was about to do great things." Another night that week a group of them met and spent the whole night in prayer.

The next weekend, January 14, 1739, Whitfield was ordained. He spent the day before his ordination in prayer and fasting, praying on into the evening. Sunday morning he arose early to pray. "When I went up to the altar, I could think of nothing but Samuel's standing as a little child before the Lord…When the bishop laid hands upon my head my heart was melted down, and I offered my whole spirit, soul, and body to the service of God's sanctuary!"[59]

Whitfield had been converted in a time of despair, after he had dropped out of the Holy Club. As he searched for truth and a personal encounter with God, the answer came in a profound divine encounter. In a ministry launched in prayer, Whitfield preached to as many as thirty thousand at one time with amazing, life-changing results. Some reported that he gave eighteen thousand sermons. He worked and preached tirelessly, but his secret was time alone with God in prayer. He usually rose at 4:00 a.m. and sometimes spent whole nights in reading and devotions.[60]

McDow and Reid affirmed the impact of prayer on the First Great Awakening: "By the turn of the eighteenth century…most believed that only united, earnest prayer could bring a divine outpouring." They show that the emphasis of preachers became prayer, rather than calling people to change their behavior. "Revival of religion became the phrase used in the 1720s," they wrote. "Ministers began calling people to seek God's face in prayer, in order that He would lead the people into revival."[61]

Long before massive prayer gatherings and movements, small groups have agonized in prayer and repentance. This is good news and encouraging for thousands of groups that have been meeting across the nation, spending time in prayer for each other and for their cities. With biblical authority, they have pushed back the pervasive darkness over their areas. This has been the pattern in our city. We have gathered with others for prayer in strategic places across the city: City Hall, a judge's chambers, the local jail, the school district office, and in two other locations in the heart of the city each week. Our monthly area-wide prayer gatherings have sometimes been small—from sixty to one hundred—but powerful.

God has answered prayer throughout history, just as He promised, when only two or three have met together in His name. Revival has come. In times when there seemed to be little change, encouragement has come from God's promise: "Be strong and courageous, for your work will be rewarded" (2 Chronicles 15:7, NLT).

Johnson recounts the sparks created by the flint of prayer across London.

> In London, although the darkness was widespread, gleams of light shone here and there, in the towns, and in country places. Spiritual religion was not left without witness. A few men and women were praying, waiting, and watching for the coming of the power of God to banish darkness, and breathe new life into the heart of the nation...Day and night the prayer went up from the faithful disciples of Christ as they witnessed the degradation, the wickedness, the brutality, and the spiritual lifelessness of their countrymen.[62]

The Second Great Awakening

Before the Second Great Awakening, wickedness reached such a crescendo that men of the cloth were despairing about the future of Christendom. Into these conditions, came Isaac Backus, a man of prayer. Known as much for his praying as his exhorting, he had an encounter with the Holy Spirit that drew him to the conclusion: There's only one power on earth that commands the power of heaven—prayer.[63]

Backus wrote a paper, "Pleas for Prayer for Revival of Religion," that was patterned after a British Prayer Plan. He delivered it to clergy of all denominations and pleaded for churches to open for prayer all day the first Monday of every month. Baptists, Presbyterians, Congregationalists, Reformed, and Moravians approved the plan, and Francis Asbury adopted it for all Methodists. Thus, America was moved to pray for revival through a network of organized prayer meetings. The united prayer effort, initiated by one lone man, brought...heaven down...In 1798 revival fires began to burn again in New England.[64]

On the frontier of America, James McGready, a staid Presbyterian pastor, heard about the movement of God's Spirit. Revival fire began to ignite in his soul, and he wrote in his journal:

> In addition to praying all day the first Monday of each month, I insisted my people also spend each Saturday at sunset to Sunday at sunrise in prayer for Revival...The depth of seeking God's

> face and repentance were amazing. The winter of 1799 was one
> of weeping and mourning with the people of God.[65]

At one point, McGready called the Church of South Central Kentucky
to a four-day observance of the Lord's Supper. Revival broke out, and
people met God in dramatic ways. A similar meeting was held in Cane
Ridge in Bourbon County, with the same results. Three months later
another area-wide communion was held. This time it was called a camp
meeting. Twenty thousand came, and thousands were converted.[66]

Prayer and the Second Awakening were joined at the hip. In 1747,
John Erskine of Scotland published an article just after the crest of the
First Great Awakening, to encourage God's people to gather in prayer
and seek Him for an outpouring of the Holy Spirit. Jonathan Edwards'
treatise, "A Humble Attempt to Promote Explicit Agreement and Visible
Union of God's People in Extraordinary Prayer for the Revival of Religion
and the Advancement of Christ's Kingdom," was based on Erskine's article. In 1784 Erskine sent Baptist leaders John Ryland and Andrew Fuller
the treatise. Thus began what was soon a "concert of prayer" throughout
England. Soon reports of revival... spread across the nation.[67]

The first sparks of revival in the Second Awakening began on college
campuses. Prayer and study meetings spread, and waves of revival soon
swept campuses into the growing tide of awakening. At Hampden-Sydney College in Virginia, a group of four students met to pray, study, and
worship. Fearing the wrath and mockery of fellow students, they met in
the woods away from the campus. John Brown Smith, the college president, had come to faith in Christ during the First Great Awakening, and
he knew the power of prayer. He offered encouragement and support,
and prayer continued and grew. The results were amazing. Revival swept
through the campus several times during the next three decades.

The Hay Stack revival at Williams College in Massachusetts was also
well-known, so named because praying students found shelter under
a haystack during a rainstorm. The passionate prayer of the students
sparked a firestorm of God like that of a haystack going up in flames.[68]

It was prayer that sparked revival at Yale. In the fall of 1796, only one
freshman, one junior, and eight seniors professed faith in Christ. President Dwight, with scholarship and passionate faith in Christ, taught stu-

dents biblical truth, and deism was demolished at the school. Story after story recorded the work of the Holy Spirit as revival spread across college campuses as a result of Dwight's influence.[69]

The New York City Prayer Meeting Revival

The Prayer Meeting Revival of 1857 is the thrilling story of a sparsely attended prayer meeting that grew into a massive firestorm. At first it was like the small spark from a flint, but it ignited an explosion of revival across New York City and beyond to other major cities and around the world. It began when Jeremiah Lanphier handed out inexpensive handbills inviting people to pray at noon. At first he thought no one would show up, but finally, several came. The little group that met in a small second story room in downtown New York multiplied to thousands who prayed together seven days a week across the city.

Add the powerful impact of Phoebe Palmer to the role of Jeremiah Lanphier, and you have built a package of dynamite. She and her husband were powerful prayer warriors as much as they were revivalists. Thousands came to their meetings in both Canada and the United States, and revival followed them.

Do we really want revival today? It is ours if we will pray. Prayer is at the center of revival. It is at the heart of the instructions for revival in 2 Chronicles 7:14. Small sparks of persistent prayer can burst into a firestorm. When the church is passionate about fervent, effectual prayer, she can declare, "Revival is on the way."

The Welsh Revival of 1904 and the Azusa Street Revival

What was the role of prayer in the Welsh and Azusa Street Revivals? It is the same story, the story of prayer. Both of these revivals were a part of the Pentecostal revival that began as early as 1900. Some believe Charles R. Parham lit the spark of the Azusa Street Revival. He took his first church—a Methodist Episcopal church in Kansas—when he was nineteen. It wasn't long, however, before he left the church to become a nondenominational evangelist. In 1900 he opened a Bible school with only one text, the Bible. Unique to the school was "continuous prayer...maintained in the tower."[70]

Prayer and Bible teaching laid a solid foundation for the revival that followed at Azusa Street. The chairman of the Rockford Renewal

Ministries board, an avid student of prayer and revival, told me the following story from his reading on the Azusa Street revival. On one occasion, after Parham gave teaching on the gifts of the Holy Spirit, the class began to pray that the gifts of the Spirit would be expressed through them. Prayer extended into the evening, and at the stroke of midnight, the class erupted with speaking in tongues. J. W. Seymour was in Parham's class.

This was the man who held a cottage prayer meeting on Azusa Street in Los Angeles, California, the setting at which the fire of God erupted. As the fire spread through similar meetings, the movement became known for what some call "Pentecostal distinctives." The meetings included prayer for healing, the experience of the baptism of the Holy Spirit, and speaking in tongues.

As a result of the Azusa Street Revival, ten million people throughout the world—2.3 million in the United States alone—held Pentecostal views by the year 1960.[71] By 1980, there were fifty million classical Pentecostals, (people who believe in the baptism of the Holy Spirit accompanied by speaking in tongues), in innumerable churches, and missionary outreaches in practically every nation of the world. Untold numbers of charismatics, in every denomination, have traced at least part of their spiritual heritage to Azusa Street.[72]

Frank Bartleman left a personal account of the movement of God at Azusa Street, and it is a thrill to read. Living in poverty and making great sacrifices (even the death of one of his children), he served God with great passion. Prayer was as central to his life as breathing. Brief sketches from history demonstrate the influence of this humble, passionate man. Listen to part of his exciting narrative.

> About the first of May a powerful revival broke out in the Lake Avenue M. E. church in Pasadena. The young men who had been dug out in the meetings in Peniel Mission…attended this church. They had gotten under the burden for a revival there. In fact we had been praying for a sweeping revival for Pasadena…then we began to pray for an outpouring of the Spirit for Los Angeles and the whole of Southern California. The Spirit is breathing prayer through us for a mighty, general outpouring. Great things are coming. We are asking largely, that our joy may be full. God is

> moving. We are praying for the churches and their pastors. The Lord will visit those willing to yield to Him. And the same is true today of the Pentecostal people. Their ultimate failure or success for God will be realized just at this point.[73]

Other snapshots of prayer power are taken from Bartleman's first-hand account. A congregation was waiting for a speaker who had just returned from the revival in Wales, and Bartleman wrote, "I started the service…on the church steps…We had a season of prayer…The evening was a steady sweep of victory."[74] Later, at the beginning of the cottage meetings, he recorded, "I kept going day and night…exhorting continually to prayer…I started a little cottage prayer meeting where we could have more liberty to pray."[75]

Just as the revival was about to break at Azusa Street under the leadership of Seymour, Bartleman wrote, "We had the devil to fight…The priests were alive unto God…through much preparation and prayer."[76] He also noted, "Brother Seymour generally sat behind two empty shoeboxes, one on top of the other. He usually kept his head inside the top one during the meeting."[77]

It was not only at Azusa Street that passionate prayer was taking center stage. During the same period of time, the people of Moody Church were passionately praying in Chicago, where two thousand members were added to Moody Church in a period of eight years. Although it wasn't part of the Pentecostal movement, it certainly was part of the prayer fuel that sparked revival across the nation.

In January 1898, at the conclusion of an entire week of prayer at the church, R. A. Torrey and the teachers and leaders of Moody Bible Institute began a weekly prayer gathering. It wasn't long before four hundred were meeting to pray for revival each Saturday evening, and they continued these meetings for three years. A passionate remnant would stay until 2:00 a.m. or longer. During this time, Torrey was "impressed in one meeting to ask God to use him to lead a worldwide revival."[78]

God answered Torrey. It was like the calling of Saul and Barnabas. The church was worshiping and fasting when God said, "Set apart for me Barnabas and Saul for the work to which I have called them" (Acts 13:2). That is what happened at Moody, and it is an example of what happens when God's people commit themselves to prayer. They become a part of a global awakening of His transforming power. For example, in 1902, Torrey spoke for large gatherings in Australia and New Zealand producing "revival-like scenes." The revival followed a Saturday morning prayer meeting of pastors and laymen that extended from 1890–1901. Torrey is known generally as a great preacher, educator, author, and evangelist, but his skills were refined in prayer. Two of his classic books on prayer are listed in the bibliography. There were over two thousand groups praying with forty thousand involved all together.[79]

God tells us what to do so revival will come. In the middle of the drift and impotence of the church in America today, he calls us to passionate prayer. It is time to quit wringing our hands and cursing the darkness. Instead, we must lift our hands in prayer and call forth the light. It is time to spark an inferno of repentance that will birth a firestorm of the Holy Spirit and sweep across America and the world. It is time for the Third Great Awakening to burst across the nation.

A haunting question stands in the shadows of revival history. Why haven't great revivals lasted longer? I have identified the reason as the pattern of drift. God's people, alive with passion for Him and for serving His redemptive purpose, become comfortable and apathetic. They take God and the moving and power of His Spirit for granted. It is just like people who do not work hard at their marriage relationship. After several years, their first love fades into ordinary routines. Communication becomes relegated to short quick-answer verbal exchanges, unless there's a fight. Then the conversation is longer, heated, and destructive. That, too, characterizes much of the church today.

And that's the way it becomes with God—times of brief praise, a little thanks and a short "gi'-me" prayer on the way to work or as we drag ourselves out of bed in the morning. Passionate prayer becomes foreign to believers and to the church. We forget the basics of Christian faith, the Great Commandment, and the Great Commission. Rather than proactive transformational outreach into the community and the world, clergy become professional doers of ministry rather than equip the saints to do it (Eph. 4:11).

Sooner or later, Christian life and ministry is reduced to, "Come to church (instead of go into the world); we have a great program." Along with these subtle changes, Satan successfully draws God's people into the culture that surrounds them. As an angel of light he introduces a lot of good busyness to replace biblical basics. The light of the gospel and the dynamic witness of authentic Christians become nearly nonexistent in the marketplace.

Competition for being the best church begins to set in, and a pecking order emerges. Verbally or silently, we ask, "Who's the greatest?" The church is divided and separated by strong walls, and the city no longer knows the gospel—the Father sent His Son (John 17:21). Because of denominational and racial differences, the church becomes divided. It fails to speak the truth in love and is therefore stunted, not growing up into the fullness of the stature of Christ. Throw in some church splits, sexual scandals, and other rumored problems, and the roots of division grow deep and strong. Darkness consumes the light.

Maxie Dunnam has told a great story that was repeated in Richard Dresselhaus's *Enrichment* magazine article, "Three Miles From the Coffee." A cowboy was camping out on the prairie. When it was time to cook breakfast, he decided to light the grass and hold his skillet over the flame. But the wind came up, and he kept moving his skillet to keep it over the flame. All seemed to be going well, but when his eggs were cooked, he was three miles from his coffee.[80]

This is a picture of church drift. We keep moving with the winds of cultural change and great programming ideas, until one day, with the latest idea on the table, we look back at Scripture to find ourselves miles from basic Christianity. Central to this drift is a neglect of passionate disciplined prayer—the key to revival and one of the keys to sustaining it. Communication is the secret of intimacy with others. Our closest friends are those with whom we communicate the most and share most deeply. Communication is the secret of intimacy with God. Prayer at its best is a profound two-way communication with God.

Having considered this third characteristic of revival, I want to pause to look more deeply at the discipline of prayer, the way to maintain revival and vital Christian faith, personally and corporately.

The more praying there is in the world, the better the world will be; the mightier the forces against evil everywhere.[1]

—E. M. Bounds

To say prayers in a decent, delicate way is not heavy work. But to pray really, to pray till hell feels the ponderous stroke, to pray till the iron gates of difficulty are opened, till the mountains of obstacles are removed, till the mists are exhaled and the clouds are lifted, and the sunshine of a cloudless day brightens—this is hard work, but it is God's work and man's best labor.[2]

—E. M. Bounds

Tomorrow I plan to work, work, work, from early until late. In fact, I have so much to do that I shall spend the first three hours in prayer.[3]

—Martin Luther

We can do nothing without prayer. All things can be done by importunate prayer. It surmounts or removes all obstacles, overcomes every resisting force and gains its ends in the face of invincible hindrances.[4]

—E. M. Bounds

7

Prayer: Fanning the Flames of Intimacy With God

DOING GOD'S WORK GOD'S WAY

Have you heard about the unique ways of the bull moose? Nationals from Northern Canada recount stories of strange behavior by these beasts during mating season. The eighteen hundred pound bulls, with massive racks and proud spirits, are tense and irritable during this time and gather a herd of cows around themselves. Nothing dare come close to them because their passions run deep. You get the picture: don't mess with their cows or their territory. The freight trains that thunder through the area are irritants, a serious invasion of privacy. As the accounts go, these bulls are known to lower their heads and charge the engines of the trains. A grinding clash of antlers, flesh, and steel follows, and—the moose loses.

What does this have to do with prayer? It seems that God's people and the church try to do God's work like a bull moose during mating season. Lower your head and charge! Pick up the pace! Gather a herd, protect it, and beat out any competition that comes close, no matter what it is. Lower your head, grab your impressive experience and degrees, and charge.

But that's not how the manual on the church tells us to build God's kingdom. The ways of man and moose do not work. God's ways are higher than our ways, and His thoughts higher than our thoughts (Isa. 55:8). It is very much like Isaiah 30:15–18, "But you would have none of it. You said, 'No'... Yet the LORD longs to be gracious to you."

If we would quit charging freight trains and do God's work God's way, the church could be vibrant and revived. If God's people would stay with the designer's manual, the Bible, they would grow in intimacy with Him and in effective service for Him. The pattern of drift would be broken, and their excitement and passion would not wash out. If you charge enough trains and survive, you should quit charging sooner or later. It would certainly be wise to find a different approach to the enemy's disturbances and irritations.

I have often told Connie, "I feel like I am running full speed into concrete walls." This comment has usually followed the frustration of making another effort to unite the area-wide church and break down the walls of denominational, gender, and racial division. Or it may have followed another passionate plea for the area church to gather for prayer and worship. Again and again, Connie and I have had to agree, *Let's keep going, but let's continue to be passionate and faithful in prayer and depend on the Holy Spirit to do what needs to be done. Let's continue to pray in strategic places across the city and call God's people together, but let's make sure we are enjoying this life and calling.*

God's Word reinforces this encouragement.

> Unless the LORD builds a house, the work of the builders is useless. Unless the LORD protects a city, guarding it with sentries will do no good. It is useless for you to work so hard from early morning until late at night, anxiously working for food to eat; for God gives rest to his loved ones.
>
> —*Psalm 127:1–2, NLT*

Here's the bottom line. We must do God's work God's way. When we do, His work gets done in His time, and we do not burn out doing it. The kingdom of God thrives, and God's people flourish as they live the abundant life. *I believe that prayer is how God gets His work done.* It is the top priority for the church, the secret of growing intimacy with God and the catalyst for unleashing the power of God.

The older I become, the more I realize that intimacy with God, through conversation in prayer is one of life's greatest treasures. For this reason, my prayer life has become longer and richer. On an average day, I get up at 5:00 a.m. and sit in my home study, in the living room with a fire in the fireplace; or, in the warmth of summer, on the deck in the backyard. I spend an hour or more in worship and weave memorized or paraphrased scriptures into my worship and prayer. This shapes my perspective for the day and for life.

After this, I read the Bible, with the use of a reading guide, and mark the texts that the Holy Spirit uses to grip my soul, fire my passion, or minister to a screaming need. I often make brief notes in the margins and record markings of my personal journey of faith from crisis or need to amazing reassurance or breakthrough. Connie joins me for prayer on many mornings and always on the weekends. I have found that there is nothing like prayer to enrich a marriage and build intimacy.

Following this wonderful time with the Lord, I often write shorter notes or longer letters to Him in my journal. When I conclude my writing, I make an asterisk in the margin and listen to the still small voice of the Father. I record what He speaks to me. Three or four days a week, I get on my treadmill for thirty minutes of passionate perspiring and list praying. I have built a podium that sits in front of the treadmill and holds my prayer lists. This enables me to pray through different lists on different days—the city, several hundred congregations, my family, our ministry and board, the nation—and also through a stack of pictures of special people for whom I have committed to pray. I never fall asleep on the treadmill. It is a great place for spiritual warfare prayer and intercession.

Communication is the secret of intimacy in all areas of life and relationships—in marriage, friendship, the professional world, and with God. Your best friend is the one with whom you spend the most time in quality communication. Prayer is communication with God. Let me say it again, as prayer is at the apex of 2 Chronicles 7:14, the instructions for revival, it must be at the heart of knowing and serving God. We must develop a disciplined contemplative life, one of prayer, worship, reading, and listening to the still small voice of the Holy Spirit (Isa. 30:21; John 10:4,16). It must be at the heart of the church, central to all she does and woven together with worship and praise. It *is* the heart of the church, and it pumps life through her body.

A number of years ago, the American auto industry slid into trouble. European and Japanese cars were flooding the American market, and U.S. auto sales were declining. Jobs, as well as American manufacturing pride, were being lost. It was necessary to make changes, or lose a substantial part of the American economy. Recognizing that the primary issue was quality, Ford Motors captured the day with the slogan: "Ford—Quality Is Job One!"

During this time I began to ask myself, *What is job #1 for the church, for followers of Jesus? Why isn't the church flourishing and pushing back the secularism and sensuality that is sweeping the nation? Why is she declining in America when tens of thousands are coming to Christ in Korea—a nation that is now over 40 percent Christian with the largest congregations in the world? Is it the neglect of the Great Commandment and the Great Commission? Why isn't the American church getting the job done? How are we to do God's work, God's way?*

Once again I read, "Apart from me you can do nothing" (John 15:5). I was reminded, "By his mighty power at work within us, he is able to accomplish infinitely more than we would ever dare to ask or hope" (Eph. 3:20, NLT). I finally concluded: Prayer is job number one—prayer that seeks God's face, not His hand; prayer that seeks God's direction and is followed by obedience.

It is important to remember that God's ways are not our ways. In fact, sometimes His ways do not even make sense. Would you choose a teenager to kill a giant nine feet tall and deliver a nation? God did! The soldiers in Israel's army were cowering under the intimidating threats of Goliath, and the king was even afraid. The entire nation was held hostage by his threats.

But God sent a teenage sheepherder to face Goliath when he was visiting his brothers with some food from home. With one rock from a creek, young David hit the giant in the forehead, knocked him out, and used Goliath's own sword to cut off his head. God's ways are not our ways. Don't expect Him to accomplish His purpose with great human ingenuity and ideas. His ways only begin to make sense when we see the incredible results.

Would you choose a man who said he couldn't talk to confront one of the most powerful rulers in the world and lead Israel out of slavery and across a desert? God did! Would you choose a man who killed someone in anger and then ran? God did! Even then, this man, Moses, asked God to get someone else. "O Lord," Moses said, "I have never been eloquent, neither in the past nor since you have spoken to your servant. I am slow of speech and tongue" (Exod. 4:10). How could he ever talk to the king of Egypt, and ask him to release the Israeli slaves?

Yet, God chose Moses. It is rather amazing as we look at this. Moses was raised and educated in the palace, more than likely groomed to be the next Pharaoh, and then spent forty years on the backside of the desert, herding sheep. This was the most menial, low class job an Egyptian could do, and it was clear that Moses had become a broken, humble person. Don't miss it. He was living in the very desert through which he would later lead God's people.

Do you recall God's brilliant military strategy for taking the city of Jericho? God told Israel to march around the city walls once a day for six days and then march around seven times on the seventh day. When they finished, the priests were to blow their trumpets and all the people were to give a loud shout. The group of escaped slaves, nomads who had wandered in the desert, obeyed in faith, and the massive walls fell down. The nomads won. *God won.*

Would you have used a boy's lunch, five loaves and two fish, to feed five thousand hungry people? The crowd had been following Jesus and listening to His teaching. Jesus' disciples were rather stunned when He told them to prepare lunch. Where was the wholesale food store? Where would they get enough money to pay for it? There could have been ten thousand or more hungry men, women, and children. Yet, everyone was fed and there was plenty left for the twelve faithless followers.

God's ways are not our ways and His thoughts are not our thoughts. Don't expect that we will ever get His work done our way. To use another ad line from Ford, "God has a better idea." It is prayer, seeking His face, receiving His specific direction, and then obeying. As we obey, God will bring revival and city transformation in His own brilliant way and in His perfect timing. God uses people who are available to Him, those who listen to His still small voice and are broken, humble, and obedient. He tells them what to do as they seek Him and listen carefully. (See Isa. 30:19–21.)

It is a thrill to remember God's work through young David and fearful Moses. There is nothing more exciting than to be a part of what God is doing. However, we have to do it with His power and in His way. It is an exciting partnership. The dynamic work of prayer builds intimacy with God and trains us to hear Him. Hearing His still small voice allows us to learn the next step in accomplishing His purpose. Prayer is how we do God's work. Don't miss it. *Prayer is job one!* Don't pick up the pace. Don't lower your head and charge. You will crash and burn.

Some may say, "Oh no! I've tried to pray, and I drift into sleep. My mind wanders. I don't have time. Prayer is an exercise in futility." I believe the answer to this is discipline. There are very few valuable endeavors that do not take hard work and discipline. We must, with tenacity and creativity, keep learning and growing in prayer until it becomes as natural as talking or relaxing with a good friend. Isaiah 40:31 says, "They that *wait* on the LORD shall renew their strength" (KJV, author's emphasis). God has wonderful things to teach us in the waiting room of His will. The disciples of Jesus saw and learned the power of prayer by watching Him speak to His Father day after day.

If God says pray, we must. To rebel against His instruction is like divination or witchcraft and even idolatry. Obedience is more important than our religious activity (1 Sam. 15:22–23). God is the all-wise, all-powerful, ever-present, Sovereign of the universe. I need to understand what He says, and do it. Have you ever noticed how often the Bible tells us to obey? The Great Commission says, "Go and make disciples...teaching them to *obey* everything I have commanded you" (Matt. 28:19–20, author's emphasis). And Luke 11:28 declares, "Blessed...are those who hear the word of God and *obey* it" (author's emphasis).

RESULTS OF PRAYER

What is revival? It is a spontaneous spiritual awakening by God the Holy Spirit—an outpouring of God's power—among God's people. It results from their humble prayers, as they passionately seek God's face, and repent of their sins. The result is deepened intimacy with God, passion for Him, holy living, evangelism, thousands coming to faith in Christ, and major social reform or city transformation.

Revival is inextricably linked to prayer. Brian Edwards, in his classic book, *Revival*, affirms this:

> You cannot read far into the story of revival without discovering that not only is prayer a part of the inevitable result of an outpouring of the Spirit, but from a human standpoint, it is, also, the single most significant cause.[5]

Listen to the words of 1 Peter 4:7: "The end of the world is coming soon. Therefore, be earnest and disciplined in your prayers" (NLT). As we near the end of time as we know it, we are commanded to pray. Many national church leaders are saying that time is short and Jesus is coming soon. Although no one knows the time, signs are pointing that way (1 Thess. 5:1–11). The end of history as we have known it is very close, and God tells us what to do—pray.

The more I have prayed, the more incredible results I have seen. As I have grown in prayer, the stories of amazing answers have multiplied. In the introduction, I shared the story of how God called us to our current ministry. I am amazed at how clearly He spoke the morning I was waiting before Him in prayer, with pen in hand. I have never ceased to be amazed at the wonderful home He provided for us, ideal for our hospitality and on what I believe to be one of the most beautiful streets in our city.

Both Connie and I have watched God heal us through major surgeries. For example, Connie had her aortic valve replaced when she was only thirty-seven years old. A childhood illness had damaged her valve, and she had been told that one day her heart would deteriorate to the degree that she could not function well. At that point, she would need to have surgery.

When we moved from California to a university position in the midwest, Connie missed her annual heart checkup. At a university board meeting, I mentioned Connie's situation to a board member who was a cardiovascular surgeon from Michigan. The doctor casually turned to me and said, "We like to operate on healthy hearts. There is a much better chance of healing and health. Come on up for vacation sometime, stay with us, and I'll have my cardiologist check her heart."

A few months later, we traveled north for vacation and spent the weekend with the doctor's family on the way home. Connie saw the cardiologist on Monday morning, and that afternoon, our doctor friend called and asked us to stay another day. When he talked to us about the test results, he said that Connie's heart had enlarged, and she needed surgery soon. She had the condition from which athletes suddenly die because they are unaware of any serious problem.

"I have an opening on Thursday," he said. "Stay with us. I'll do the surgery, my wife will take care of your three children, and when you are strong enough to travel you can use our large car to return home."

We accepted his generous offer and began to make calls to family, friends, and colleagues across the country. As we found out later, hundreds began to pray. The night before the operation, Connie planned to write good-by letters to the kids, just in case she didn't make it through the surgery. However, her peace was so overwhelming, that she never wrote them. She came through surgery fine.

But there is more to tell. Connie was given a carbon steel valve because the long-term results of other options were not recommended for someone so young. The steel valve, we were told, would only last fifteen to twenty years. Connie continued her annual check-ups, and when we moved to Rockford, Illinois, her cardiologist began ordering an echocardiogram every six months. Her valve was leaking, and her heart was enlarging.

The doctor suggested that it was time to begin thinking about another surgery, and we began to pray for a miracle. We asked others to pray, and many did. A wonderfully gifted African American doctor anointed her with oil and prayed for her healing one morning when we were visiting his church. Soon, Connie's doctor reported that her heart was no longer enlarging. Appointments were extended, and today she remains at the annual check-up level. It has been twenty-four years, and Connie is doing fine.

Financial support for our prayer and revival ministry has been one of the greatest challenges, much more difficult than when we raised support for international ministry to missionaries and national pastors. For example, shortly after we launched our faith ministry, we faced a day when we had eighteen hundred dollars worth of bills in envelopes, nicely stacked on the desk, ready to be mailed. However, we did not have enough money to cover the checks.

I attended a meeting at a nearby church on the morning of the need. After the meeting concluded with prayer, the pastor of the church turned to me and asked, "Do you need money? The Lord just told me to write you a check."

Smiling and fighting back tears, I simply said, "Yes; bills are waiting to be paid." He gave me a check for one thousand dollars.

As I returned home from the meeting, and pulled into our driveway, another car pulled up behind me. A retired doctor greeted us. He had served on the mission board that Connie had previously led as the staff missions director. He came in for a brief chat and then handed us an envelope with five hundred dollars in it. "I just had the sense that you might need this," he said.

It was turning out to be a wonderful day. Not much later the mail came. It included the remaining amount we needed to mail the bills on time.

The longer we have been with Rockford Renewal Ministries, the higher the stakes have become, a larger budget and a greater financial need. At the end of 2004, our ministry was behind financially by over twenty thousand dollars. God began to send in large gifts, and by year-end, we had received twenty-five thousand dollars. With this breakthrough, Connie and I felt new encouragement. We believed that God had renewed our call and had given us a new mandate to pursue the vision He had given us. The year 2005 broke upon us with new energy, hope, and no ministry debt.

At our previous church, I managed the benevolence funds. On one occasion, a handicapped young man needed a car with an automatic transmission. Someone had donated a small car for him, but it had a stick shift, which he couldn't operate. I gave him our family car, which was well maintained, had an automatic transmission and was just right for him. The church, in turn, gave us the donated car, which required a lot of repairs to keep it running. One day our mechanic said, "Don't fix it again. It is not worth it."

Not knowing what to do, we asked, *Now what, Lord? We need a car.* I happened to be having lunch with a new board member, and I mentioned the car situation. He generously offered to give us five thousand dollars for a down payment.

The following week I was meeting a businessman for lunch. When the conversation somehow got around to cars, I said, "Strange, isn't it? I have a down payment for one."

He responded simply, "I'll make the payments. Go get a car." Thus, with tight finances and living by faith, Connie and I had a new car for the ministry.

I could write an entire book about answers to prayer, but let me tell you one more story. This one may blow your cognitive and spiritual circuits, but I want to take the risk. Connie and I had been counseling with someone who was sold to Satan before birth. Some Ephesians 6 principalities and powers had manifested in some of our counseling sessions, and we knew we were dealing with things way over our heads and far from our experience. Our learning curve was nearly straight up. Out of sheer helplessness and desperation, our prayer life and passion to hear the Lord grew by leaps and bounds during those years.

We did everything possible to be spiritually protected. On one occasion, after ministering for hours, we were exhausted, perspiring, and at the end of our strength. We were doing battle with one of the major principalities who was claiming the life of the one with whom we were working. It was a life and death battle. All we knew to do and all our desperate praying was not helping. I had read about Michael the Archangel in Scripture. Now, as I called out to God in my weakness, I heard God speak to me, *Call Michael.*

"Michael, come! Help!" I called out. The battle was suddenly over. Our friend was still and at rest, free from the evil influence. God answered! Glory to God!

I am nearly over the hill now, as some would say. Perhaps I am just at the crest of the hill. The longer I live and serve the Lord, the more convinced I am that prayer is really the secret of intimacy with God and the catalyst for unleashing His power. Reflect on the following scriptures about intimacy with God. Psalm 145:18 says, "The LORD is near to all who call on him." And James 4:8 counsels, "Come near to God and he will come near to you."

The only way I know to draw close to God is in conversation with Him, both talking and listening. It is the same with anyone we love. We have to spend time together to enrich our relationship. God lives within us, but we have to be aware of Him and practice a conversational relationship with Him. Deuteronomy 4:7 clinches it: "What other nation is so great as to have their gods near them the way the LORD our God is near us whenever we pray to him?"

Prayer releases or engages the power of God. Jesus said, "Until now you have not asked for anything in my name. Ask and you will receive, and your joy will be complete" (John 16:24). He also taught, "If you remain in me and my words remain in you, ask whatever you wish, and it will be given you" (John 15:7). James 4:2 reminds us, "You do not have, because you do not ask God." These powerful promises function in the context of obedience.

THE PRIORITY OF PRAYER IN THE SCRIPTURE

You may be questioning if prayer is really as important as I have just presented it. *Is* it the secret of intimacy with God? *Does* it release the power of God? *Can* it sustain revival? A careful reading of the Bible proves that prayer is to be the top priority in the life and ministry of the Christian.

First, Luke 18:1 says, "[We] should always pray and not give up." First Thessalonians 5:17 adds, "Pray continually." I like to think of this as a conversational relationship with God, step-by-step, day-by-day, in every situation. It is what Brother Lawrence, the monk assigned to washing dishes in the monastery, urged. The title of his book, *Practicing the Presence of God*, says it all.

Consider the great apostle Paul's instructions to his understudy, Timothy:

> I urge, then, *first of all* [my emphasis to reflect that this is the top priority], that requests, prayers, intercession and thanksgiving be made for everyone—for kings and all those in authority, that we may live peaceful and quiet lives in all godliness and holiness. This is good, and pleases God our Savior, who wants all men to be saved and to come to a knowledge of the truth. I want men [and women] everywhere to lift up holy hands in prayer, without anger or disputing.
> —*1 Timothy 2:1–4, 8*

What is the top priority of the church? What should characterize her? Jesus said, "My house will be called *a house of prayer*" (Matt 21:13, author's emphasis). He was angry—tipping over tables and driving moneychangers out of the temple. The place had become a lot of things, but it was not a house of prayer. Does this sound familiar? Who would Jesus be kicking out of the church today? What would He be tipping over? Sometimes when I hear church announcements, I wonder how close we are to what bothered Jesus at the temple. What would Jesus say today? Would He be angry?

In Acts 13:2, the church was worshiping and fasting. That's when the Holy Spirit said, "Set apart for me Barnabas and Saul for the work to which I have called them." With fasting and prayer, they laid hands on them and sent them out. These two men, anointed and appointed, turned the known world upside down for Jesus Christ and His kingdom. Prayer gave the church strategic direction. It was a house of prayer.

Acts 14 tells how Paul and Barnabas appointed elders, then with prayer, sent them out. Prayer gave the new elders a solid foundation. I think this was meant to be the model for launching church leadership. How many congregations have you known that spend time in fasting and prayer for newly appointed elders and leaders?

The Bible clearly teaches that prayer should capture the devotion and disciplined obedience of God's people. Romans 12:12 says, "Be...faithful in prayer." This, however, is a far cry from the priorities that have won the devotion of today's church in America. I suspect that prayer would be quite low on the list for many congregations and leaders. If I were a betting man, I would wager that sports and watching television are given more time than prayer.

Am I being too harsh? If our neighbors are going to hell, if Jesus is coming back soon, if we want to do God's work God's way, we need to get back to basics, to the priority of prayer. Is this why the church and her people are not penetrating the darkness today? Is this why enemy walls and strongholds are not coming down? Is this why we are living in a post-Christian era? Have we as proud Americans done things our own way? That was the story of Isaiah 30:15–18.

> This is what the Sovereign LORD, the Holy One of Israel, says: "In repentance and rest is your salvation, in quietness and trust is your strength, but you would have none of it. You said, 'No, we will flee on horses.' Therefore you will flee! You said, 'We will ride off on swift horses.' Therefore your pursuers will be swift! A thousand will flee at the threat of one; at the threat of five you will all flee away, till you are left like a flagstaff on a mountaintop, like a banner on a hill. Yet the LORD longs to be gracious to you.
> —*Isaiah 30:15–18*

God does not smile when we depend on others or on ourselves.

> Woe to those who go down to Egypt for help, who rely on horses, who trust in the multitude of their chariots and in the great strength of their horsemen, but do not look to the Holy One of Israel, or seek help from the LORD.
>
> —*Isaiah 31:1*

Consider the concern Samuel voiced in 1 Samuel 12:23. In his address to Israel after Saul was confirmed as their king, he said, "As for me, far be it from me that I should *sin against the LORD by failing to pray for you*" (author's emphasis). I believe that each of us has a radius of responsibility and influence in our prayer ministry, and we must be creative in fulfilling the job God has given us.

As a city-reacher, I want to pray for about two hundred fifty pastors and congregations. To accomplish this, I try to go away to a quiet place once a month for a time of fasting and prayer. My favorite place is about an hour and a half north of my home, and I have found that I can pray for these pastors and churches before I arrive at the cabin. More recently, I have begun to pray through this list as I walk on my treadmill early Sunday mornings.

I also want to pray once a week for our board members and intercessors and through a small pile of prayer cards from missionaries and friends. On early Sunday mornings I pray for these, as well as a list of area concerns and people. I make all this effort to weave my prayer life into all I do in a creative significant way. Since I work out four times a week in a routine that includes a brisk thirty-minute walk on a treadmill, it is a perfect time to list pray. And, by the way, I never fall asleep.

So what's the point? Each of us must decide what our priorities are, and then create a plan to give them the time and effort they deserve. Is prayer our top priority? How else will we do God's work God's way?

Congregations must learn how to make gatherings for prayer some of the most strategic, God focused, exciting, and energized meetings of the church. Worship and praise must set the pace. Creativity and the leadership of the Holy Spirit must keep us from the doldrums of disappointing prayer meetings. The Brooklyn Tabernacle, led by Pastor Jim Cymbala, has learned how to do this. Prayer is a top priority for the church and one of the largest gatherings of the Tabernacle during the week.

Acts 1 presents a powerful picture of pristine Christianity. Before the church was born, before the Holy Spirit came at Pentecost, before thousands came to faith in Christ on the streets of the city, Christ's followers obediently went to an upper room to pray. They followed the instructions of Jesus and prayed and waited until they were clothed with the promised power of the Holy Spirit. They probably didn't know exactly what they were waiting and praying for, but they obeyed. When the church was born, the people in this core group were devoting themselves to prayer, waiting on the Lord in unity.

What a thrilling story! The Holy Spirit was poured out, and a mighty rushing wind swept through the room and through the city. It made so much noise that people visiting Jerusalem for the feast of Pentecost were drawn to the scene, where they saw tongues of fire resting on the heads of Christ's followers. They heard the gospel in the various languages of the areas where they lived, as the one hundred twenty people in the upper room spoke in languages they had not learned. *Do it again, oh, Lord. Do it again.*

In Acts 12:1–5, a crisis hit the church. The whimsical and self-serving Herod had killed the apostle James. Because this pleased those who opposed Christ's followers, Herod decided to go two-for-two. He had Peter seized and thrown into prison, and verse five says, "the church was earnestly praying to God for him." If you know the story, you remember that an angel appeared in the prison, and light filled the cell. When the angel awakened Peter, the prisoner's chains fell off. The angel told Peter to get dressed, and then walked him out the gate, right past the guards. Finally, an iron gate opened by itself, and Peter walked out on a city street in freedom.

When Peter realized what had happened, he headed to Mary's home, where the church was praying for him. Although the group was exercising considerable faith, it would be an understatement to say that they were surprised! They didn't believe Rhoda, the servant girl who heard Peter knock, answered the door and ran in to tell them the good news, "Peter is at the door!" (v. 14). Iron gates yielded against the power and tenacity of passionate prayer. Peter's life was spared.

Prayer has a high priority in Scripture. It is the way God accomplishes

His work. In 1 Chronicles 5:20 God defeated Israel's enemy because His people cried out to Him during a fierce battle. The text says: "He answered their prayers, because they trusted in him." They *trusted* Him.

Israel's great King David received the most honorable epitaph anyone could desire: "a man after God's own heart." Why? If you have read 1 Samuel, you have noticed his humility, his commitment to God, and his faith. You have read about his tenacity, patience, and character. But have you read David's psalms recently? His life was centered in prayer, praise, and worship. To read the psalms is to read his personal journal. Yes, he was an adulterer and murderer, but David knew God would be merciful, gracious, forgiving, and redemptive as he mourned and repented of his sin.

David was not shy in prayer. He poured out his heart to God and had an intimate relationship with Him. David has stood as a great king and a great model for prayer. Although he bore the scars of his sin, he grew in greater intimacy with God through his life experiences. David knew God, lived in intimate fellowship with Him and worshiped and loved Him with all his heart, soul, mind, and strength.

Elijah was an ordinary man like you and me. He prayed, and it didn't rain for three and a half years. Through prayer, God can change the weather. Do you remember the story of Mt. Carmel and the prophets of Baal in 1 Kings 18? As Elijah prayed, fire fell from heaven and consumed the offering—and the water, the soil, and the rocks, and the prophets of Baal, probably the Asherah prophets, too. Eight hundred total were killed.

After this great miracle and answer from God, it was time to pray for rain. In faith, Elijah told Ahab to get ready. Then he bowed his head between his knees and began to pray. Here again is the human-divine partnership. God promised, and Elijah prayed passionately and earnestly. He waited and prayed...prayed and waited. Then a small cloud, the size of a man's hand, appeared. The exciting answer—an abundance of rain—was on the way. The drought was over, and Elijah's prayers were answered. Prayer brought fire from heaven, destroyed false prophets, honored God, and returned rain to the land.

Later Elijah panicked because of Jezebel's threats to kill him. Feeling alone, he ran for his life. In a desert place outside of Beersheba he prayed again—that he might die. God answered with encouragement and great strength. He traveled another forty days and nights until he came to the mountain of God. There he waited before God until he heard His gentle whisper. God spoke to him as he waited in stillness and listened. God told him what to do.

In 2 Chronicles 20, Judah and her godly king, Jehoshaphat, was under the threat of imminent attack by a coalition of armies. Many great kings would have mounted their steeds, called up the army, and faced the onslaught—but not this king. He had followed and served the One who could win battles. He knew he was powerless before the advancing army. Jehoshaphat called the nation to fast and pray. He personally bowed in prayer to lead them, his face to the ground.

God answered through a prophet, gave Jehoshaphat and Judah a proper perspective, and told them what to do: "Do not be afraid or discouraged because of this vast army. For the battle is not yours, but God's" (2 Chron. 20:15). How often these words have encouraged me! There was great victory that day. Amazingly, the instructions called for the musicians to lead the army. God's ways were not what any military leader would have advised. I'll follow a leader like Jehoshaphat. Send him on.

Ephesians 6:10–18 emphasizes the high priority of prayer when it teaches us to put on the full armor of God. This is not the result of a quick, "I put on the full armor" prayer as I run out the door in the morning. No, it is praying through the great truths of the armor, which I discuss more fully in Appendix III. An example of this kind of prayer follows:

> *Holy Spirit, You who remind me of truth, give me great skill with your Word today, just like Jesus when He was confronted by the half-truths of Satan in the wilderness.*

The armor of God is strategically important for the personal and spiritual battles we face every day. However, notice in these verses that the armor is not enough! After the description of the armor, at the end of this text on warfare, is the command to "pray...on all occasions with all kinds of prayers...always...for all the saints" (v. 18). Having your armor on without prayer is like launching a battleship in a mud puddle. It is a gun without a bullet; a computer without a hard drive. Prayer is strategic to winning the battles of each day and the wars of life.

Where was the church born? *It happened in a prayer meeting* and on the streets of a great city. Where will the church be reborn? *It will be in a prayer meeting!* Revival will be the result of passionate prayer and repentance. If we will do our part, God will do His. Prayer has a high priority in Scripture, and it is the way we do God's work. Prayer sustains a vibrant, intimate relationship with God, and keeps a church congregation on the cutting edge of impact for God's kingdom.

PRAYER AND THE PROMISES OF GOD

Ephesians 3:20 teaches that God promises to do "immeasurably more than all we ask or imagine." We need to dream; we need to ask. Jeremiah 32:17 gives a no limit description of God's power: "Ah, Sovereign LORD, you have made the heavens and the earth by your great power and outstretched arm. Nothing is too hard for you." God wants us to ask, and He tells us to ask. In John 16:24, Jesus says, "Until now you have not asked for anything in my name. Ask and you will receive, and your joy will be complete."

Our God is the God of the impossible. Luke 18:27 says, "What is impossible with men is possible with God." God makes this very clear in Jeremiah 33:3: "*Call* to me and *I will answer* you and tell you great and unsearchable things you do not know" (author's emphasis). Of course, as a loving Father, God will not allow us to ride our bikes on the freeway, especially at rush hour. He will not deny the truth of His revealed Word, and we can't ask Him to bless our sin. His love is incomprehensible, and His timing is always precise. It doesn't seem like it sometimes, but when we look back, it is amazing to trace His plan.

God loves to give us the desires of our hearts as we delight in Him (Ps. 37:4). The psalmist also said, "No good thing does he withhold from those whose walk is blameless" (Ps. 84:11). The New Living Translation renders the last phrase of Psalm 84:11 as "…who do what is right." The promises of God are amazing. To obey Him is to know the best life possible. It is called the abundant life, life "to the full," in John 10:10. God's love is beyond comprehension and unconditional, but His blessings are based on our obedience. His amazing answers come in the context of obedience.

When it came to prayer, Jesus provided the best example. During His life He learned what the Father was doing and joined Him. (See John 8:28; 5:19.) In every case, His perspective was, "Yet not my will, but yours be done" (Luke 22:42). We see this most graphically in the Garden of Gethsemane the night before the crucifixion. It was there that Jesus asked the Father if He could escape the horrors of "this cup"—the crucifixion, with its torture, and worst of all, the hideous sin of all history, which would be laid on Him. He knew what was coming. It was the purpose for which the Father had sent Him.

I can't imagine the horrific battle Jesus fought in His prayer to His Father. The capillaries of His skin broke under the intense spiritual and emotional pressure, as He sweat blood in prayer. However, when it was over, He was equipped to do what He came to do—what He chose to do—knowing the horror of it all. Jesus went through a trumped up trial in front of both the religious and the civic leaders. He didn't even need to open His mouth, but stood securely and confidently before the courts and the mockers. For the joy set before Him He endured the mocking, the hideous torture, and the cross.

Will we need to sweat blood in the spiritual warfare of ministry and the stress of life? We probably will. As we do our sweating and bleeding in prayer, we will know great victory and security. Jesus is our best model of passionate prayer in all the circumstances of life—in the routine and mundane, in ministry, and in the most difficult battles.

It is important that we have the same attitude Jesus expressed in His prayer to the Father. As He showed, the Father's will is always the best answer, even if it is not what we want. To learn what the Father is doing and join Him is the best of all ways to live. If God promises something, then we need go after it aggressively, in spiritual warfare and tenacious prayer. When young Mary, the mother of Jesus, was told that she would become pregnant with God's Son by the Holy Spirit, she said, "May it be to me as you have said" (Luke 1:38). Often I quote or read a text of Scripture and pray, "May it be to me as you have said."

We need to break any powers of darkness that delay God's answers. Daniel 10 tells of an instance when the Prince of Persia was resisting the messenger who brought an answer to Daniel's prayer. Michael was dispatched to help him (vs. 13). We need to pray like Elijah did on Mt.

Carmel, with our head between our knees, warring against the enemy until the answer comes.

Review some of God's amazing promises with me. Let your faith grow, and dream big. As Romans 10:17 says, "Faith comes from hearing the message, and the message is heard through the word of Christ." Some of these texts are "Griffin paraphrases." I have italicized some thrilling phrases.

> Don't worry about anything; instead, *pray about everything.* Tell God what you need, and thank him for all he has done. If you do this, you will experience God's peace, which is far more wonderful than the human mind can understand. [Prayer and peace go hand in hand. Prayer is the antidote to the poison of anxiety.]
> —*Philippians 4:6–7,* NLT, *Author's emphasis*

> So let us *come boldly to the throne of our gracious God.* There we will receive his mercy, and we will find grace to help us when we need it.
> —*Hebrews 4:16,* NLT, *Author's emphasis*

> Confess your sins to each other and *pray for each so that you may be healed. The earnest prayer of a righteous person has great power and wonderful results.*
> —*James 5:16,* NLT, *Author's emphasis*

> *Keep on asking,* and you will be given what you ask for. *Keep on looking,* and you will find. *Keep on knocking,* and the door will be opened. For *everyone who asks, receives. Everyone who seeks, finds. And the door is opened to everyone who knocks.* You parents—if your children ask for a loaf of bread, do you give them a stone instead? Or if they ask for a fish, do you give them a snake? Of course not! If you sinful people know how to give good gifts to your children, how much more will your heavenly Father give good gifts to those who ask him.
> —*Matthew 7:7–11,* NLT, *Author's emphasis*

> The LORD hates the sacrifice of the wicked, but *he delights in the prayers of the upright.* The LORD is far from the wicked, but *he hears the prayers of the righteous.*
> —*Proverbs 15:8, 29,* NLT, *Author's emphasis*

At that time you won't need to ask me for anything. The truth is, *you can go directly to the Father and ask him, and he will grant your request because you use my name.* You haven't done this before. *Ask, using my name, and you will receive, and you will have abundant joy.*
—*John 16:23–24,* NLT, *Author's emphasis*

You didn't choose me. I chose you. I appointed you to go and produce fruit that will last, so that *the Father will give you whatever you ask for, using my name.*
—*John 15:16,* NLT, *Author's emphasis*

The LORD longs to be gracious to you; he rises to show you compassion. For the LORD is a God of justice. Blessed are all who wait for him! O people of Zion…you will weep no more. *How gracious he will be when you cry for help! As soon as he hears, he will answer you.* Although the Lord gives you the bread of adversity and the water of affliction, your teachers will be hidden no more; with your own eyes you will see them. Whether you turn to the right or to the left, your ears will hear a voice behind you, saying, "This is the way; walk in it."
—*Isaiah 30:18–21, Author's emphasis*

Jesus replied, "I tell you the truth, if you have faith and do not doubt, not only can you do what was done to the fig tree, but also you can say to this mountain, 'Go throw yourself into the sea,' and it will be done. *If you believe, you will receive whatever you ask for in prayer.*
—*Matthew 21:21–22, Author's emphasis*

Take delight in the LORD, and he will give you your heart's desires.
—*Psalm 37:4,* NLT

For the eyes of the Lord are on the righteous and *his ears are attentive to their prayer.*
—*1 Peter 3:12, Author's emphasis*

As we just noted in James 5:16, "*the prayer* of a righteous man is powerful and effective." James illustrates this from the life of Elijah, an ordinary man who prayed passionately that it wouldn't rain. It didn't—for three and a half years. He prayed again, and the sky poured rain. The earth responded with tremendous crops. Why did Elijah need to pray? Why does God ask us to pray? He certainly doesn't need us, although it is exciting to be a part of what He is doing. The only logical answer is that *God has chosen to work through His people as they pray.* He has chosen us to be in partnership with Him. Without God, we can't; without us, God won't.

The challenge of understanding the interaction of our part and God's part is one of those areas I call "creative tension." In the western world, most of us reason in Roman or Greek ways, with everything lined up in a logical and orderly way. We have a hard time seeing how two seemingly opposite things can be true at the same time. In Hebrew thought, however, this is common. There is a general understanding that people will never understand God and His ways.

It is like the creative tension between God's sovereignty and our responsibility. Both are true at the same time. Both God's sovereignty and our responsibility make great sense to me. If I move over too far toward the responsibility side, I can easily crumble under the load. On the other hand, if I move too far toward the sovereignty side, I have a tendency to become apathetic. My efforts do not matter or change things. The Bible helps us understand that these are areas where faith is required. The apostle Paul says:

> For we know *in part* and we prophesy *in part*, but when perfection comes, the imperfect disappears…Now we see but a poor reflection as in a mirror; then [in heaven, in God's presence] we shall see face to face. Now I know *in part*; then I shall know fully, even as I am fully known.
> —*1 Corinthians 13:9–10,12, Author's emphasis* .

God has chosen us to be a part of what He is doing. Our prayers can bring revival and healing transformation to a city or a nation. Satan's strongholds can be brought down. His agenda can be cancelled and his plans thwarted. It is all God's power, but we have a necessary and strategic role to play. Prayer is how God accomplishes His work, and we are privileged to be a part of what is happening as we serve His redemptive purpose.

E. M. Bounds put it this way:

> The possibilities of prayer are found in its allying itself with the purposes of God, for God's purposes and man's praying are the combination of all potent and omnipotent.[6]

Psalm 145:13 promises, "The LORD is faithful to all his promises and loving toward all he has made." Isaiah 46:11 confirms it: "What I have said, that will I bring about; what I have planned, that will I do." The "wait" work of prayer produces the necessary muscle to handle God's answers humbly and without pride. It builds faith, muscle, and strength to handle awesome assignments and great victories. We learn in waiting and trusting, and we grow in faith and intimacy with God. Waiting for God's answers is the difficult part of faith. We must understand, especially in our quick-paced, fast-food, western world, that God is not into microwaving, but into marinating.

Is it really true that God promises to answer prayer? In John 14:14, Jesus said, "You may ask me for anything in my name, and I will do it." The apostle John affirmed:

> This is the confidence we have in approaching God: that if we ask anything *according to his will*, he hears us. And if we know that he hears us—whatever we ask—we know that we have what we asked of him.
>
> —*1 John 5:14–15, Author's emphasis*

THE PATTERN OF PRAYER IN THE LIFE OF JESUS

As I have said before, prayer must be the top priority in the life of the Christ-follower and the church if we are to do God's work God's way. The promises of God are incredible. They are all in place. When I think of the strategic role of prayer, I am drawn to the pattern of prayer in the life of Jesus. Are we following Him? Are we taking His example seriously? Are we becoming like Him? Let's consider this.

> During the days of Jesus' life on earth, he offered up prayers and petitions with loud cries and tears to the one who could save him from death, and he was heard because of his reverent submission.
>
> —*Hebrews 5:7*

Let's look at Jesus' prayer life from the beginning of His ministry. After He was baptized, He spent forty days in the Judean wilderness, alone with the Father in fasting and prayer. He went into hand-to-hand combat with Satan, who hit Him with subtle half-truths, and He won every skirmish by speaking the truth of the Word of God. From this ministry launch, we see Him in prayer often.

In Mark 1:35, after a long and busy day of ministry and people, Jesus was up early the next morning—before dawn—to pray. I love this text. For most of my life the early morning has been my best time and my greatest opportunity to be with my heavenly Father. If you have not been a morning person, this could be scary. However, you can take heart and be encouraged by Matthew 14:22–23. He also prayed late at night.

Prayer was woven into the events of Jesus' life and ministry. In Matthew 14:13, He went off to be alone with the Father after He heard that John the Baptist had been beheaded. He prayed before He fed the five thousand (or as many believe, ten thousand to fifteen thousand with women and children) in Matthew 14:19. In Luke 6:12, when He was facing threats against His life and just before He chose His twelve disciples, Jesus prayed all night long.

Have you ever faced the threat of death? I have. It is a good time to talk with God the Father. At times I have wondered if I would return from an overseas trip because of the dangers involved. Just before Christmas 2004, I was diagnosed with cancer. It caught my attention, and I wondered how long I had to live. To face the possibility of death or even to suffer, usually causes considerable reflection on what is important, and this has been true for me. I have been excited to watch a new adventure of faith unfold and also experience an opportunity for greater intimacy with God. My theology of healing has been tested in the fire of personal experience.

Luke 11:1 says, "One day Jesus was praying in a certain place. When he finished, one of his disciples said to him, "Lord, teach us to pray." This is one of the places where Jesus gave us a model prayer—the Lord's prayer. It is not one that He prayed, but it is for us to pray. Why did the disciples ask Jesus to teach them to pray? If I had been following Jesus day after day, I would have asked Him how to raise the dead, heal withered hands, or make fish sandwiches for thousands. The only thing that makes sense to me is that the disciples were connecting the dots of His miracles with His prayer life and His intimacy with the Father.

The eternal Son of God who came to us in human flesh was a person of prayer. Luke 5:16 summarizes it: "But Jesus often withdrew to lonely places and prayed." What is Jesus doing now? According to Hebrews 7:25, His life is still characterized by prayer because He "lives to intercede for [us]." He is joined by the Holy Spirit who "intercedes for us with groans that words cannot express" (Rom. 8:26). Jesus is still praying and interceding for us at the right hand of the Father. If we are in hot pursuit of Jesus, really wanting to follow Him and to be like Him, prayer will be a priority in our lives. We will be in prayer often, conversationally intimate with the Father.

Jesus said, "My house will be called a house of prayer" (Matt. 21:13). If this is still an important directive and instruction, prayer must characterize the church. Is it happening? What's the least attended meeting of most congregations? I really believe that if we did God's work God's way, we would see the results that characterized the life of Jesus when He was on Earth.

Prayer was Jesus' work; ministry was His reward! As Jesus modeled, intimacy with God the Father comes before productivity for Him and His kingdom. Prayer is not something to be added to our other duties. Prayer and intimacy with God are to be the center of our lives. Prayer integrates and shapes all of life. It is the way God accomplishes His work through us. Prayer is how we do God's work God's way. Prayer is job number one.

A BIBLICAL PERSPECTIVE ON POWER

We often hear about the anointing of God for ministry—the power and gifting of God to serve His purpose and impact the lives of people for God's kingdom. In the Old Testament, leaders received the Holy Spirit when they were called to serve a special appointment. An example of this was when Elisha received the mantle and anointing of Elijah. Since Pentecost, we receive the presence of the Holy Spirit when we trust in Christ as Savior and Lord. I believe that we can have special anointings or empowerings beyond this.

Some believe that there is a second work of grace whereby the Holy Spirit gives greater power and gifts. I don't disagree. All I have to do is read through the Book of Acts. I believe that there are, in reality, many fillings and empowerings of the Holy Spirit, as we grow in Christ and seek Him. I am sure of one thing: *prayer is the catalyst for unleashing the power of God* through our lives and ministries.

Once again, we have a creative tension. We know that God's power is unlimited, and nothing is too difficult for Him. But what about our power? Oh, we might have some wonderful gifts—spiritual gifts to grace others, (the Greek word for *gifts* comes from the same root word as grace)—and natural abilities, but they fade in significance next to God's power. Our power and ability are miniscule in comparison to God's power and the name of Jesus. However, God's power is more than enough for anything God may ask us to do or be.

What does the Bible say about God's power? Ephesians 3:20–21 says that God is able to do far beyond anything we can think or even imagine. In Ephesians 1:19, Paul prayed that we would know God's incomparably great power, the same power that raised Jesus from the dead and seated Him in the heavenly realms at the right hand of the Father (resurrection power). We are seated with Jesus at this place of honor, power, and authority in the intangible world of spiritual reality. He is above all rule and authority, power and dominion, in this age and the age to come!

Paul prays that we will be strengthened by this incredible power, by the power of the Holy Spirit residing and working in and through us. Imagine it! He is able to do exceeding abundantly beyond all we can ask, think, or imagine. What are your dreams?

First Corinthians 3:7 reminds us of the limitations of our spiritual power when it says, "So neither he who plants nor he who waters is anything, but only God, who makes things grow." Ephesians 6:10 adds that we are to "be strong in the Lord and in his mighty power," not our own. Hosea 10:13 warns about the terrible result of trying to do God's work with our power or strength. It says that God's people planned wickedness, reaped evil, and ate the fruit of deception because they depended on their own strength. A few chapters later, in Hosea 14:8–9, God spoke through the prophet and said, "Your fruitfulness comes from me. Who is wise? He will realize these things."

In my years of serving the Lord, and most recently with passion to see our city transformed, I have often pondered Psalm 127:1: "Unless the LORD builds the house, its builders labor in vain. Unless the LORD watches over the city, the watchmen stand guard in vain." When the church in an area is swept by a great firestorm of revival and the city is transformed, it is done by God's power. God comes with wind and fire—with great revival—when a growing number of His people seek Him passionately in prayer and repentance (2 Chron. 7:14). As we, by faith, listen to God, follow Him step-by-step, and unify in passionate prayer, God's power will be released. Our role is small, but necessary.

Spiritual power has little to do with our ability. First Thessalonians 5:24 says, "The one who calls you is faithful and he will do it." Remember the great king, Jehoshaphat, when a coalition of armies was about to attack him and his nation? As they were standing in prayer, God told them, "The battle is not yours, but God's . . . stand, wait and see what I will do" (2 Chron. 20:15, 17, author's paraphrase).

It seems that preaching and teaching have taken the primary place when the people of God gather. While these form a very important characteristic of revival, I wonder what would happen if equal time and energy were given to prayer. First Corinthians 4:20 hints at an answer when it says, "The kingdom of God is not a matter of talk but of power." If prayer took its rightful place in the churches of America, I believe that revival would be just around the corner.

We are at war against a very skillful enemy (Eph. 6:12). Satan is the god of this world. Yes, it is true that "The earth is the LORD's, and everything in it, the world, and all who live in it" (Psalm 24:1; 1 Cor 10:25–26). However, Satan is a massive monkey wrench in the affairs of government, including church polity and politics. Can you recall a conflicted church business meeting or a church split?

Satan is subtle and very good at what he does, as he goes about to steal, kill, and destroy. He is a master of deception, a liar of the first order. I will deal with his power and ways later, but for now, it is important to understand we have very little to fight him in our strength. The apostle Paul gives us a key that will unlock the secret of victory in spiritual warfare.

> For though we live in the world, we do not wage war as the world does. The weapons we fight with are not the weapons of the world. On the contrary, they have divine power to demolish strongholds. We demolish arguments [Satan is a liar] and every pretension that sets itself up against the knowledge of God, and *we take captive every thought* [Satan is a deceiver] to make it obedient to Christ.
>
> —*2 Corinthians 10:3–5, Author's emphasis*

I recall what Jill Briscoe once said to a group of university students and faculty: "Our nothingness gives God a chance to fill us with His something-thingness, and blow the devil away." She is right. We have divine power available to us, and it can demolish Satan's fortresses, whether they be large or small, over cities, or quietly tucked away in our souls. We don't trust in ourselves because the necessary power to do battle against this enemy is not our own. Psalm 146:3–6 warns, "Do not put your trust in princes, in mortal men, who cannot save…Blessed is he whose help is in the God of Jacob, whose hope is in the LORD his God, the Maker of heaven and earth."

Satan has no power against God. No plan of man or Satan can succeed against the Lord. Proverbs 21:30–31 tells us, "There is no wisdom, no insight, no plan that can succeed against the LORD. The horse is made ready for the day of battle, but victory rests with the LORD." As we obey and follow Jesus, do His work His way, we will see great things accomplished by His power and ability. Listen to the words of Isaiah:

> All that we have accomplished you have done for us.
>
> —*Isaiah 26:12*

> Those who hope in me will not be disappointed.
>
> —*Isaiah 49:23*

> He gives strength to the weary and increases the power of the weak.
>
> —*Isaiah 40:29*

God promises to give us all the power we need. Second Peter 1:3 says, "His divine power has given us everything we need for life and godliness through our knowledge of him." A bit earlier, Peter writes, "If anyone serves, he should do it with the strength God provides" (1 Pet. 4:11). A contemporary Christian music group takes the name, "Jars of Clay." They have discovered the great truth of 2 Corinthians 4:7: "But we have this treasure [the gospel and God's truth] in jars of clay to show that this all-surpassing power is from God and not from us."

Because I come from a very broken background, I often feel inadequate to serve God. Frequently I am haunted by the question, *How could God ever use me?* It really is grace that God would choose to adopt me and use me. God chooses to use people like you and me. We are all broken to one degree or another. Those who have led a rather pristine life have the great challenge of dealing with too much comfort, apathy, and pride. And yes, when broken people see God working through them, they too have to deal with the pride monster, sometimes even more.

God has encouraged me with the truth of 1 Corinthians 1:26–31 many times. I have come to remember the text and its teaching by the following acrostic: God does not use W.I.N.ners—the **W**ise, **I**nfluential, and **N**oble. He uses the foolish W.I.L.D.—the **W**eak, **I**n Christ, **L**owly, and **D**espised. Paul knew the power of this firsthand. Remember, it was Paul who held the coat of Stephen when he was being stoned to death by an angry religious mob. It was Paul who obtained permission to imprison the followers of Christ in Damascus—before God's light and fire fell on him. Here's what Paul said:

> Brothers, think of what you were when you were called. Not many of you were *wise* by human standards; not many were *influential*; not many were of *noble* birth. But God chose the *foolish* things of the world to shame the wise; God chose the *weak* things of the world to shame the strong. He chose the *lowly* things of this world and the *despised* things—and the things that are not—to nullify the things that are, so that no one may boast before him. It is because of him that you are *in Christ* Jesus, who has become for us wisdom from God—that is, our righteousness, holiness and redemption. Therefore, as it is written: "Let him who boasts boast in the Lord.
>
> —*1 Corinthians 1:26–31*

Who does God's work? We do, as God works through us. Psalm 37 says, "Commit your way to the LORD;...Be still before the LORD; wait patiently for him...trust in him...he will do this." Zechariah 4:6 teaches that it is "not by might nor by power, but by my Spirit says the LORD." In John 15:5 Jesus said, "I am the vine; you are the branches. If a man remains in me and I in him, he will bear much fruit; *apart from me you can do nothing*" (author's emphasis). That doesn't do much for a proud ego.

It is no wonder that Jesus told the disciples in Luke 24:49, "Stay in the city until you have been clothed with power from on high." Because one hundred twenty followers of Christ obeyed these instructions, God sent the great firestorm of Pentecost—the birth of the church—when over three thousand came to faith in Jesus from all over the known world. What was behind it all? It was the dynamite that brings revival, God's power through *prayer* (Acts 1:14) and His *unified* people (Acts 2:1). If there were a place large enough to handle the area-wide church, I would love to see this happen in our city. The fire of the Holy Spirit would fall again.

Oswald Chambers is often quoted as follows:

> Prayer does not fit us for the greater work; prayer is the greater work. The measure of the worth of our public activity for God is the private profound communion we have with God.[7]

Dr. Martin Lloyd Jones once said:

> Prayer is the highest activity of the human soul, and therefore it is at the same time the ultimate test of a man's true spiritual condition (there is nothing so much as prayer life that tells the truth about us as Christian people). Everything we do in the Christian life is easier than prayer.[8]

E. M. Bounds declared, "Prayer is our most formidable weapon, the thing which makes all else we do efficient."[9] It is true, my fellow followers and servants of Jesus, *intimacy with God comes before productivity for God.*

One of my all-time favorite stories comes from Washington State, and her logging industry. As a boy, I lived in Port Angeles, Washington, which boasted several large paper pulp and lumber mills. Huge logging trucks frequented our highways. Long before the days of chain saws and the heavy equipment that now harvests lumber, logging crews looked for men who were skilled with a double bladed ax. Wherever the logging industry flourished, a man's man was a lumberjack, not a three hundred-pound lineman for a professional football team or a Michael Jordan of Chicago Bulls fame.

As the story goes, a young man had often dreamed of working in the woods. After graduating from high school, he decided to drive up to a logging camp where a crew was felling trees for a lumber mill. He had purchased a "professional" double bladed ax as soon as his dad—or should I say his mother—would let him. He had honed his tree felling skills as carefully as he had learned to keep his ax sharp as a razor's edge.

When he found the job foreman, he asked if he could come to work, at least for the summer. The big burly veteran of the woods looked down his nose at him and said, "Son, we only hire men on this job, men who can handle the big trees." No matter how much he urged and begged, the boss wasn't about to let the boy work with the crew in the woods. Finally, after producing his double-edged ax, the young man desperately asked if he could show him what he could do.

It was about lunchtime, so the foreman gathered some of the men around a large Douglas Fir tree to see what the boy could do. Of course, it was partly in humor, a little comic relief from the hard work of the day. With amazing skill and with his razor sharp ax, the boy shaped a perfect back cut. Rounding the tree, he skillfully finessed the front cut, and the tree fell perfectly. He skinned off the branches in short order, then stood, sweat pouring down his face and back, to wait for a response. What would the big boys say?

They were amazed. With some cheers and some "way to go kid" compliments, they recognized that a prima donna of the woods stood before them. The young man had convinced not only the foreman, but the crew as well. The summer in the woods began with great hope.

However, trouble was just around the corner. As the first few days on the job passed, the young hero worked slower and slower. After giving the boy a warning, the foreman called the wanna-be-woodsman into his trailer. "Here's your check, kid," he said. "You're slowing down the crew. You just can't keep up."

With pleas of despair, the young buck begged to stay on. It was then that the seasoned foreman leaned back in his rickety old chair to ponder what was happening. Finally, scratching his head, he asked, "Son, did you forget to sharpen your ax?"

The response was immediate, defensive, and quite revealing. "Yes," he said. "I was afraid to take the time. I didn't want to hold up the crew."

With a deep sigh, the foreman said to him, "Son, that's exactly what you did. You must sharpen your ax every morning, and several times during the day. Get back out in the woods. Keep your ax sharp, and you will do fine."[10]

Prayer keeps the ax of ministry sharp, so it can cut through the culture with the Holy Spirit's power. Satan has done a masterful job of thwarting the forward progress of God's kingdom because our ax is dull. It is time to pray—in the morning, at night, in between, and in special unified gatherings in upper rooms and large arenas. We must keep our axes razor sharp. In Appendix III, I have included some tips on prayer to help us do this.

As Dutch Sheets says:

> We can run our churches and ministries from the boardroom or the prayer room. The first produces the works of man, the other births a move of God.[11]

When God's people become untethered from truth, they begin to float purposelessly on their whims or speculation. They are easily drawn into the culture or philosophies that surround them. It is the pattern of history.

—Dr. Bob Griffin

8

Great Storms of History: Characteristic 4

WHEN I WAS a boy, we heated our home with a large wood-burning stove in our living room and cooked our food on an iron stove in the kitchen. Sometimes, it was necessary to stir a neglected fire, and I remember getting dizzy as I tried to blow sparks back into flame. Although we didn't have a bellows on our farm, I later learned that the power of a few pumps with the bellows was all I needed to produce a new flame from the embers of a fading fire.

Bellows might connote the old idea of "blowing hot air," but this is not true of the fourth characteristic of revival—the powerful preaching and teaching of the Bible, the Word of God. Through great preaching, God burns conviction into the soul, to fan new spiritual flame into the hearts of people. The truth sets people free (John 8:32; Hebrews 4:12). It burns off impurities—the old dross of cultural drift—and calls God's people to the pure gold of holiness that reflects Jesus.

God's truth is alive and powerful. It penetrates deeply into the soul like a double-edged sword. It discerns what is going on inside. It brings conviction of sin and renewed spiritual life. It is no wonder that the preaching and teaching of the Word of God takes center stage in revival. Consider the following declaration of the apostle Paul:

> All Scripture is inspired by God and is useful to teach us what is true and to make us realize what is wrong in our lives. It straightens us out and teaches us to do what is right. It is God's way of preparing us in every way, fully equipped for every good thing God wants us to do.
>
> —*2 Timothy 3:15, NLT*

This is the power of the fourth characteristic of revival.

CHARACTERISTIC 4:
BIBLICAL PREACHING: THE BELLOWS THAT
FAN THE FLAME

> Revival rested upon the powerful proclamation—preaching and teaching—of the law of God and His Word. Many revivals were the result of a return to Scripture.

God raises up great preachers, evangelists, and teachers to lead revival. Some call God's people to prayer and repentance while others set the stage for preaching by their passion for prayer and revival. When these leaders are anchored in biblical truth, the Word of God shapes the movements they spark. God's truth or law must guide revival to keep it in balance, under the direction of the Holy Spirit. All too often, extremes begin to rise under the manipulation of the enemy himself.

At first glance, some might wonder if the Word of God really did play a major role in the New York City Prayer Meeting, Welsh, and Azusa Street revivals. In the first, prayer seemed to stand alone without preaching. In the second, it could appear that Evan Roberts didn't give adequate attention to Scripture. Some have even said that the revival was brief for that reason. Some might also question the significant role of preaching or teaching in the Azusa Street Revival. However, if we take a broad view, we find that great preaching and teaching were central to all three.

Look at the role preaching has played in post-biblical revivals. The First and Second Great Awakenings were known by the effective preachers whose stories we have already told and by the powerful preaching that wove its way through the warp and woof of the revival tapestry. The strong presentation of Scripture brought the "living" (Heb. 4:12) and active impact of God's Word in evangelism and drew the fire of conviction from heaven. Thousands responded by streaming forward at invitations to receive Christ as Savior. Believers were convicted of sin that so easily had beset them or entangled them (Heb. 12:1).

What was the role of Scripture in the New York City Prayer Meeting Revival? J. Edwin Orr, one of the greatest revival historians, saw the New York City Revival as part of a much wider movement of God's Spirit. He wrote:

Finney became the literary mouthpiece of revivalism, and his works were soon spread all over the world, bearing fruit to this day…Finney lived to see the greatest religious revival of all time, the Great Revival which broke out in Canada in 1857 [as part of the New York City Prayer Meeting Revival] and swept through the United States, Northern Ireland, Scotland, Wales, England, South Africa, Scandinavia, Switzerland, and many other evangelical countries, adding millions to the professing church.[1]

Revival meetings that swept the country were initiated by prayer. However, as the Holy Spirit began to work among God's people, preaching and teaching either ran alongside the prayer movements or followed closely on their heels. Orr said:

Although prayer-meetings were the greatest vehicle of blessing in the Awakening of 1858, preaching was by no means as neglected or discarded as some writers insist…There was truly a great revival of the ministry of preaching.

Noon prayer meetings were dominant in the New York City revival, but, Orr shows, "The interest…was immediately captured and used by the evening preaching services. The…awakening was a revival of preaching."[2] The ministry of D. L. Moody began during the first part of the New York City Awakening of 1857 and, as Orr reports, later became a powerful force in Britain as well as America.[3]

Although prayer was the central characteristic in the Prayer Meeting Revival, thousands upon thousands returned to church and therefore to biblical instruction. How many returned to the church? Orr stated that there were thirty million people in the United States in 1858. When all statistical figuring was complete, probably one million of them converted to Christ within twenty-four months of the first outbreak.[4] In summarizing the larger sweep of the revival he says that approximately two million converts were added to the various churches. "The quality of the conversions was excellent and abiding."[5]

What was the role of preaching and teaching in the Welsh revival of 1904? The revival was associated with Evan Roberts, and it was generally true that he was "an exhorter rather than an expositor, and he neglected preaching and teaching the Bible." However, others played important roles. Rosina Davies was known for singing and preaching the Word of God. Jessie Penn-Lewis led Bible classes and set up the Welsh Keswick movement in 1903, a great movement centered in teaching the Bible. Seth Joshua, a Welsh Presbyterian, was an effective evangelist and held Bible conferences to teach believers about a deeper life in Christ. Joseph Jenkins, the pastor of a congregation in New Quay, had a passion to stop spiritual decline.[6]

I enjoy the way Dr. Relfe wrote about the Welsh revival:

> Though [Evan Roberts was] loudly scorned by some staid ministers for being a "youthful see," within five months 100,000 Welsh had been added to church rolls, and many more nominal church-goers had been soundly converted. The Chapels in Wales were crowded day and night for about two years...the need for additional chairs...in the aisles for another twenty years. A survey indicated that 80% of those born again during the revival of Wales, five years later, were still steadfast Christians.[7]

Revival draws people back to a deep love for God and then to the nurture of His Word. Evan Roberts was deeply impacted by Scripture. One observer reported that he was not an orator or even widely read except for the Bible. It was clear that he knew it from cover to cover—probably through the maps. When Roberts was working in a coal mine, he took his Bible to work. He kept it close on a ledge or beam, ready for any pause or break where he could read it.[8]

Bible sales mushroomed during the Welsh revival, and there was a decline in the purchase of other literature. People were purchasing Bibles in large quantities, especially pocket Testaments, which were snatched up by young men. One bookstore owner had his supply of Bibles in "dead stock" before the revival, but soon he had to pull them out to sell. He ran out of Bibles as revival came. Some who had never owned a Bible, "carried one off as a hoarded treasure."[9]

Localized revivals happened independent of Roberts' ministry. For example, special preaching services were held in Llanerchymedd. The first night, sixty-seven received Christ and on the second night, one hundred eleven came to Christ. The preacher spoke on the Holiness of God.[10]

In the Azusa Street Revival, teaching became very important. Careful teaching was needed to support Pentecostal experiences that, for the most part, were new or reborn across the church. It became important to show that the baptism of the Holy Spirit, prophecy, and speaking in tongues were biblical. Parham had established Bible schools for teaching the Word, and revival leader, Seymour, was a product of one of these schools. The Azusa Street meetings grew out of cottage meetings where Bible study and prayer were central.

The Word of God has been central to every revival. It either formed the solid foundation, (along with a renewed passion for prayer), or it followed a prayer movement. As revival came, so did the teaching and study of the Word of God.

When God's people neglect truth, they begin to float purposelessly according to their whims and speculations. They are easily drawn into the culture and philosophies that surround them. This is the pattern of history, and I believe it is where much of the church is today. The truth sets people free today just as it always has. A careful reading and a basic understanding of the Word of God opens the door to people so they can walk into the life God has designed for them; the abundant life (John 10:10).

One of life's central questions is, What does the Bible say? One of life's most important decisions is the choice to do what it says. The Bible answers the question Francis Shaeffer used years ago as the title of his popular book *How Shall We Then Live?* The Word of God is the manual on life, given to us by the Engineer of the universe. It is alive and active like yeast in dough. It discerns and corrects the thoughts and attitudes that breeze through our minds (Heb. 4:12). This is why I have chosen to include the next chapter on God's Word. It is time to embrace the theme of the *Back to the Bible* radio ministry.

A word of caution is necessary here. Being nurtured or fed by the Word of God must be balanced by exercising its truth in obedience. Elizabeth O'Connor's book title, *Journey Inward, Journey Outward*, gives us the proper balance. Our journey inward must be balanced by our journey outward. Too much journey inward can be as destructive as too much food intake without a balanced plan of exercise. It produces spiritual obesity and poor spiritual health. Some congregations, perhaps even denominations, reflect this poor health and, in fact, disobedience to the Word of God. To modify a popular saying, "All truth and no action, makes Christian Johnny a dull boy." And his church is limited in its impact for God's kingdom.

Sink the Bible to the bottom of the sea, and man's obligation to God would be unchanged. He would have the same path to tread, only his map and his guide would be gone; he would have the same voyage to make, only his compass and chart would be overboard.[1]

—*Henry Ward Beecher*

The Bible is God's chart for you to steer by, to keep you from the bottom of the sea, and to show you where the harbor is, and how to reach it without running on rocks or bars.[2]

—*Henry Ward Beecher*

9

The Word of God: An Amazing Strategic Weapon

S I WRITE, America is at war. The date, September 11, 2001 (9/11), sends flashbacks—if not chills—across the hearts and minds of most Americans. On that terrible day, religious terrorists penetrated the security of our nation and inflicted devastation and death. Militant Muslims, commandeering two commercial planes attacked the Twin Towers in New York City. One moment the towers stood as the proud symbols of America's financial strength, international economic superiority, and architectural creativity. In a brief moment of time, they became a pile of rubble and bodies, symbolizing the vulnerability of a nation that thought her security was impenetrable.

A third plane hit the Pentagon, the headquarters of the nation's military. A penetrating question swept through our minds. *How can this be possible? We are the most powerful military nation in the world.* A fourth plane was probably targeting the White House. Thankfully, brave passengers wrestled it away from the terrorists, and it crashed in a field, killing all the passengers on board. They gave their lives for their nation.

America's pride and security were reduced to fear and uncertainty, and thousands died. Marriages were mangled as partners slipped into eternity, and children were left with only one parent. Churches were opened, and prayer became popular again. For two months it looked like America might turn back to God. For a brief time, "In God we trust," the motto printed on American coins, became true again. In the grief and horror following the attack, the Bible was quoted and embraced, as millions found comfort in God and His truth. The liberal secular press and the American Civil Liberties Union were silent. On a political level, America responded with a massive military buildup and war against terrorism.

If you are a follower of Jesus Christ—a Christian—you face a terrorist every day. He is Satan, the god of this world, and he goes about as a devourer, to steal, kill, and destroy (see John 10:10). No one is exempt from his evil ways. Each day we face perilous attacks and deception from this enemy—the devil—and his hierarchy of principalities, powers, and rulers in dark and wicked high places. Satan prowls around like a lion, like those who quietly used our airlines to wreak death and destruction in our land. He is sometimes a roaring lion, too. However, when he roars, it is only to strike fear in people, to intimidate them.

The principalities, powers, and demonic forces that carry out Satan's horrors are subtle, sadistic, and evil. We face battles that are psychological and emotional, cultural and cross-cultural. Our eyes and ears are inundated with enemy rhetoric from secular media and lies—often presented as cunning half-truths of Satan. He is an angel of light. His New Age subtlety is magnetic and appears to be good. His redefinition of tolerance opposes the presentation of truth and the gospel.

Christians, we are fighting in enemy territory. We are away from our eternal home, living as aliens and foreigners in a secular and sensual society where cultural values are far from biblical. Our nation, once considered generically Christian, is now nearly controlled by enemy advances. We live in a post-Christian world and have come untethered from biblical truth like that of the Ten Commandments. The culture in which we live is floating on the sea of secularism, guided by those who most convincingly capture the media. A small vocal minority sometimes shapes values simply by gaining a hearing with the press or government. Today many believe right and wrong are relative.

Our nation has highly regarded secular gods. One of the most powerful is the god of tolerance, which has nearly reduced dialogue about Christian truth and values to silence. Tolerance used to mean that people could try to convert each other to their faith or point of view and still live together civilly. It implied respect for the differing beliefs of others. Now, it is inappropriate to speak out with the intent to convert others to Christian faith. It is considered intolerant.

We experienced problems related to tolerance when, in a grand litany, we declared Jesus Lord and King over Rockford, Illinois in an area-wide prayer gathering at our city's grand historic Coronado Theater. The name *Coronado* means "place of coronation," and the so-named theater was a fitting place to publicly affirm that Jesus is Lord. Those "Christians" who had embraced the new definition of tolerance came out of the theological woodwork and used newspaper editorials to condemn what we had done. They said it was not only intolerant, but also arrogant and lacking in humility.

It seems that we are becoming like the culture of Judges 17:6: "In those days Israel had no king, so the people did whatever seemed right in their own eyes." No longer do the majority of people openly worship the God of Abraham, Isaac, and Jacob. Many who profess faith in God and even claim salvation through Jesus Christ, ignore obedience to even basic truths of the Bible.

The war in which we are engaged began eons ago. The enemy, Satan, with ego in hand, tried to take over God's throne and was kicked out of heaven. With him went a host of lesser spirits, a hierarchy of leaders, and a host of demons. A battle raged in the Garden of Eden after man was created, and Satan won. Man's fellowship with God was broken by sin, and Adam and Eve had to leave the beautiful pristine Eden, God's artistic natural masterpiece and perfect environment.

Man, as he had been warned, was separated from God, the holy and righteous One. God's righteousness required Him to keep His Word even as He loved us unconditionally with incomprehensible love. Sin had to have a payday. Nature fell with the terrible consequences of hard labor and pain in childbirth, and life became sweat, blood, and tears.

Spiritual war continued throughout Israel's history. In chapter 3, we learned how Israel was called to be a vibrant community of faith, a witness to all the nations around them. She was to tell the story about the love and grace of the one true God. After many centuries, suffering time and again from the disease of drift, she was declared a prostitute (see Ezekiel 16:15). She worshiped and served other gods and went through the pattern of revival many times until God's patience ran out.

Warfare became more intense when Jesus was born. King Herod, whimsically evil and under the influence of Satan, tried to win a decisive, once-for-all victory by wiping out the Messiah. Herod missed his target and tragically destroyed many other young innocent lives. Furious fighting raged as Jesus began His public ministry. He went head to head with Satan in the Judean wilderness after He fasted and prayed for forty days, and He took a decisive victory. Satan finally departed in defeat, but continued looking for a more opportune time (see Luke 4:14).

The enemy found an avenue of attack through the religious leadership of the day. At Gethsemane, Jesus fought His final battle to submit to the Father's will and accept the bitter cup of the cross. He endured hideous torture and abuse at the hands of religious and civic leaders and was convicted by affirming that He was God. Jesus went confidently to Golgotha, the place of the skull.

His walk to that hideous place was nearly deadly because of His loss of blood from gaping wounds. He crumbled under the weight of the Roman cross He was forced to carry and on which He would die. Satan thought he had won a historic victory when Jesus gave up His life, but Satan was wrong. It was all part of God's plan to provide redemption through the resurrection of Jesus from the grave. Sin's debt was paid. Death died that day. Glory to God!

The very people Jesus came to save were the ones who took His precious life. It was terrorism, brutal torture, and the worst of battlefield realities and nightmares. When a sword pierced Jesus' side a flow of blood and water poured out. Some believe this indicates that Jesus died of a broken heart. Satan had laid out the worst he had in his awful arsenal. The celebration had more than likely begun among the hateful hordes of hell when three days after Jesus' death, word came that He was alive!

It was the pinnacle of redemptive history. War had been waged, and Jesus had won. Satan, death, and hell were defeated for all time. Satan was disarmed (Col 2:15) and condemned to hell, with all his evil cohorts. In time he will be thrown into the lake of fire. However, in God's plan, Satan continues to be operative within a limited sphere of influence—tethered, as it were, on a long rope—until Jesus returns for His church.

Jesus' death provided eternal life for all who believe in Him. He made eternity with God possible: a new home in heaven...abundant life until then...the opportunity to serve the righteous and redemptive kingdom of God. Our Lord gave us—the saints of God—the unfathomable gift of eternal life and the honor to serve our Creator, along with myriad's of angels, in great worship and praise for all eternity.

We are engaged in a war for the souls of mankind. We are fighting a defeated enemy, and we have the assurance of Christ's unconditional and incomprehensible love, His presence, and powerful help through all life's battles. However, we tend to forget this and we soon find ourselves living in defeat or slavery. It is the problem of drift that has plagued God's people throughout time.

Time and again, God's people throughout history have drifted into the attitudes and actions of the surrounding culture. Even though they pay terrible consequences, they become numb to the truth or deny its validity. Materialism, sensuality, self-centeredness, and power-plays take center stage, even in the church.

The church needs to return to the Word of God, to the truth that sets people free (John 8:32). The Word of God is powerful. It is no wonder that the fourth characteristic of revival is a return to the Word of God and its preaching and teaching.

> The word of God is living and active. Sharper than any double-edged sword, it penetrates even to dividing soul and spirit, joints and marrow; it judges the thoughts and attitudes of the heart.
> —*Hebrews 4:12*

Why has the church failed to sustain revival? People quit praying. They become busy with the excitement of revival and taking care of new believers. They become prosperous and blessed—and apathetic. Drift sets in.

Again, I ask, why has the church failed to sustain revival? God's people move away from the disciplined study of the Bible and particularly its application to daily life. Obedience drifts into tolerance and a comfortable apathy. Revival, including the blessings of God that flow from it, has to be aggressively given away.

Prayer and the Word of God are the two primary strategic weapons in the war we are fighting. They are the keys to sustaining a historic move of God. Before I discuss the remaining characteristics of revival, I want to suggest a wonderful victory strategy. I believe it is critically important if we are going to see revival sweep our nation and the world before Jesus returns.

GOOD NEWS

Spiritual warfare rages around us each day. Recognizing this and understanding our need of equipment to fight, we turn our attention to 2 Peter 1:3–4:

> His divine power has given us everything we need for life and
> godliness through our knowledge of him who called us by his
> own glory and goodness. Through these he has given us his very
> great and precious promises, so that through them you may par-
> ticipate in the divine nature and escape the corruption in the
> world caused by evil desires.

These verses remind us that we have been given everything we need
for life and godliness. This is good news as we face the enemy day-by-
day. If we try to win battles with our own wisdom or the strategies of the
world, we lose. The apostle Paul warned us that though we live in the
world, we do not wage war as the world does. Our weapons are superior.
With them, we have divine power to demolish or bring down enemy fortresses or strongholds (2 Cor. 10:3–4). These strongholds are a central
strategy of the enemy.

Paul told us how to demolish strongholds. We demolish arguments and
every pretension that sets itself up against the knowledge of God... Here's
the secret: "We take captive every thought to make it obedient to Christ"
(2 Cor. 10:5). When we tie this text to John 8:31–32, we have a phenomenal truth and a winning combination. In these verses, Jesus—the Great
Warrior—said that *if we hold to His teaching*, we really are His disciples,
His followers. Then, holding on to His truth, we can be set free. Notice
the implication that if we do not hold to His truth, we are not His disciples, and we will remain captives.

We must *take captive every thought* and the lies of Satan by replacing them with truth. *Take captive* is an aggressive, intentional, pro-active
phrase. Most of what Satan says to deceive us is a half-truth. We would
probably discern a bold-faced lie, but we must be on guard for the subtleties of Satan's sneaky deception.

The Bible warns about choices that would open the door to Satan's
control in our lives—enemy camps in the territory of our souls. "In your
anger do not sin: Do not let the sun go down while you are still angry,
and do not give the devil a foothold [or stronghold]" (Eph 4:26–27).
Notice that the battlefront is our soul—our conscious and subconscious
mind and our will and emotions. Anger is the example in this text, but I
am convinced it is only one of many door openers for Satan, one of many

potential areas of disobedience and sin.

This is strategic war counsel: Watch out for strongholds. The primary battleground is our mind. Paul wanted us to know this, and he wrote:

> You were taught, with regard to your former way of life, to put off your old self, which is being corrupted by its deceitful desires; to be made new *in the attitude of your minds;* and to put on the new self, created to be like God in true righteousness and holiness.
> —*Ephesians 4:22-24, Author's emphasis*

Satan is a masterful liar, and we must replace his lies and deception with biblical truth. This is exactly what Jesus did when He went head to head with Satan in the wilderness. After each half-truth, Jesus came back with, "It is written" (Matthew 4:4). James 4:6–7 says that if we resist the devil he has to flee from us. Jesus resisted him with truth, and he slithered away.

We have the power—in Jesus' name—to do just as Jesus did. He is in us, and He is greater than our enemy, who is in the world (1 John 4:4). This was not true before we invited Jesus to take up residence in us. According to Ephesians 2:5, we were dead in trespasses and sins before that decision. We were not only dead, but we were owned and duped by the enemy. At salvation, however, we were raised up into heavenly places, the intangible spiritual world, and seated at the right hand of Jesus.

In Ephesians 1:19, Paul tells us that God's power—resurrection power—is available to us who believe. He continues in verses 20–22 and explains that Jesus is the head over all principalities and powers. We have incredible resources in Him. When we speak in the name of Jesus, Satan must listen. When we resist Satan, he must flee. Paul wrote to the Galatian Christians and said, "It is for freedom that Christ has set us free" (Gal 5:1). Sin's power over them was broken, and the same is true for all believers. Paul concluded this declaration of freedom with a serious warning: Keep standing in freedom. Do not be subject again to a yoke of slavery.

We not only have war wisdom; we also have strategic weapons. The power we have available in Christ is incomparably great (Eph 1:19). Jesus promised in Matthew 18:18–19 that whatever we bind on Earth will be bound in heaven. Whatever we loose on Earth will be loosed in heaven.

Job 1:10 and Hosea 2:6 mention God's hedges, His protection. I believe God has set a hedge of protection around each believer, and I ask for it to be strengthened each day.

The Bible makes over three hundred references to angels. Psalm 91:9–12 says that angels serve us and guard us. They pick us up lest we dash our foot against a stone. Psalm 34:7 encourages us, "The angel of the LORD encamps around those who fear him, and he delivers them." Isaiah 59:19 declares, "When the enemy shall come in like a flood, the Spirit of the LORD shall lift up a standard against him" (KJV).

Several years ago, I was in charge of the intercessory prayer team for a major city outreach in what we called the "war zone," an area of high crime and homicides. Local pastors presented the gospel every half-hour, and Christians distributed a large quantity of food and provided many social services. The day before the big event, a group of intercessors gathered with me to commit the park to God and ask for His protection from any enemy efforts to destroy or distract from the outreach. At each corner we anointed the ground with oil, a symbol of the Holy Spirit. We also took communion at each corner and asked for the protection of the blood of Jesus—like in the Exodus of Israel from Egypt.

On the day of the outreach, things were going very well. Hundreds gathered from the local housing projects and neighborhoods, and many were coming to faith in Christ. The intercessors were on duty with me praying the entire day. At mid-morning, as we stood in a circle and prayed under a large oak tree, an older man walked down the street, entered the park and joined our circle. At one point he interrupted our praying. "You may think I am crazy," he said, "but as I walked up to the park a few minutes ago, I saw four massive angels, each with long swords raised, standing at the four corners of the park. I just wanted to let you know." Isn't that exciting? What he described was exactly what we had requested.

There is, always has been, and always shall be great power in the blood of Jesus. I believe this is very strategic truth in the battle against Satan and his kingdom, and we must apply it to the best of our understanding. Do you remember the story of Israel's escape from Egypt? In the last plague, a death angel was released to kill the first-born boys of the Egyptians. God's people were told to kill a lamb and place the blood at the top and sides of the doorway to their homes. This was a picture of the cross on which, in time, the eternal Lamb of God—Jesus—would die to save us from sin, Satan, death, and hell.

Revelation 12:11 reports that the saints defeated Satan by the blood of the Lamb. In the dedication of the tabernacle in the Old Testament (Ezekiel 45:18; Exodus 29:19) and in the dedication of the priest's garments, a lamb was killed and its blood was sprinkled strategically, according to God's instructions. How does this relate to us? I believe we can, by faith, apply the blood of Jesus to ourselves—body, soul, and spirit—and also to our dwellings. Doing this provides special spiritual protection. (See Appendix II.)

Colossians 2:15 says that Jesus disarmed the powers and authorities of evil and made a spectacle of them, triumphing over them by the cross. Satan and his cohorts are disarmed and toothless, and the only power they are able to use is deception. This is how the enemy brings God's people under his influence. He is able set up camp in their souls and create strongholds by tempting them to sin and then not deal with it. However, we have all the armor and strategic weaponry we need to live in victory over him.

BAD NEWS

In spite of the good news that God has provided all we need for our spiritual warfare, we must also face the bad news: We can lose the battle. If we do not manage our mind and emotions with truth, the enemy can establish strongholds within our souls. Satan can never touch our spirit because it is the Holy Spirit's dwelling. Picture a target with three rings and a red bull's eye in the center. For the purpose of this word picture, the bull's eye represents our spirit. That is where the Holy Spirit comes to reside when we ask Jesus Christ to be our Savior and Lord. We belong to Him, and He possesses us. The Christian can never be demon-possessed.

The next ring depicts our soul. This is the area of our conscious and subconscious mind, our emotions and will. It is where Satan can enter and bring some perpetuating demonic forces to camp out. We can't be demon-possessed, but we can be demonized and suffer from this kind of evil influence. As we mentioned above, Ephesians 4:26–27 warns us not to let the sun go down on our anger or we will give the devil a foothold. The third and final ring is our physical body, the house in which we live.

In our "Good News" section, we looked at Galatians 5:1 and its instructions to keep standing firm and not to be subject again to a yoke of slavery. These words communicate a terrible potential: We can lose our freedom in Christ and become enslaved again. In his letter to the Galatians, Paul warns against the law that enslaves people. The Holy Spirit gives life, but legalism—our best efforts to keep God's law and our accompanying failures—brings death (2 Cor. 3:6). Many people try and fail, try and fail. They do not seem to understand that it is not about trying. Instead, it is about trusting God, His love, mercy, and grace.

The Christian life is not about arriving at perfection; it is about laying aside the past and pressing ahead to the wonderful calling of God. As Paul shares in his testimony in Philippians 3:12–14, it is not about arriving, but being on the way and pressing on toward God's high calling. It is all done in the power of the Holy Spirit, growing in Christ and His lavish love.

It is important that we identify our strongholds and get rid of them. We must also identify generational sins and curses that have been passed on to us, renouncing them in Jesus' name, and casting away any and all perpetuating demonic activity. Obedience brings God's blessings, but disobedience invites curses, as we learn in Deuteronomy chapters eleven and twenty-eight.

Exodus 34:6–7 describes God's love to a thousand generations, but it also teaches that the sins of the fathers are passed on to the third and fourth generation. (Also see Exodus 20:6; Deuteronomy 5:9–10.) For example, children who have been abused often grow up to be abusers. Promiscuity, divorce, violent behavior, alcoholism, and drug abuse seem to pass from one generation to another.

Over the past several years Connie and I have become aware of generational curses or strongholds that were passed on to us. As we have discerned their identity, we have renounced them and broken them. We discovered that they were like a ball and chain around our ankles. They hindered our efforts to run the Christian race and stretch for the prize of God's high calling. We were able to receive guidance and help for these spiritual struggles by praying with very discerning intercessors.

We urge every believer to be very intentional about getting rid of generational sins and curses. If you have been engaged in sexual sin, sexual bonds must be broken and renounced. Patterns of addiction, abusive talk or behavior, divorce, fear, anger, and depression could indicate generational strongholds or curses. All of God's people need to be aggressive about spiritual house cleaning or soul cleansing.

Jesus wants all His people to be free, really free. A very helpful tool for this purpose is *Seven Steps to Freedom,* a work and prayer booklet written by Dr. Neal Anderson. It is also helpful to read Neal's book, *The Bondage Breaker,* which is listed in the bibliography. This material is proving to be powerful and effective for many people who desire to grow into a much deeper level of freedom in Christ. It is a wonderful beginning place. (See Appendix IV.)

Sin's power over us is broken, but we can once again be subject to its power. Satan has no right of ownership or authority over us, and he is defeated. However, he is bound and determined to keep us from understanding the truth. He knows he can block our effectiveness as individuals, or as a church, if he can deceive us with his lies.

Paul warned the believers in Corinth about this. In 2 Corinthians 11:3–4, he said, "I am afraid that just as Eve was deceived by the serpent's cunning, your *minds* may somehow be led astray from your sincere and pure devotion of Christ" (author's emphasis). Paul was also concerned about the Thessalonians and wrote, "I sent…to find out about your faith. I was afraid that in some way the tempter might have tempted you and our efforts might have been useless" (1 Thess. 3:5).

I fear that the church is ineffective because of Satan's subtle work in the lives of believers and church leaders. Satan loves to quietly grow fat calluses of sin and compromise over the sensitivities of God's people. Or he quite logically convinces us to do church our way, not according to God's Word. Simple instructions, like the Great Commandment and the Great Commission, easily take a backseat to other agendas. We speak to people about *coming* to church, when God's instructions say more about *going* into the world with the gospel.

God's love is unconditional and incomprehensible, but His blessings depend on obedience. As a pastoral counselor, I meet professing Christians whose lives are a disaster. Some of their stories are like a sensual soap opera. Others who come for help are angry with God because it seems that He hasn't kept His word. After listening to their stories, I discover that they have lived lives of quiet and sometimes overt disobedience. They tragically illustrate the fact that disobedience is deadly in the lives of God's people.

However, Jesus gave the solution for brokenness that comes from disobedience. In John 8:31–32, He said, "You are truly my disciples if you keep obeying my teachings. And you will know the truth, and the truth will set you free" (NLT). To live a life of obedience as a Christian is the only way to live the Christian life. God is the engineer of life and living. We must grow to know His manual, the Word of God, and press ahead, growing in understanding and obedience.

Spiritual warfare is not always a power encounter, but it is always a truth encounter. This principle is very important because Satan's power to oppose us is in his lies. He deceives the whole world and leads it astray. He also accuses believers—you and me—night and day. When we sin, he jumps all over us. If we are not careful and alert, we can easily believe his condemnation.

However, God has a much better plan for us. He invites us to confess our sin—agree with God that we have sinned—and embrace the wonderful truth, love, and grace of 1 John 1:9. In this amazing verse, the apostle John says, "If we confess our sins, he is faithful and just and will forgive us our sins and purify us from all unrighteousness." Once we have confessed our sin, we must lay it down and grow on.

The entire world is under the influence of Satan (1 John 5:19). He goes about to steal, kill, and destroy. In contrast, Jesus comes to give us life—a life described as abundant (John 10:10). I wish we could lock in on this truth when the enemy tells us the non-believing world has it so much better than us. That's a lie! There is enjoyment in sin for a short time, but the end result is terrible—today, and especially in eternity. Satan's deception has caused incredible brokenness, even among professing Christians who are looking for the good life (Prov. 10:23; 21:17; 2 Tim. 3:4).

In the Old Testament, King Saul had great potential. However, he flagrantly disobeyed God, and it cost him the throne. King David, who was called "a man after [God's] own heart" (1 Sam. 13:14; Acts 13:22) followed him. He sinned too, but returned to God with a repentant, broken heart.

God restored David to Himself, but even then, his life and his family bore the scars of sin. The Bible is clear, the rich blessing of God is promised to those who "hunger and thirst for righteousness" (Matt. 5:6).

The church today desperately needs revival because too many of God's people believe the lies of Satan and the culture in which they live. "Be a good religious person," the enemy tells us, "but don't be a prude or take the Bible too seriously. You might offend someone." As a result, preachers and teachers hesitate to declare God's truth about sin and repentance. The church no longer pushes back the darkness and is no longer attractive to the nonbeliever. Although it has religious ritual and form, it is not obedient. First Samuel 15:22 speaks to this very pointedly and says, "To obey is better than sacrifice."

In John 15:14 Jesus said, "You are my friends if you *do* what I command" (author's emphasis). Can we conclude that those who are not pursuing obedience are just casual acquaintances of Jesus? In the same chapter, the obedience of Jesus to His Father is presented as the ultimate example for us (vv. 9–11). The Old Testament proverb puts it this way: "One who turns away his ear from hearing the law, Even his prayer is an abomination" (Prov. 28:9, NKJV).

The covenant blessings of God are for those who obey. Obedience and the pursuit of holiness are not burdensome (1 John 5:3). Instead, they offer wonderful freedom and the abundant life. God was very clear with His instructions to Joshua (Josh. 1:1–9). Paying careful attention to God's law and obeying it guarantees success.

We must pursue truth because it liberates us from Satan's subtle deception. We must also declare God's truth to ourselves, to the culture around us, and to Satan himself. This is how we gain victory over the world, the flesh, and the devil, the three primary sources of lies and deception. I have found it helpful to pray truth into my soul and my behavior through the apostolic prayers in Ephesians 1:17–23; 3:16–21, and Philippians 1:9–11. I have also been strengthened by confessing my way through Galatians 5 and by asking the Holy Spirit to fill and control me so that His fruit is produced in me.

Most of us have heard that God has a wonderful plan for our lives (Jer. 29:11), and this is true. The Christian life is abundant and God does promise to meet our needs. However, this does not mean that we will live free from problems and spiritual warfare. We will not necessarily always have everything we ever wanted or demanded. As I look back over many years of following and serving Jesus, I can say that it has been an absolutely abundant and blessed life—very, very good. On the other hand, it has been very, very difficult at times.

I have noticed that my most difficult times have produced the most faith and growth. The apostle Peter taught that we are like gold that is being refined by heat (1 Pet. 1:7). The more pure the gold, the more perfectly Jesus is reflected in our lives. Jesus' words in John 16:33 offer us some growth producing wisdom: "I have told you these things, so that in me you may have peace. In this world *you will have trouble*. But take heart! I have overcome the world" (author's emphasis).

It helps to remember that this life is brief, and that I am heading home to glory soon. Life is abundant. I am privileged to be a part of what God is doing. God has given me everything I need for this life and for godliness. He will never leave or forsake me, and in my case, He is the best Father anyone could ever have. Yes, we fight a defeated enemy whom Jesus conquered by His death and resurrection. Jesus, who lives in you and me, is greater than the enemy who is in the world (1 John 4:4).

Very Good News

The fact that we are at war may seem like very bad news. However, let me share some very good news. Listen to the powerful and progressive logic of the Bible: We can know the truth and the truth will set us free (John 8:32). Jesus is the way, the truth, and the life (John 14:6). The Holy Spirit guides us into all truth, and He lives inside us (John 16:13). Jesus' prayer for us is that we will be set apart—sanctified—in and through the truth. God's Word is truth, and it keeps us strong against the enemy of our soul until we are taken out of this world (John 17:15, 17).

We have all the resources we need through the Word of God, through God's resurrection power within us, and through the spiritual armor He has provided for the daily battle (Eph. 6:10–18). God has given us wonderful biblical truths, and we can focus our minds on them and take captive every thought (2 Cor. 10:5). When we do, we will know God's peace. The apostle Paul counseled us to manage our minds well.

> Finally, brothers, whatever is true, whatever is noble, whatever is right, whatever is pure, whatever is lovely, whatever is admirable—if anything is excellent or praiseworthy—*think about such things.* Whatever you have learned or received or heard from me, or seen in me—*put it into practice.* And the God of peace will be with you.
>
> —*Philippians 4:8–9, Author's emphasis*

According to Romans 15:4, "everything that was written in the past was written to teach us, so that through endurance and the encouragement of the Scriptures we might have hope." We cannot expose Satan's lies by our reasoning, but by God's revelation! Faith does not create reality; it responds to reality. Faith is choosing to believe God's revealed truth and being set free.

Have you ever noticed that the armor of God includes only one offensive weapon? Although the preparation of the gospel, given as our footwear for walking in victory day by day, may be considered an offensive weapon, the primary offensive weapon is the sword of the Spirit, the Word of God. This sword is an amazing, strategic weapon! The psalmist celebrates it in Psalm 19:7–8 and describes it as "perfect, reviving the soul…trustworthy, making wise the simple." Its commands are radiant, and they give light to the eyes. This sword is more valuable than pure gold. It can warn us, and we have great reward if we use it wisely (Ps. 19:7–11).

It would take an entire book to unpack the incredible truths of Psalm 119, with its 176 verses devoted to the sword, the Word of God. One of its significant teachings, in verse nine, is that a young man (and old man) can keep his way pure by living according to the Word of God. This truth needs to be powerfully driven into the souls of our Christian men today. Also, in verse eleven we are told that hiding the Word of God in our heart will help us live in victory over sin.

Jesus was steeped in Scripture. When Satan tempted Him in the wilderness, He quoted the Word of God. When He went to Nazareth at the beginning of His ministry, He quoted Isaiah's prophesy about Himself (Isa. 61:1–3; Luke 4:18–19) and when He was hanging on the cross, He quoted Psalm 22:1 as He carried our sin and suffered the eternal judgment we deserved (Matt. 27:46).

Martin Luther, who penned the great hymn, "A Mighty Fortress Is Our God," knew the power of the Word. The truth of the Word of God moved him so deeply that in 1517 he nailed his "Ninety-Five Theses" to a church door for all to see. It revolutionized the church and corrected the course of history. Recall those great words.

> Still our ancient foe doth seek to work us woe, his craft and power are great, and armed with cruel hate, on earth is not his equal. Did we in our own strength confide, our striving would be losing…We tremble not at him. His rage we can endure. One little Word will fell him.[3]

When the Greek word *logos* is translated "word," it speaks of the entire Scripture. The Greek word *rhema* is also translated "word," but it pictures a small dagger for close fighting. In my early years of discipleship, as I worked to overcome my broken past—Satan's lies and my own—I recorded key Scripture verses on note cards. I carried these "rhemas" in my pocket, and, in the heat of the battle, I would pull them out and speak the truth in the face of the lies. In time the little stack of cards became too large for my pocket, and I began to list scriptures in categories.

Today I carry twenty-four pages of strategic texts in my briefcase, and every few months I read and pray through these verses of transforming truth in my devotional time. It is like downloading God's Word onto the computer of my soul so that when I hit the proper icons or keys, God's truth and promises come up on the screen of my mind. If you face specific battles, I suggest that you do the same. It will set you free and keep you from sin. God's truth will help you take captive every thought. It has the power to change feelings. Romans 10:17 teaches that "faith comes from hearing the message, and the message is heard through the word of Christ."

The personal study and application of the sword of the Spirit, the Word of God, is very important for spiritual warfare. You may benefit from a list of texts on our web page at www.rockfordrenewalministries.org. The scriptures are categorized under the following topics:

1. God's power and ability
2. God's perspective; His love, character, and care; His promises

of provision through prayer; my object of trust

3. God's principles for life, ministry, and growth
4. Spiritual disciplines
5. Managing the mind
6. The Word of God; the truth, the manual on doing life
7. God's financial provision and promises
8. Healing scriptures. Appendix V gives the introduction to this list and presents scriptural truth I tell myself before I read it.

If revival is to come, the preaching and teaching of the Word of God will be a central characteristic of it. The church will have to return to a serious commitment to Scripture, from the superficial level of merely learning information to the intentional posture of seeking a heart understanding and living it out day by day. God's people will have to exercise radical obedience that makes no room for excuses. If revival is going to be sustained, it will be the result of disciplined growth in intimate relationship with God and the practice of His Word.

The degree to which we are mature in Christ is the degree to which our lives reflect the fruit of the Holy Spirit listed in Galatians 5:22–23. As we consider this truth, it is important that we evaluate if our lives are on the growing edge of a closer relationship with God. Are we becoming holy—totally God's in every way and used only for His redemptive purpose? Are we growing in holiness, becoming more and more God's possession, looking and acting more like Jesus?

Greg Frizzell's book, *Returning to Holiness*, describes the sad state of the church in America and urges God's people to return to holiness. After reading this book, I created an evaluation list I entitled "The Hot Pursuit of Holiness." I carry a small version of this in my Day-Timer and have a larger version at my treadmill where I do a lot of praying. As I pray through the list several times a week, I confess my sin and reinforce the ministry of biblical truth in my heart. Perhaps you will find it helpful to do this. The list is printed below.

THE HOT PURSUIT OF HOLINESS

This list of questions is offered as a resource for daily reflection and repentance and an instrument that will promote intimacy with God. It is not intended to be an exercise in legalism, but a guide to help you personally apply God's Word to your life. Obedience to Scripture will result in blessing, as shown in Deuteronomy chapters eleven and twenty-eight. Your spirit will be strengthened and renewed in Christ as you write out the apostolic prayers of Ephesians 1:17–23, 3:16–21, and Philippians 1:9–11 in a helpful paraphrase and pray them regularly.

> The fruit of righteousness will be peace; the effect of righteousness will be *quietness and confidence forever;*
> —Isaiah 32:17, *Author's emphasis*

- What are my thoughts? Are they out of line with Scripture and the Holy Spirit?

- What are my attitudes? Do they reflect Jesus and His Word?

- What kind of words am I communicating? Do they honor God?

- What relationships are not right in my life? Where is there a need for reconciliation and healing of stress? Where do I need to give or receive forgiveness?

- What are my sins of commission—things I did that I should not have done?

- What are my sins of omission—things I failed to do in obedience and honor to Christ?

- Where and when am I living in self-rule or self-reliance?

- How am I dealing with the lust of the *flesh*, the lust of the *eyes*, and the *pride* of life?

- How well am I resisting the *world*, the *flesh*, and the *devil*?

- How well am I progressing on my growing edge—for example, faith instead of worry or fussing?

- My growing edge(s) is (are):

  _____

- How well do I reflect the fruit of the Spirit and the Spirit's filling and control?

  (The fruit of the Spirit is love, joy, peace, patience [long-suffering], kindness, gentleness, goodness, faithfulness, and self-control.)

- How well and how passionately am I loving God, with all my heart, soul, mind, and strength? How well am I loving others as myself?

- How well am I practicing the beatitudes, which bring God's blessing?

  Being poor in spirit, realizing my desperate need of God;
  Mourning over my sinful spiritual condition and mourning with those who mourn;
  Being meek, gentle, and lowly, with managed strength;
  Hungering and thirsting after righteousness, that which is right and good;
  Being merciful, going beyond justice (James 2:13);
  Being pure in heart and soul: my conscious and subconscious mind, my will, and my emotions;
  Being a peacemaker, not a troublemaker;
  Being persecuted because of righteousness;
  Being insulted, persecuted, falsely accused with evil because of Jesus; Am I glad? Do I rejoice?

Oh, that it would happen again in America, that the walls would come down, that followers of Jesus would love and serve each other in unity. The world would know the Father sent the Son. It would thrill the heart of God and many who are calling the church to unity across the nation.

—Dr. Bob Griffin

10

Great Storms of History: Characteristics 5–10

M Y LIFETIME HAS seen the use of four-letter words become defiled with cursing and evil. However, some powerfully posi- tive four-letter words *do* have great significance. Consider the word *save*. Think about the power of the words *true*, *life*, *love*, and *care*. Each one is loaded with great meaning.

Another four-letter word that is woven throughout the Bible could very well stir up a negative response or at least distaste in many who claim to be followers of Jesus. It is the key to enjoying the good gifts of God, but it requires that we stand strong against the cultural tide. This source of God's promised covenant blessings is the powerful little four-letter word and command, *obey*. God's love is incomprehensible and immense, beyond measurement, but if we want to enjoy all God has for us, we must trust God and obey Him. When I was a boy, our little con- gregation sang these truths.

I have heard many Christians complain about the problems in their lives when I meet with them in counseling sessions. Life has unraveled, and they have come for help. As I listen to them, I begin to coach them toward repentance and a life of obedience. This is what God, the engineer who designed us and wants us to enjoy His wonderful love and gifts, tells us in His manual.

The fifth characteristic of revival is a return to first love: intimacy with God and a deep, growing, commitment to holiness and obedience. The result of this is a renewed commitment to serve God's kingdom purpose, and Christian leadership must disciple and equip people to do this. When God's people are motivated and mobilized to serve Him, they move out to love others and change their world.

CHARACTERISTIC 5:
EQUIPPING THE SAINTS TO SERVE GOD'S PURPOSE

Revival in the Old Testament reflected the work of God the Father to awaken His people, Israel, to a restored relationship with Him, to obey Him, and serve His purpose. Revival in the New Testament and post-biblical history reflected the work of the Holy Spirit in miracles and the equipping of people for ministry. It resulted in the spread of the gospel and the growth of the church.

This characteristic describes a newly revived church that is motivated and mobilized to ministry that eventually draws thousands to faith in Christ as Savior. In all five of the post biblical revivals, the church grew in great numbers. Church buildings that once served a handful of faithful saints became full to overflowing. Out of this electrified spiritual environment, many were called into vocational ministry and/or missionary work at home and abroad.

One of the exciting results of the First Great Awakening was the creation of new approaches to evangelism. Itinerant preachers were common and even those in more stable ministries often took a leave of absence to travel and speak. As the church came out of her four walls, and into the streets, incredible social impact resulted. Many schools and orphanages were birthed, and the moral climate of the colonies was changed. Jonathan Edwards left a fervent piety to be modeled alongside excellence in intellectual pursuits.[1]

Mary Relfe, writing in her unique and flamboyant style, said:

Multitudes of new Christian Protestants addressed social sins with such compassion and mercy, that enemies of the state were unable to incite unrest among the poor and needy.

The Christian conscience permeated society after this Great Revival as yeast does dough. Education was Bible-oriented again…Believers, as in prior years, began caring for the elderly in their homes, and an intense sympathy was created for the poor. Genuine national prosperity followed. It was called the Industrial Revolution.[2]

Winke Pratney described how the great preacher/scholar Jonathan Edwards was concerned that some of the emotional extremes in meetings, were merely expressions of the flesh. Edwards wanted concrete results, not just emotion. In genuine results Edwards warned, there must first be a demonstration of "aversion to judging other professing Christians." There must be "a very great sense of the importance of moral social duties and how great a part religion lay in them." With these results, "There was such a new sense and conviction of this beyond what had been before that it seemed to be as it were a clear discovery was made to the soul."[3]

Henry Johnson described what was happening in the United Kingdom as God called and equipped gifted revivalists for the hour.

> They awakened thousands of nominal Christians to realize the true meaning of the Divine revelation in Jesus Christ. They induced thousands of persons to read and study the Bible, which had been regarded by multitudes as a mere fetish, by other large numbers as a book intended only for parsons, and which to a majority of the rural population was practically unknown. They were the means of raising up bands of lay-preachers, on fire with love and zeal, for disseminating the Gospel among the poor and the laboring classes of towns and villages....They were the means of the conversion of hundreds of ministers, in the established church and in the nonconformist church, from neglect, coldness, and dead works, to serve with heart and soul the living God. Then, when the conscience of the churches had been illumined, and it grasped its immense responsibility, and realized the world-embracing evangel of the cross, there came into existence agencies for the spread of the Truth—Missionary, Bible, and Tract Societies, and Sunday Schools. The social and political results are manifest to all who have studied history.[4]

Warren A. Candler's book *Great Revivals and the Great Republic* reports that more than fifty thousand came to faith in Christ as a result of the First Great Awakening. Candler decried the lostness of not only the clergy, but most of the people in churches and said, "If the sons of Levi were thus without God, what must have been the condition of the unofficial membership of the churches?" However, he explained that "the

Great Awakening changed all that." Both church members, and pastors, were saved by the thousands "to be blessings to the land."[5]

Candler affirmed the beginning of many new ministries and the advancement of education. Many colleges like Dartmouth and Princeton were born. A new spirit between England and the American Colonies was created and a "moral revolution of the most beneficent sort."[6] As the deep feelings of war over the revolution began to mellow and heal, God's people on both sides returned to kingdom priorities.

It is amazing to see what happens in the church and in society when God's people are revived and mobilized out of their religious, cultural, and traditional ruts. Like the First Great Awakening, the Second Great Awakening is a great example of this. Listen to what Candler wrote about the revival at Yale.

> In 1802, a revival at Yale College, shook the institution to its center, and it seemed for a time that the whole mass of students would press into the kingdom, and nearly all the converts entered the ministry.[7]

One of the most significant movements of God's Spirit was at Cane Ridge, Kentucky in 1801. Twenty thousand people attended a six-day camp meeting, and according to Pratney, the revival that resulted spread like a prairie fire. It was set "ablaze. The Presbyterians and Methodists immediately caught fire, and then the flame broke out among the Baptists in Carroll County on the Ohio River."

Great leaders like Peter Cartwright, Charles Finney, and the Methodist circuit riders emerged from the revival. Baptist revivalism was birthed, and camp meetings spread all over eastern America. The wild frontier—with its gambling, cursing, and vice—were transformed into genuine Christianity.

> It was God's great hour. Revival stopped skepticism in its tracks and returned the helm of the country to the godly...The revivalists linked conversion and spiritual growth directly to the alteration of society.[8]

Relfe described the results of the Second Great Awakening on the

American frontier in glowing terms. "It turned drunkards, horse thieves, gamblers, cock fighters, and murderers into evangelists," she wrote. Many who were converted east of the frontier moved west and took the frontier for Christ. The missionary movement grew and spread. The roots of the abolition of slavery and the roots of popular education were both products of the awakening. More than six hundred colleges were founded and "the church began influencing the world once more."[9]

These results continued for many years, and phenomenal church growth occurred. For example, the Presbyterians grew four times larger than they were before the move of God. Stretching the dates of the awakening to 1850, the Methodists grew to 1,323,361.[10] The American Bible Society was born, and many Christian magazines began publication. The American Tract Society was formed, and the American Sunday School Union was created to support the growing Sunday school movement.

The YMCA was birthed. At the beginning, it was a Christian ministry to nurture young believers, but it has drifted to become a secular organization, a social recreational and educational club. Many other agencies sprang up across America. Historian Robert Lacy concluded that the revival actually saved the young nation from French skepticism, crass materialism, rapacious greed, godlessness, and violence on American frontiers.[11]

The church of Jesus Christ became alive and mobilized in transformational ministry as a result of the Second Great Awakening. The equipping of God's people for ministry—the fifth characteristic of revival—was evident. The church flourished, and as it did, society was changed. America had returned to her biblical, God-centered roots.

The results of the New York City Prayer Meeting Revival were the same. It spread nationwide and eventually, worldwide and mirrored the impact of the First and Second Great Awakenings. J. Edwin Orr wrote, "It became world-wide and lasted fifty years, something that could not be said of...any other movement in America except the Great Awakening of the eighteenth century."[12] He estimated that at least one million people came to faith in Christ in America, and about the same number received salvation when the revival jumped across the Atlantic.[13]

Candler reported the same mushrooming results and said that this began "the era of lay work in American Christianity."[14]

J. Edwin Orr referred to others who documented amazing results from the New York Revival. One person stated that it was "a great training school for laymen" and brought great leaders like D. L. Moody to the world. One of the most encouraging results of the revival was unity. "With scarcely an exception, the churches were working as one man." Even more amazing were reports related to doctrinal and denominational differences. "Armenians and Calvinists ignored their differences...doctrinal controversies were left alone" Orr wrote, "At last the world was able to say, 'Behold, how these Christians love one another.'"[15]

Once again, the world knew again that God the Father had sent Jesus, His Son (John 17:23). Oh, that it would happen again in America, that the walls would come down and followers of Jesus would love and serve Him and each other in unity. It would thrill the heart of God and many who share His desire. We would have a new understanding that there is only one church—with many congregations—in a city.

Some writers believe that the Civil War postponed missionary advance in America. After the war a great missionary movement broke out and spread God's people across the world. Writing about England, Orr said, "Free from war, the oppressed at home were liberated." Many Christian organizations and the creation of new ones "brought a flood of blessing down the old channels and broke through obstacles to form new rivers of Christian enterprise." An author from the British Isles stated, "Humanitarian activity was the characteristic form in which their religious piety expressed itself."[16]

The Welsh Revival of 1904 demonstrated the fifth characteristic all over again. George T. B. Davis, in his book, *When the Fire Fell,* gave a firsthand report from Wales. "Evidences of great renewing and the mobilization of the church were reflected in a rash of Bible sales unseen for eighteen years." Others simply report "faith and fervor and...forsaking sin."[17]

William Stead, the editor of the *Pall Mall Gazette* and one of the most powerful men of London, visited the Welsh Revival. He was asked if the results would be lasting, and although he was not known to be a Christian or even religious, he answered this way:

> Nothing lasts forever in this mutable world...But if the analogy of all previous revivals holds good, this religious awakening will be influencing for good the lives of numberless men and women

who will be living and toiling and carrying on the work of this God's world of ours long after you and I have been gathered to our fathers.[18]

The move of God at Azusa Street launched the Pentecostal movement. As we have already mentioned, fifty million classical Pentecostals were in uncounted churches and missions in practically every nation of the world in 1980. Also, many of the charismatics scattered in Christian denominations could trace at least part of their spiritual heritage to the Azusa Street meeting.[19]

It is widely accepted that Pentecostal and Charismatic believers have made an amazing impact around the world. Many of the largest and fastest growing churches in the world are charismatic. Although they have not been without controversy, the Pentecostal and Charismatic movements have ignited passion and emotion across the church. They have brought balance to the more cognitive, unemotional part of the church.

CHARACTERISTIC 6:
THE CHURCH AFLAME RETURNS TO WORSHIP

Revival was marked by a return to the worship of God.

Nothing characterizes revival more than worship. As people see their sin in the light of God's holiness and respond to this revelation with repentance, they are deeply moved to praise and worship. The people of Israel fell on their faces at the dedication of Solomon's temple when they saw God's firestorm consume the sacrifices and His glory fill the house. In revival, hearts and emotions explode with praise. Hands are lifted in adoration, and feet dance with excitement. This is the sixth characteristic of biblical and post-biblical revival.

The five post-biblical revivals are great examples of worship, and three of them stand at the apex of this characteristic. They are the New York City Prayer Meeting Revival, which was known more for prayer than for preaching; the Welsh Revival, which was sometimes criticized for a lack of preaching and teaching; and the Azusa Street Revival.

Many of the worship songs we sing in traditional congregations were written during the five revivals that spanned the history of the church from 1726 through the early twentieth century. At first the new forms of praise and worship choruses came from the more charismatic and Pentecostal denominations. It didn't take long, however, until these songs were springing up across the entire church.

The great hymns written by the Wesley brothers—Charles being the primary songwriter—have endured through time. The Methodist movement was at the center of the First Great Awakening, and some have said that it laid the foundation for the Second Great Awakening. The ministry of the Wesleys bridged both.[20]

Writing about the First Great Awakening, Jonathan Edwards is known to have said that the worship was a deep longing for two things, to be more perfect in humility and more perfect in adoration.

> The flesh and the heart seem often to cry out, lying low before God and adoring Him with greater love and humility…The person felt a great delight in singing praises to God and Jesus Christ, and longing that this present life may be as it were one continued song of praise to God. There was a longing as one person expressed it, "to sit and sing this life away."[21]

Great worship and praise music was central in the First Great Awakening. Sovereignly orchestrated by the Spirit of God, new songs of praise captured the hearts of His people and turned their souls to singing songs of love and worship. Isaac Watts created much of this great music. Brian Edwards wrote:

> Revival under Whitfield and Wesley gave a strong boost to hymn writing…Singing was so central to the Methodist movement that John Wesley wrote, "Rules for Methodist Singers." Charles wrote more than 6000 hymns.[22]

In his description of both the First and Second Awakenings, Pratney said, "God restored…facets of His awesome nature and supernatural power, allowing Him due worship in spirit and truth."[23]

In the New York City Prayer Meeting Revival, the worship often took the form of testimonies. People stood to praise and thank God for answering prayers for the conversion of their friends and family and for the changes God had made in their lives.

Under the preaching of Evan Roberts in the Welsh revival, the services were described as "go-as-you-please for two hours or more...People pray and sing, give testimony; exhort as the Spirit moves them." Catch the excitement from the writing of Brian Edwards:

> So when the Spirit came to Wales, there were frequent outbursts of praising at the preaching services. Sometimes the preachers were interrupted and not able to continue because the praising was so great. On the other hand, a little before this, in Dundee, an awful and breathless stillness pervaded the assembly, "each hearer bent forward in the posture of rapt attention."[24]

The Azusa Street Revival created a worship paradigm shift of immeasurable proportions, and worship in the Christian church has not been the same since. Even in the most traditional and formal churches, leaders, by sheer necessity and demand, have been forced to offer contemporary worship in at least one of their services. Some have blended the former rich hymnody with choruses or with what has become known as contemporary Christian music. Hymnals have been disappearing as words to songs are projected on screens or walls. Grand organs have become rare in churches. Praise and worship bands have taken center stage.

Brian Edwards wrote about worship as a primary characteristic of revival. He described the sense of the presence of God in revival and how people were spontaneously drawn to worship with songs of praise.

> Singing almost always forms a significant part of a true spiritual revival. Jonathan Edwards...described...the First Great Awakening. "Public praises were then greatly enlivened; God was then served in our psalmody...They sang with unusual elevation of heart and voice."[25]

There is rarely great passion for God without great expressions of adoration, worship, and praise. It spills out of hearts too full to contain it and springs heavenward like Old Faithful in Yellowstone National Park, right on time when revival sweeps through the hearts of God's people.

Passionate relationship between lovers results in heartfelt expressions such as love songs, poetry, and romantic creativity. This is what happens when God's people return to their first love for Him.

CHARACTERISTIC 7:
THE CLEANSING, PURIFYING WORK OF GOD'S REFINING FIRE

> Revival led to the destruction of idols and ungodly preoccupations and also to separation from personal and corporate sin.

When the firestorms of the Holy Spirit sweep across the church, His refining fire purifies His people. Time-robbing cultural preoccupations are replaced with balanced priorities and a passion for personal holiness and kingdom service. Spiritual growth and personal holiness become priorities. Understanding the Word of God and walking it out in life take on new importance. The fruit of the Holy Spirit becomes the measure of maturity. This is the seventh characteristic of revival.

As worship becomes the expression of revival, repentance, and a return to holiness characterize the church. Brian Edwards put it this way, "Revival is always a revival of holiness. And it begins with a terrible conviction of sin." He added that sometimes it is "crushing. People weep uncontrollably, and worse... There is no such thing as a revival without tears of conviction and sorrow."[26]

Consider this moving account of the passionate repentance that came to Scotland in the First Great Awakening.

> I found a good many persons under the deepest exercise of soul, crying out most bitterly of their lost and miserable state, by reason of sin; of their unbelief, in despising Christ and the offers of the gospel; of the hardness of their heart; and of their gross carelessness and indifference about religion, not so much... from fear of punishment as from a sense of the dishonor done to God.[27]

Edwards also reported what happened toward the end of the Second Great Awakening, in a meeting in Tuckingmill, England. "Hundreds were crying for mercy at once." In this weeklong gathering, those repenting or crying out for mercy would remain "in great distress from one to fifteen hours before the Lord spoke peace to their souls."[28]

The New York City Prayer Meeting Revival attracted multiple thousands. As people gathered in the prayer meetings, deep conviction of sin fell across the crowds, and with it, open passionate confession and repentance. J. Edwin Orr wrote:

> The promise of renewal given Solomon in the days of the Kings (2 Chron. 7:14), has made it clear that the humbling of the people of God, their diligence in intercession, their seeking of the Divine Will, and their turning from recognized sin—these are the factors in Revival, bringing about in God's good time an answer to their prayers, forgiveness of their sin, and a healing of their community. And these were the real factors recognized at the time by authorities qualified to judge, rather than the notions of facetious journalists of the day or opinions of the prejudiced a century or so later.[29]

In the Welsh Revival of 1904, the central message of Evan Roberts came in four clear, confronting statements. As he spoke to crowds from place to place, these statements became the essential standards to be met if revival was going to fall. They were the fuel for the fire of the Holy Spirit as the firestorm swept across Wales.

- You must put away any unconfessed sin.

- You must put away any doubtful habit.

- You must obey the Spirit promptly.

- You must confess Christ publicly.

Accounts from the Azusa Street Revival reported that people's "hearts were being searched as with a candle in a dark room. Inner secret motives were being exposed as well as behavior." Nothing could escape God's conviction as Jesus was "lifted up."[30]

Mark it! Know it! Spread the word, and shout it from the platforms of the church! We will never have a great sweep of revival across America or the world without repentance and a return to holiness and biblical living. A Third Great Awakening—with thousands coming to faith in Christ and cities being transformed—will never come until the drifting church is anchored again to biblical truth, first love, and personal holiness.

CHARACTERISTIC 8:
A FRESH UNDERSTANDING OF CHRIST'S REDEMPTIVE WORK

> Revival brought a return to the offering of blood sacrifices in the Old Testament and a concentration on the death, resurrection, and return of Jesus Christ—celebrated in the Lord's Supper—in the New Testament.

The disease of drift has infected God's people from the beginning. It began with Adam and Eve in the pristine environment of Eden, when they responded to Satan's temptation by disobeying God. From this tragic fall of man, the pattern of drift has woven its way throughout Israel's history and has continued all the way to the modern day church. She is no longer distinct from her pagan post-Christian culture. The church could have learned from history how to avoid Israel's wrong choices, but she didn't. Paul the Apostle wrote:

> I do not want you to be ignorant of the fact, brothers, that our forefathers were all under the cloud and that they all passed through the sea. They were all baptized into Moses in the cloud and in the sea. They all ate the same spiritual food and drank the same spiritual drink; for they drank from the spiritual rock that accompanied them, and that rock was Christ. Nevertheless, God was not pleased with most of them; their bodies were scattered over the desert. Now these things occurred as examples to keep us from setting our hearts on evil things as they did. Do not be idolaters, as some of them were.
>
> —*1 Corinthians 10:1–7*

In the Old Testament, the blood sacrifices were a dramatic picture of what would happen to the perfect Lamb of God, Jesus Christ. The night before His death, Jesus instituted the Lord's Supper, saying, "Do this...in remembrance of me" (1 Cor. 11:25). Jesus gave us the Lord's Supper—Communion or the Eucharist—as a meaningful way to remember His death and reflect on our sin. It was to be central and frequent in the life and worship of the church.

When Israel was in trouble spiritually, the sacrifices in the Old Testament became rote and religious, if not neglected altogether. Similarly, when the church has been adrift in the culture, away from her first love, the observance of Communion has become a religious activity that is void of deep passion. Before the end of the first century Paul had to write to the Corinthian church about her abuses of this sacred meal. She had become twisted with greed and formality and no longer celebrated the meaning and significance of the Lord's Supper.

The memorial meal Christ gave us was intended to keep God's love and redemption fresh in our hearts. We need it because the heart of the gospel—the death, burial, resurrection, and soon return of Jesus Christ—is too easily forgotten or taken for granted. In times of revival, God's people are deeply moved by conviction and return to an understanding of what it took to rescue and save them. They once again become sensitive to the plight of fallen and hell-bound sinners who are hopelessly lost, apart from God's mercy and grace. God reminds them that His amazing grace and mercy is the necessary antidote for those who are far from the righteous requirements of a holy and perfect God.

In revival, the thousands who repent and return to Christ are essentially returning to the cross, the apex of human history. The cross is where eternal salvation and the forgiveness of sin was purchased at an incredible price. There, at the terrible place called Golgotha—meaning "The Place of the Skull" (Matt. 27:33)—the amazing grace and love of God was demonstrated. And there, as fallen sinners kneel and meditate today, their soul is overwhelmed with great love and deep gratitude for all that Jesus has done for them.

In times of great awakening, those who do not know Christ as Savior and Lord are convicted by the knowledge that they have fallen far short of God's righteous requirements. They come by the thousands to the cross with an overwhelming conviction that they have been floating anchorless from the God who created them and sent His Son to die for them.

All five great revivals are characterized by the preaching of the cross. We can have no great awakening apart from a fresh look at what Jesus did for us during the dark days of His torture and sacrificial death. He is indeed "the way and the truth and the life. No one comes to the Father except through [Him]" (John 14:6).

Mel Gibson's movie, *The Passion of the Christ,* spread across America and the world in 2004 and drew millions into a new awareness of Christ's sacrifice for sin on the cross. The first time I saw the film, I fought back tears and anger until the scene when Mary, the mother of Jesus got close to where He walked. Bent under the heavy cross, with blood dripping and wounds laid bare, Jesus turned and said, "I make all things new!"[31] In that powerful moment, I could no longer hold back my tears. That's also when my anger eased and the unspeakable tragic torture made just a little sense—it was all for me! And it was for you, too.

Paul the Apostle explained it to the Christ followers in Rome.

> But God demonstrates his own love for us in this: While we were still sinners, Christ died for us. Since we have now been justified by his blood, how much more shall we be saved from God's wrath through him! For if, when we were God's enemies, we were reconciled to him through the death of his Son, how much more, having been reconciled, shall we be saved through his life! Not only is this so, but we also rejoice in God through our Lord Jesus Christ, through whom we have now received reconciliation.
> —*Romans 5:8–11*

According to McDow and Reid, the tragic condition of the church before the First Great Awakening was that of a two-headed monster— "deviant orthodoxy and dead orthodoxy or laxity in devotion or compromising the Word of God."[32] In this setting, Theodore Jackobus Frelinghuysen, a Dutch reformed pastor, was one of the first preachers to see revival sparks fly in his ministry. He "determined to bring a fresh vigor to the faith through...preaching, church discipline (especially the observance of the Lord's Supper), and zealous visitation."[33]

Brian Edwards, writing from his understanding of historic revival, said that the blood of Jesus and His cross took central stage in preaching. He explained, "Perhaps this is why many records of revival refer to the special blessings experienced at communion services when the blood of Christ is preached both from the Word and through the bread and wine."[34]

Edwards recounted several examples from the First Great Awakening and Wales. In Cambuslang in 1742, Scottish Presbyterians held two consecutive communion services and experienced revival in both of them. At the second, twenty thousand attended, and only a few thousand were able to participate. However, many came to Christ. Edwards wrote, "One writer has concluded that the root of the Methodist revival lay in the Lord's Supper."

The ministries of Whitfield and Wesley found that although the preaching of the cross was hated, it was what drew many to faith. Thousands found justification in the blood of Christ, redemption, propitiation, peace, reconciliation, and cleansing, even if they did not understand all those terms. When Joseph Kemp returned from the Welsh revival of 1904, he reported that "the dominating note of the Welsh revival was "redemption through the Blood.'"[35]

Wesley Duewel gave one of the most exciting accounts of the Lord's Supper in revival. In the First Great Awakening following, Whitfield came to Edinburgh, the village of Cambuslang, a suburb of Glasgow, on July 8, 1742. Two thousand seats were provided in a park, and he preached several times a day there. Revival fires burned, and for days he preached long hours, even into the night.

On the tenth of July a communion service was held, and thirty thousand gathered to hear Whitfield. Only seventeen hundred were able to take communion. A second communion service was held in August, and twelve ministers helped to administer the elements in three different tents. Only three thousand were able to take communion in a crowd that numbered between thirty and fifty thousand.[36]

Relfe reported similar crowds in the Second Great Awakening. At the turn of the nineteenth century, revival broke out after James McGready, a Presbyterian pastor, called for a four-day observance of the Lord's Supper, the third community-wide communion service he had held. The meetings were so unusual that another communion service was held a month later. Approximately eleven thousand people flocked to the small church.[37]

In the Second Great Awakening, Devereux Jarratt (1733–1801), an early Methodist revivalist, accepted a call to pastor a church. He was the product of the great and powerful preaching of John Wesley and George

Whitfield, and the theme of his preaching was "man's depravity by the Fall and his inability to be saved by works." With the bad news of man's desperate need, His powerful preaching trumpeted the Good News, "salvation in Christ's redemptive work, to be received by faith." Revival broke out in the church in 1776. His ministry illustrates the power of preaching about the cross, one of the primary passions of great revivals.[38]

The New York City Prayer Meeting Revival of 1857 saw the conversion of approximately one million people in America, and one million in Europe. There is no conversion without the gospel—the good news of the death and resurrection of Jesus Christ. This message was central to the revival as the Lord's Supper once again took a prominent place in the churches.

Like the other revivals, the Welsh Revival and the Azusa Street Revival were centered on the cross of Christ. The massive sweep of revival in Wales drew God's people back to the churches where services were alive, dynamic, and crowded. As revival moved across the nation, so did a return to the Lord's Supper. It was the same with Azusa Street. The primary leader was William J. Seymour, an African-American pastor. Bartleman wrote:

> The "color line" was washed away in the blood. A. S. Worrell, translator of the New Testament, declared the "Azusa" work had rediscovered the blood of Christ to the church at that time. Great emphasis was placed on the "blood," for cleansing, etc. A high standard was held up for a clean life. Jesus is being lifted up, the "blood" magnified, and the Holy Spirit honored once more.[39]

The cross of Jesus Christ stands at the apex of human and redemptive history. Is it any wonder that it also stands at the apex of revival? Is it any wonder that it was central to the sacrifices of the Old Testament and was restored to its significance when God drew His wandering people back to Himself? In revival, the human soul comes under the deep conviction of sin by the power of the Holy Spirit. In this state of desperation, thousands rush to receive the good news of salvation and embrace the glorious remedy of God's amazing grace. This is the eighth characteristic of revival.

CHARACTERISTIC 9:
THE THRILL OF REVIVAL: GREAT CELEBRATION AND JOY

> Revival resulted in an experience of exuberant joy and gladness among God's people.

"Freedom!"—the shout of William Wallace, the mighty warrior played by Mel Gibson in the movie *Braveheart*—is that for which brave hearts are willing to die.[40] And nothing is quite so wonderful as knowing freedom from Satan's bondage, our personal brokenness, and "the sin of [our] fathers" passed on to us (Exod. 20:5–6). Few things in life match the deep excitement and joy of being fully forgiven and set free from the sin that has separated us from God.

To know this deep sense of well-being and renewed hope is to know peace with God and the peace of God. To ponder eternal salvation and freedom in Christ spills tears of joy and relief down faces. It brings shouts of praise and thanksgiving to God, and deep levels of commitment to serve God's purpose. Regardless of how it is expressed—in a celebrative spirit or in the solitude of meditating on the richness of redemption—joy is the ninth characteristic of revival.

Consider this story of great joy from a report on the ministry of Jonathan Edwards in the First Great Awakening:

> From day to day, for many months together, might be seen evident instances of sinners brought out of darkness into marvelous light, and delivered out of a horrible pit and from the miry clay, and set upon a rock with a new song of praise to God in their mouths...The town seemed to be full of the presence of God—it never was so full of love, nor so full of joy...It was a time of joy in families on account of salvation being brought to them—parents rejoicing over their children as newborn, and husbands over their wives, and wives over their husbands.[41]

The same thing was going on at the great camp meetings of the Second Great Awakening. Pastor Barton Stone had gone to Kentucky from the Northwest to see firsthand what was happening. He wasn't used to seeing the manifestations of God's power, and he wrote,

> The scene was new to me and passing strange. It baffled description. Many, very many, fell down as men slain in battle, and continued for hours together in an apparently breathless and motionless state, sometimes for a few minutes reviving and exhibiting symptoms of life by a deep groan or a piercing shriek, or by a prayer for mercy fervently uttered. After lying there for hours, they obtained deliverance. The gloomy cloud that had covered their faces seemed gradually and visibly to disappear, and hope in smiles brightened into joy. They would rise shouting deliverance, and then would address the surrounding multitude in language truly eloquent and impressive. With astonishment did I hear men, women, and children declaring the wonderful works of God and the glorious mysteries of the gospel.[42]

These are the things that cognitive critics and the theologically constrained criticize in their response to revival. They can shout without restraint at their child's soccer game or when their favorite baseball player hits a grand slam to win a close game in the bottom of the ninth inning. They can become very excited when the kicker puts the pigskin between the uprights to win a football game as time is running out. Some can even get a little goofy at a party with friends. But it just doesn't seem right to be emotional about the redemption and long-awaited freedom of a sinner turned saint or a powerful manifestation of the Holy Spirit!

Revival is messy, and we may be tempted to fear what people outside of Christ think about it. I have nothing against scholarship and educational discipline and excellence, but we who have committed ourselves to the study of theology and the attainment of advanced academic degrees, must be careful that these gifts do not quench our openness to God. We must let God be God and allow His people to rejoice and celebrate.

God cannot be contained in a formal box of religion or even in the best of theological constructs. When it comes to eternal life, the stakes are high—heaven or hell. Breakthroughs of eternal significance and incredible freedom call for great joy and celebration. And sometimes God's people are knocked to the ground by the same lightning power of the Holy Spirit that fell at the dedication of Solomon's temple and also on Saul when he was on his way to Damascus.

Regardless of how people meet God—dramatically in revival, or in a quiet faith encounter—they enter into the glories of heavenly hope and the promise of heaven. I can relate more easily to the more reflective part of God's family because I am one of them. While I can quickly weary of loud worship and praise, I long for the glory of God to flood my soul in solitude. My eyes still become teary when I sing great historic hymns of faith like "Amazing Grace" and "Great Is Thy Faithfulness." I cut my worship teeth on these songs when I was a child and a young pastor, and I have to stretch to embrace the louder, more exuberant expressions.

An antique California grape tray on the wall of my home study bears my personal painting of some very helpful counsel my older brother, Chas, once gave me. "Don't make a principle out of your experience," he said. "Let God be as original with others as He has been with you." This is good revival advice. In response to this, I pray that I will not be among the cognitive naysayers of great revival. My heart says: *God, I am ready. Bring on the out-of-the-box and exuberant manifestations of the Holy Spirit in revival. Bring on the loud praise and worship music—especially worship music. Help me, Lord, to dance with others in the aisle. May I never try to keep You in a box of my experience or preferences.*

Wise leadership must guide revival, but it must not quench the work of the Holy Spirit. In our city, leading pastors are meeting as gatekeepers. This diverse group is building relationships and trust so that it will be able to guide revival when it sweeps the area.

Revival is celebrative and exuberant because of the great breakthrough it brings. When revival comes, it is time to shout and dance in the light of the Holy Spirit's fire. It is time to rejoice in the amazing grace and goodness of God.

J. Edwin Orr, the great revival historian, recorded firsthand accounts of many conversions in the New York City Prayer Meeting Revival. To be prayed for in one of the prayer meetings nearly guaranteed one's conversion. Orr included the case of a father who stood to request prayer for his three unconverted sons. Communication was difficult in those days, but the man later reported that "each son wrote to his father to give an account of his conversion." Another account read:

> The exultant Miller led two other friends to Christ before he left Massachusetts for New York City. Upon his return…the now-rejoicing restored backslider sought out his cousin in that city and informed him of the united prayers of the newly converted family for his spiritual condition. The cousin smiled broadly, only to say that…he, too, had become a disciple of the Master.[43]

An eyewitness report from David Matthews described the meetings of the Welsh Revival and the ministry of Evan Roberts this way: "Confronting and surrounding me was a mass of people, with faces aglow with a divine radiance…Others, who had received 'the blessing,' were joyous in their newfound experience."[44] Another observer called the Welsh revival "a storm center that was sweeping over Wales like a cyclone, lifting people into an ecstasy of spiritual fervor."[45] Davis describes what he observed in Evan Roberts.

> My attention was riveted on Evan Roberts who stood in the pulpit and led the music with face irradiated with joy, smiles, and even laughter…He seemed just bubbling over with sheer happiness, just as jubilant as a young man at a baseball game.[46]

Many firsthand stories of joy and wild excitement were recorded at the Azusa Street Revival. Bartleman recounts the time he received a special gift of song from the Holy Spirit. "The Spirit dropped the 'heavenly chorus' into my soul…It was a spontaneous manifestation and rapture no earthly tongue can describe."[47] Riss recorded the experience of a Baptist pastor who was hit with a similar rush of the Holy Spirit. The pastor said:

> As brother Seymour preached, God's power seemed to be increasing…Near the close of the sermon, as suddenly as on the day of Pentecost, while I was sitting in front of the preacher, the Holy Spirit fell upon me and literally filled me. I shouted and praised the Lord and incidentally, I began to speak in another language. Two of the saints quite a distance apart saw the Spirit fall on me.[48]

Joy and gladness has been characteristic of the restoration of God's people throughout Scripture. David danced before the Lord "with all his might" as the Ark of the Covenant came home (2 Sam. 6:14–15). Oh yes, a sophisticated naysayer—David's wife, Michal—was watching, and she rebuked David when he came home. However, in verses 21–22, David told her, "I will celebrate before the LORD. I will become even more undignified than this." God disciplined Michal severely, and she never had a child.

In Psalm 30:11–12 David testified to the Lord, "You turned my wailing into dancing…clothed me with joy, that my heart may sing to you and not be silent." This song, more than likely, became a part of what turned into a two-week celebration at the dedication of the temple. Scripture set the pattern long ago. In account after account, smiles and dances weave their way through the stories. It is no wonder the psalmist wrote in Psalm 85:6, "Will you not revive us again, that your people may rejoice in you?"

CHARACTERISTIC 10:
THE TESTIMONY OF SOCIAL TRANSFORMATION

> Revival was followed by a period of blessing and area-wide trans-
> formation that produced social reform.

George Otis of the Sentinel Group is producing some of the most exciting documentaries in recent church history. The documentaries tell of revival that is breaking out around the world and reflect the presence of the ten characteristics we have identified. Revival begins in the womb of dark and difficult times, and the agonizing labor and travail of prayer and repentance in time brings forth new spiritual life. Each characteristic of revival follows, and in the end, one of the most exciting aspects of revival brings the story to an exciting climax—area-wide, citywide, national, and international transformation.

As I write, revival is sweeping the Fiji Islands. Government leaders are committing themselves and the nation to Christ and His kingdom. Warring insurgent criminals are coming to faith in Christ, and fighting and insurrection are lessening. Social and economic reform is exploding, and the poor are being fed. Once-polluted streams are flowing crystal clear, and once-dead coral is returning to life. With it, the depleted fishing industry is flourishing again, and the economy is turning around.

Crops that were once devastatingly small are now abundant.[49]

The Sentinel Group has documented other stories. One of them comes from Almolonga, Guatemala, which the secular press calls the "City of God." Over 90 percent of the population is genuinely Christian, and the church is unified. Two jails, once overcrowded, are now closed, and the illegal drug traffic and crime that ruled the city are nearly a thing of the past. The ground is producing mammoth vegetables, such as carrots the size of a man's forearm. These amazing vegetables are being shipped to markets further and further away.[50]

In 2 Chronicles 7:14, God promises not only to forgive His people but also to heal their land. This is the grand climax of revival—the tenth characteristic of revival. When God's people are revived, they are mobilized redemptively. Social reform follows, and societies, nations, and cities are radically transformed. Economies flourish, and the ground produces abundantly. When God's people are revived and live in vital relationship with Him, His powerful light beams through them and dispels the darkness of Satan's death and destruction.

Mary Stewart Relfe, a student of revival and an authority on prayer and economics, has written about the radical social reformation of revival in her book *The Cure of All Ills*. Although some might consider her remarks to be overstatement, she has proven credibility as the president of the League of Prayer, a popular conference speaker in the Assemblies of God movement, and a guest speaker for Dr. Paul Yonggi Cho of Seoul, Korea. Writing on the results of the First Great Awakening, Relfe describes the phenomenal impact.

> God sought for a man among them, Ez. 22:30, and found a wealthy German, discerning enough to sense the need of the church universal and unselfish enough to organize prayer groups to cry unto God for it. Count Ludwig von Zinzendorf initiated Herrnhut, The Lord's Watch, with a small band of Moravians (persecuted believers who had fled for their faith and found asylum in the Count's estates in Saxony). The rebirth of Western Christian Culture can be traced back to the prayers, which ascended from the altar at Herrnhut. The Wesley brothers and George Whitfield owe their conversion to Moravian Bishop Peter Bohler at Aldersgate.
>
> The revival of 1735 brought about a transformation of condi-

tions, which reversed the social, moral and political declines. The prevailing vain philosophy, Deism, which denied the need of God, was stopped abruptly. Only those dedicated to godly principles were elected to public offices. This Spiritual Awakening returned the reins of the "West" back to God, decency and honesty.[51]

Historian Elie Halevy believed that the stability of eighteenth century England was the result of the Wesleyan Revival. French-styled revolution did not sweep England like the riots and bloodshed that characterized the continent. A Christian conscience permeated the nation, and there was passion for the poor. National prosperity emerged. There was "such a reversal of conditions, that though their problems were many, the revival proved to be their solution."[52]

In his book *Great Revivals and the Great Republic,* Warren A. Candler listed nine results of the First Great Awakening. They include the following transformational developments:

1. A new catholicity was born among churches—unity!
2. Education was promoted and advanced.
3. A new bond of affection was established between the British Isles and the America Colonies.
4. There was a unifying of the Anglo-Saxon peoples of the earth.
5. A moral revolution regenerated and unified the colonies. It prepared the way for the political unity of Christian states.[53]

McDow and Reid stated that the Log College that was established during the First Great Awakening, dedicated to training converts, was the forerunner of the modern seminary. Whitfield's tabernacle, which was built for his meetings, was a charity school and then became the home of the University of Pennsylvania. A charity school established for Indians eventually became Dartmouth. Orphanages sprang up to care for homeless children. The revival had a unifying impact on the colonies and changed their moral climate. "The awakening prepared the colonies for the struggle to become a nation later in the century."[54]

The Second Great Awakening produced the modern missionary movement—and so much more. The abolition of slavery emerged, as well as popular education. Six hundred colleges were founded. Relfe said:

> Chastity was in vogue again. Honesty and integrity were the rule rather than the exception. Decreased crime, gambling and drunkenness provided a backdrop for a period of genuine national prosperity.[55]

Many new societies and agencies were born. Among them were the American Bible Society, The New York Missions Society, The Missionary Society of Connecticut, the Massachusetts Society, The American Board of Commissioners for Foreign Missions, the General Missionary Convention of the Baptist Denomination, the American Home Missions Society, the first Sunday School Union in Philadelphia, the New York Sunday School Union, and the American Sunday School Union. Christian magazines were birthed from the revival, particularly to support the growing Christian Education movement.[56]

The Second Great Awakening, particularly the Methodist movement changed peoples thinking and their hearts. It was a spiritual revolution. Candler commented:

> It affected the destiny of the Great Republic, and in fact, the history of all mankind...reinvigorating the moral and religious life of the nation...inspiring invention, quickening industrialism and saving it from revolutionary tendencies, by averting perils from within and turning back dangers from without.[57]

What would social transformation look like today? Without exaggeration, I believe we would see a return to the Ten Commandments as the ethical base for American life. Biblical marriage would be re-established, rooted in obedience to God and centered in men loving their wives unconditionally and women respecting their husbands (Eph. 5:21–33). Thousands of couples who are living together outside of marriage would get married. The sensual plague of Sodom and Gomorrah that has increasingly swept America and the world would be over. The epidemic of pornography would come to a screeching halt, with a return to committed human love, according to God's design.

The tragic infanticide of pre-born and partially born babies would come to an end. Churches across the nation would be packed once more and would mobilize God's people to meet the crying needs of the hungry, the homeless, and the addicted. America would enjoy a return to a Judeo-Christian consensus. Now the most powerful nation in military and financial capability would also return to being a spiritual and moral light.

> *Oh, God, bring revival. Cause Your people to cry out to You with repentance and unity in the cities and across the nation. Revive Your church. Transform the nation for Your glory and honor. Do it, Lord, in our day as you have done it in the past, in Your Word and throughout history.*

The New York City Prayer Meeting Revival changed the social and financial landscape of America, and it had the same impact when it jumped across the ocean. In her unique style, Relfe described it as a cure for social ills.

> The Revival of 1857 restored integrity to government and business in America once again. There was renewed obedience to the social commandments. An intense sympathy was created for the poor and needy. A compassionate society was re-birthed. The reins of America were returned to the godly. Yet another time, Revival became the solution to the problems, the remedy for the evils, the cure of the ills.[58]

The international impact was similar. Virtues of honesty, sobriety, and integrity were kindled. Courtesies were reborn. Gentle, modest restraints kept men in order again. Women were able to blush again, and children were taught obedience. Around the globe, decency returned to government and business. Values for good and for God arose in the hearts of mankind everywhere as God wiped the spit from the face of the earth once more.[59] Clearly, the results of the New York City Prayer Revival produced a social and moral cleansing.

As we look at our world today, we can see a lot worse than spit. In fact, it is mixed with blood in some cases, as hostilities increase between the West and the radical sector of the Muslim world, and the remaining holdouts of communism. Major denominations have gay and lesbian parades at their national conferences, and we wonder if we are seeing a replay of Sodom and Gomorrah. Many who profess the name of Christ stand against any constitutional amendment that would say marriage in America is to be only between a man and a woman. Yes, we desperately need revival. How bad must it become? How far from basic biblical truth can the church go and still claim to believe the Bible is God's revealed truth?

Returning to the writing of Relfe, we learn that the mining pits were aflame with revival. There was a general consensus that 90 percent of the mining community was converted to faith in Christ. A moral revolution occurred, and pornography was nearly eliminated. Illegitimate births declined, and certain destructive theatrical companies were shut down. Saloons were emptied; the courts were too, as court calendars cleared with no cases to try. Bible sales escalated, enemies became friends, and the ministries of women and men were honored equally.[60]

What a thrill it is to read the accounts of social transformation that follow revival! J. Edwin Orr has told us more about the results of the New York City Revival. Think of what this would mean for America today. Imagine what American historians would write.

> Socially, the Nineteenth Century Awakening gave birth to a litter of active religious and philanthropic societies, which accomplished much in human uplift, the welfare of children, the reclamation of prostituted women, of alcoholics, of criminals and the development of social virtues. Certain effects of the Awakening were not immediately apparent—the relation of the conversion of hundreds of thousands who developed an insatiable desire for education, to the passing of the 1870 Education Act: or the evangelical conversion of Keir Hardie under Moody's ministry and the introduction of that evangelical spirit into the Labor Movement in contrast to the atheism of Continental socialism. The great Evangelical Revival...was also effective in all three spheres of life: it saved Britain from the bloody Revolution; it produced the Evangelical order within the Church of England and Methodism, and revived Nonconformity without; and it changed the social order by stages, spectacularly in the abolition of slavery.[61]

In a later book, *The Fervent Prayer: The Worldwide Impact of the Great Awakening of 1858*, Orr included two chapters on social impact. He gave

England the lead in social reform while America struggled through the Civil War. However, in the post-war years, American Evangelicals began to address social problems related to "the homeless and hungry, the drunkard, criminal and the harlot." And there was more: "A school of Christian philanthropists soon arose, seeking to go straight to the heart of the slums with its practical Samaritans, yet always ready to cooperate in all wise legislative improvements."[62]

Industrial Extension Acts brought reform for the needs of workers, and other social changes including educational reform, the establishment of orphanages, reform on behalf of incarcerated criminals, the rehabilitation of prostitutes, and efforts to remove slavery. The impact on world missions was revolutionary. Orr wrote, "No other voluntary agency in all the world has achieved so much good and so little harm. Hence missionaries have stayed on where civil power evacuated." He highlighted great achievement, not only in presenting the gospel but also in sparking efforts for reform in industrialization, medical services and hygiene, education, and agriculture.[63]

The impact of the Welsh Revival of 1904 followed the same pattern. Riss wrote that employers were amazed at the improvement in the quality of work their employees produced. Waste was reduced, and there was less drinking, idleness, and gambling. The employees worked with joy. The mine ponies in Wales could no longer understand the commands of the miners because their language had improved so much. They had quit cussing and kicking the ponies, and the poor little burden bearers didn't know what to do.[64]

Another account of transformation was given by the Chief Constable of Cardiff and recorded in Judge Gilym Williams' quarterly report. It showed that there was a decrease of 1,364 in the number of people brought in for "nonindictable offenses. This improvement arose mainly from the decrease of drunkenness, especially in quarters where Mr. Evan Roberts had held revival services."[65]

Although it is more difficult to define the social impact of the Azusa Street Revival of 1906, we can conclude that its impact was without measure. Pratney stated that there were one hundred thousand recorded healings in the first five years of the revival, and this was certainly a major impact.[66] Recorded accounts also tell how people were raised from the dead. Beyond this immediate result, the impact of Azusa Street was like time-released social salt scattered across the world, with fifty million Pentecostal adherents by 1980[67] and many more Charismatic followers scattered throughout many denominations.

Some of the largest, most rapidly growing and most impacting missions societies and mega congregations today are Pentecostal. In three years of international travel, speaking to missionaries and national pastors, Connie and I can affirm their impact. Many Pentecostal denominations that were born after the revival are still strong and growing. For example, when Pratney wrote in 1983, the Four Square Gospel denomination claimed 783 congregations, 2,000 missionaries, 32 day schools and Bible schools, and 117 daily or weekly radio broadcasts in the United States and 27 in other countries.[68]

Revival changes history, and its social and economic impact is immeasurable. Our need for revival is becoming desperate as we feel ourselves picking up speed in our slide down Satan's slippery slope. One hundred years is far too long to wait for a move of God across the church in America. We see brush fires of revival, but we have not experienced citywide or area-wide revival. Will the church in America rise out of her current apathy, darkness, and impotence to humble herself, pray, seek God's face, and repent? Many are calling the church to prayer and fasting. Is it too late? *It is never too late.*

George Otis, Jr., whose videos have presented story after story of revival and transformation, has compiled a list of markers that he believes mark transformation. As the church humbles herself in prayer and repentance, she can expect these results.

1. Political leaders publicly acknowledge their sin and dependence on God (2 Kings 11:17–18; 23:2; Jon. 3:6–9).

2. New laws and business practices are put into effect (2 Chron. 19:10; Neh. 10:31).

3. The natural environment is restored to its original life-nurturing state (Lev. 26:4–5; 2 Chron. 7:14; Ezek. 34:27; 36:29–30).

4. Economic conditions improve and lead to a discernable lessening of poverty (2 Chron. 17:3–5; Ps. 144:14; Isa. 60:5; Amos 9:13).

5. There is marked change in social entertainment and vices as kingdom values are integrated into the rhythm of daily life (Ezra 10:4; Neh. 8:10; Eccles. 10:17; Acts 19:17–20).

6. Crime and corruption diminish throughout the community (2 Kings 12:13–15; Neh. 5:6–12; Isa. 60:17–18).

7. Volunteerism increases as Christians recognize their responsibility to heal and undergird the community (Isa. 58:10–12; 61:1–11).

8. Restored hope and joy leads to a decline in divorce, bankruptcy, and suicide (Neh. 12:27–28,43; Isa. 54:11–14; 62:3,7; Jer. 30:17–19, 31:11–13; Hos. 2:15).

9. The spiritual nature of the growing socio-political renewal becomes a hot topic in the secular media (2 Chron. 20:29; Neh. 6:16; Isa. 55:5; Ezek. 36:36; Acts 19:17).

10. Overwhelmed by the goodness of God, grateful Christians take the embers of revival into surrounding communities and nations (2 Chron. 17:9; Isa. 61:6; Acts 11:20–26).[69]

This list fans the flame of passion that burns hot in my bones for revival and the transformation of our area and America. Can you picture how your area would look if these things were happening? I am deeply grieved and sometimes angry about the desperate, dangerous conditions in our world: Crime, homicide, corruption, economic problems, sensuality, the growing trend to remove godliness and Scripture from the public square, and the tragic unraveling of the home and family. George's list calls me to hope again and to make a deeper commitment to the prayer of 2 Chronicles 7:14.

In late December 2004, history's greatest natural disaster occurred after a powerful earthquake that was centered in the Indian Ocean. A massive tsunami hit the surrounding nations in wave after wave of destruction, and over three hundred thousand people lost their lives. One island in the Indian Ocean was moved one hundred feet. The newspapers were full of reports about generous financial support, as individuals, organizations, and nations began to provide aid and relief. The entire story will take years to tell, especially for the nations that were hardest hit.

Many people asked questions about God's role in this awful tragedy. Was it a natural disaster, or was it God's judgment for the purpose of returning the nations to righteousness? David Wilkerson, the pastor of Times Square Church in New York City, reflected on America's response to the disaster in a January 17, 2005, letter he sent to his national constituents.

> America is a giving nation and very compassionate. Thank God for the response of so many who are praying, giving and going to help. But something deep within my soul troubles me. The magnitude of the disaster is not sinking in. We seem to be numbed, stupefied by it all.
>
> Just today it was announced that the U.S. confidence level has increased. I thank God for good reports for the blessings. But if we cannot be brought to our knees—if we cannot humble ourselves before such unleashed power, after witnessing the worst natural disaster in world history, our entire globe trembling—what will it take to silence the God-mockers? Are we now shock proof?
>
> Think of the expulsion of God from our society in the name of political correctness...secularism and materialism...a church growing more worldly than the world itself...more violence and apathy than in Noah's day...the Bible no longer being accepted as God's Word, a day "when everything that can be shaken is being shaken," when power is unleashed that was one million times more powerful than the atomic bomb dropped on Hiroshima...when thinking men everywhere have an intuition that "somebody is tinkering with nature, something is happening that cannot be explained away"...when society moves on without a single "God pause," without even a thought that God will not be mocked. THAT IS WHEN I SAY WE HAVE COME NEAR OR CROSSED OVER A LINE INTO A SPIRITUAL STUPOR THAT NO AMOUNT OF DIVINE MERCY CAN AWAKEN.

> God is merciful, gracious and ready to forgive. Christ died to save this lost world; he did not come to destroy, maim or pour out wrath. Out of the terror and pain of the passion of Christ, redemption came. May Christ demonstrate his love and compassion through his disciples, in this hour of mass destruction.[70]

As I pondered the meaning of the tsunami disaster, I recalled the End Time description Jesus gave in Luke 21:25–28 (author's emphasis):

> There will be signs in the sun, moon and stars. On the earth, nations will be in anguish and perplexity at *the roaring and tossing of the sea*. Men will faint from terror, apprehensive of what is coming on the world, for the heavenly bodies will be shaken. At that time they will see the Son of Man coming in a cloud with power and great glory. When these things begin to take place, stand up and lift up your heads, because your redemption is drawing near.

No one knows the exact time of the Lord's return, but scriptures like this stop me in my tracks. What disaster will come next? Where will it fall?

Now is the time to respond like the king of Nineveh, when he called his nation to prayer, humility, and fasting. "Who can tell?" he cried. "Perhaps even yet God will have pity on us and hold back his fierce anger from destroying us." (Jon. 3:9, NLT). This is how revival comes.

Malcolm McDow and Alvin L. Reid's book, *Fire Fall: How God Has Shaped History Through Revivals*, is a call to prayer. Commenting on revival between 1901 and 1910, they said:

> The story of revival coming at the dawn of a new century offers hope for our generation. Surely we can follow the example of those before us to set aside special times of prayer and fasting to seek the Lord.[71]

Church of Jesus Christ, it is time to pray. How we will respond?

You say the little efforts that I make will do no good;

They never will prevail to tip the hovering scale

Where Justice hangs in the balance.

I don't think I ever thought they would,

But I am prejudiced beyond debate.

In favor of my right to choose which side

Shall feel the stubborn ounces of my weight.[1]

—Bonaro Overstreet

11

A Tale of Three Cities

CHARLES DICKENS'S WELL-KNOWN novel, *A Tale of Two Cities*, begins with an even better known first line. "It was the best of times—it was the worst of times."[2] Though this was Dickens's description of the time of the French Revolution, I believe it could also be said of America today.

Some wonderful things are happening in this "best of times." A prayer movement is growing across the nation. God's people are beginning to stir as they see the rise of secularism against biblical truth and values. A movement is working to establish a constitutional amendment that will define marriage as a relationship between a man and a woman.

Thousands are coming to Christ in China, Africa, and Latin America every day. Modern technology gives us an unprecedented ability and opportunity to communicate the gospel around the globe. In some parts of the world multiple thousands have been gathering in stadiums to renounce sins of the past, and to declare that they will be a people who follow Jesus Christ. Uganda and Fiji are two nations that are experiencing revival.

After the U.S. was attacked on September 11, 2001, war preparations captured the nation's attention. As a result of warfare in Iraq and Afghanistan, new democratic governments have been taking shape in Iraq and Afghanistan; both have held democratic elections for the first time. There has been growing hope that one day new democracies will stand tall in that part of the world.

As I write, the American economy has been turning around. Unemployment has been declining, and renewed hope for better times has been growing. Violent crime has decreased significantly. The 2004 national elections placed an outspoken Christian president in the White House for four more years and gave him a strong majority in the Congress.

I believe it reflected the prayers of the church across the nation and the world.

In spite of all this, many believe that we face "the worst of times." It could be that the contrast between darkness and light is increasing, that the light is growing brighter and the darkness is becoming darker. As hope for revival and a return to God grows in the hearts of many praying believers, the darkness seems more penetrating.

Dr. Meg Meeker's book, *Epidemic: How Sex Is Killing Our Kids*, draws our attention to one disturbing expression of the darkness in the world today. When I was young, there were three or four sexually transmitted diseases. Today, however, hundreds have emerged, and many of them are deadly. HIV/AIDS has been a pandemic across the world. Millions have died, and we have only begun to reap the terrible harvest.

America has not escaped. According to Meeker, eight thousand teenagers in America are contracting an STD each day. HIV has been one of the most dangerous, but it is only one of many that will in time produce death. Although some STDs have been treatable or manageable, there has not been a cure for many. Dr. Meeker has identified one STD that is responsible for 99.7 percent of all cervical cancers in the nation. America has been reaping a harvest of wild oats from the sexual revolution of the 1960s.[3]

We knew America was slipping before we launched into the new millennium because news headlines told the story. The cover of the *U.S. News and World Report* published on November 22, 1999 said, "Cheating, Writing, and Arithmetic: A New Epidemic of Fraud is Sweeping Through our Schools."[4] On December 6 of the same year, in Angie Cannon's article, "Crime Stories of the Century," she states, "Criminal acts tell us much about the times in which they were committed; the morals of the day illuminated by their violation."[5]

Our schools have become centers of violence and death, and armed police now patrol public high school hallways attempting to prevent further violence in schools. In April 2005, a student who called himself an angel of death killed nine people in a Minnesota school before he killed himself. As it had done after previous school shootings, the nation responded with shock and grief.

Ironically, at the same time as the above school tragedy, the judicial system ordered the slow death of Terri Shiavo by removing her feeding tube. Although she was responsive, she was considered brain dead. Her parents pleaded unsuccessfully to keep her alive, even though they did everything that was legally within their power to keep the courts from removing her feeding tube.

Abortion clinics in nearly every sizable city have profited from the death of babies in the womb. Since abortion was made legal by Roe v. Wade in 1973, over forty million pre-born children have been killed.[6] In recent days, legislatures have discussed and floated a bill to allow a baby to die if an attempted abortion failed. According to a speech Alan Keyes gave when he was running for the Illinois Senate in 2004, this would be after a birth certificate has already been written.[7]

I have read about debates on the right of a child to live, even after months of life. Should a mother have the right to terminate her child's life if she decides she doesn't want it? One university ethicist suggested that this would be morally sound. Such debates and proposals have trampled on America's Bill of Rights, not to mention biblical teaching.

Millions are hooked on pornography in America. One of the fastest growing industries, it now attracts billions of dollars annually. America is sensually sick. Catalogues, ads, television, the Internet, and films are used to sell sex. More than at any previous time, people are coming to me for counseling with sexual addictions and sordid stories of sexual abuse and sexual affairs. Most of them profess to be Christians.

The Ten Commandments, as well as public manger scenes, are being removed from most public settings. As we have tossed the Ten Commandments in the ethical trash, we have also trashed our moral compass. American history has been rewritten to eliminate the Pilgrims' interest in finding religious freedom in the New World. Many Christmas programs in public schools have not included traditional Christmas carols, and Christmas vacation has been renamed Winter Break. And sadly, America leads the world in gambling, out-of-wedlock births, the use of alcohol and illicit drugs, and the number of people who are incarcerated.

Once the church of Jesus Christ lifted anchor from the rock of revealed truth—the Bible—she, the nation and the cities she served, set sail aimlessly on the uncertain sea of relativism and humanism. In these waters, leaders who shouted the loudest shaped the culture and standards of morality. As a result, a redefined tolerance has become America's most worshiped deity. It is a tolerance that means no one can say anything significant about any real issue, lest they offend another biblically untethered soul.

God is not pleased with this, and He has called us, the disciples of Jesus Christ, to speak the truth in love. As we do this, we grow up into His full stature—the second incarnation on earth (Eph. 4:13). We are able to present the living Jesus on earth wherever the church exists.

The Importance of Our "Little Efforts"

I introduced this chapter with a brief paragraph by Bonaro Overstreet. It came to me on a small card enclosed in a birthday note I received years ago from Dr. Vernon Grounds, the former president of Denver Seminary and a godly model and mentor I continue to regard highly. At the time I received it, I was wondering if the sacrifices of radical discipleship were worth the struggles and pain. I decided they were—even to death—and I cherish Overstreet's words about the importance of our "little efforts." They are framed in a prominent place in my study and in my soul.

We have the power to radically transform our nation and our cities. We have the power to answer Jesus' prayer for unity in John 17:20–23. If we will unify, our nation and our communities will know that the Father sent Jesus His Son. They may reject this simple gospel truth, but it will prevail over the culture. Some say that unity is impossible. But wait! Nothing is impossible for God.

As my friend, Apostle Don Lyon says, we must pray for harmony. Unity sometimes has the connotation that we must all be the same, but this is not true. Ephesians 4:1–16 describes the church as a body of Christ-followers who have unity in diversity and stand together in mutuality. As we practice speaking truth to each other in love, we grow up to look like Jesus, the second incarnation.

I believe that we reap what we sow; Leviticus 26, and Deuteronomy 11 and 28, clearly state God's covenant blessings and His covenant curses. And I can't say enough about the importance of growing in obedience. In 1 Samuel 15:22, we are advised that it is better to obey than to practice religious rituals or sacrifice. Dare I suggest that this includes the busy externals that have encrusted the church of our day, or the things that keep us from living out the Ten Commandments and the Great Commission?

A Tale of Three Cities

Jesus said that we would be His friends if we would obey (John 15:14). Obedience characterized the incarnate life of Jesus, and it must characterize the church (John 15:9–11). Notice the desire of God's heart for His people, as He expressed it after He gave them the Ten Commandments. "Oh, that their hearts would be inclined to fear me and keep all my commands always, so that *it might go well with them* and their children forever" (Deut. 5:29, author's emphasis).

Liberalism has swept through much of the church, and it is hard to recognize biblical Christianity in many congregations. I recently heard about a pastoral candidate who was seeking the senior position at a large mainline, historically Orthodox church. When she was asked in the interview if Jesus was the eternal Son of God, she replied, "Certainly not!" She was approved for the position. Much of the mainline church has embraced Universalism. How sad this is! The early martyrs for Jesus did not die for a nice compassionate guy or a man with great ideas to debate. They died professing Jesus Christ as Lord and standing for biblical truth.

We need revival to sweep the church. We have discussed the ten characteristics of revival, and we have learned how revival happens. We know at least two major things that will sustain revival: passionate prayer, and the truth of the Word of God. *What will be our response?*

Tommy Tenney of *God Chasers* fame first alerted me to the fact that two cities in the Bible demonstrate two very different responses to God's provision of revival. Tommy Tenney's book, *The God Chasers*, has sold over a million copies since its publication. Tenney has created "The God Chasers Network.[8] We can respond to Jesus like His hometown of Nazareth did when He returned for a visit, or we can respond to God like Nineveh when Jonah finally obeyed God and called the city to repentance. The way we respond will determine if revival will sweep our nation.

Nazareth

Nazareth was the home of Mary and Joseph, who had each received an angelic visit. The angel Gabriel had spoken to Mary and told her that God the Holy Spirit would miraculously conceive the Lord Jesus Christ, the Savior of the world, in her womb. After Mary became pregnant, an angel also appeared to Joseph and told him to take Mary, the woman to whom he was engaged, as his wife.

Mary was "highly favored" (Luke 1:28), and her song of praise to God (Luke 1:46–55) demonstrated amazing maturity, wisdom, and intimacy with God. She knew Old Testament history, as well as the love and acts of God. Her heart was full of love and adoration for God, and she was submitted to Him and His will. Joseph came from the royal line of King David, the man after God's own heart. Like David, his heart was sensitive to hear and obey the voice of God.

It was this couple who became the earthly parents of the Christ child, the incarnate, eternal Son of God. They loved and obeyed God as they fulfilled their unique responsibilities from the day of Jesus' birth. Scripture tells how they took Jesus to be circumcised when He was eight days old, as the law required. Every year they went to Jerusalem for the Passover feast. When Jesus was twelve years old, they couldn't find Him among the other travelers in their group when they were on their way home. After searching for Him, they found Him back in Jerusalem in the temple courts, listening to, and talking with the rabbis.

Jesus grew up in Nazareth and spent thirty years of His life there. A synagogue was there, and that is where Jesus went when He came home after He had begun His earthly ministry. Luke 4:16–30 tells the story. Jesus' reputation for performing miracles and speaking with wisdom had spread through the entire countryside (Luke 4:14). He had visited many synagogues, and everyone was praising Him.

When He stood up to read Scripture in Nazareth, He chose Isaiah 61:1–2, a prophecy about the Messiah, and used it to show that the Spirit of the Lord was on Him. He was anointed "to preach good news to the poor" and sent by God to "proclaim freedom for the captives and release from darkness for the prisoners."

Jesus' hometown crowd knew what He was talking about. Jesus was announcing the Messianic age and saying that He was the Messiah. All eyes were glued on Him. He had made it clear, "Today [right now] this Scripture is fulfilled in your hearing."

However, the people of Nazareth could not believe this. They knew Jesus and His family. "Isn't this Joseph's son?" they asked.

Jesus responded to this by saying, "No prophet is accepted in his hometown" (Luke 4:24). He let them know that disbelief had closed their door of opportunity to know His messianic, Spirit-filled, miraculous ministry among them—just as it had in Israel's past. He reminded them of other times when lack of faith had stopped the wonderful work of God. It had happened in Elijah's day, when the widow of Zarephath in Sidon—not the people of Israel—saw God's miracles during the great years of famine. Many in Israel had leprosy in Elisha's time, but it was Naaman—a leader from Syria—who was healed.

Matthew 13:58, a parallel passage to Luke 4:16–30, sums it up: "And he did not do many miracles there because of their lack of faith." The sick could have been healed and the dead raised. They could have sat at the feet of the Son of God and listened to eternal truths. A strong vibrant community of followers of Jesus, the Messiah, could have been formed.

It is a sad story. At the reminder of their faithless history, the hometown folks became enraged and drove Jesus out of town. Their plan was to kill Him by throwing Him off a cliff, but He "walked right through the crowd and went on his way" (Luke 4:30). What had Jesus done to deserve such treatment? He had disturbed them by His clear declaration of who He was and what He had come to do; His convicting words about the history of Israel had angered them. Later He would be brutally tortured and killed for claiming to be the Son of God.

The tragic experience of Nazareth is still happening today. Among those who claim to be God's people, some deny that Jesus is the Messiah, the Eternal Son of God who came to earth in human flesh. They run Him out of town, or at least out of their churches. They know about Jesus, but they really don't know Him personally. Failure to believe that Jesus is the Son of God, the Savior of the world, is to reject Him. It means there will be no miracles, no healing, no full and meaningful life. To reject Jesus is to deny who He really is and therefore be destined to eternity in hell.

We either believe what Jesus said about Himself, or we don't. Anyone who tries to come to God apart from Jesus, is in deep spiritual trouble in life and for eternity. Jesus made it clear in John 14:6, "I am the way and the truth and the life. No one comes to the Father except through me." In John 10:1, those who try to come to God by a way other than Jesus, are called thieves and robbers. We *either believe Jesus, or we don't.* Each person must make his or her own decision. The consequences are presently and eternally significant.

Unbelief put a lid on Jesus' desire to minister in His hometown of Nazareth. It stopped a move of the Holy Spirit, a revival of heart relationship with God through the long-awaited Messiah—Jesus! Those who claimed to belong to God through their religion could have been transformed through intimacy with Christ and the demonstration of His presence and power. But in the nice religious city of Nazareth, they rejected the Savior.

NINEVEH

Nineveh is the second city in our tale. The capitol of the Assyrian Empire in what is now called Iraq, was not known for worshiping God. The Ninevites were pagan, famous for war crimes and violence, and known to make monuments of their victims' heads, stacking them as a warning to their enemies. They were constantly at war with Israel. The city was large for its day and had a population of one hundred twenty thousand. Jonah 3:3 says that it took three days to go through the whole city.

God told Jonah, a patriot of Israel, to go to Nineveh with the message that the people must repent of their sin or suffer destruction. How must have Jonah felt when God called him to do this? Most of us would have gone the other direction like Jonah did. These were violent people. Would it be too much to compare Jonah's call to preaching repentance to the terrorists behind the September 11 attacks on America? Or, what about the comparison of a call to preach to a city of radical Muslims who want to annihilate the nation of Israel?

When Jonah ran the opposite way, trying to avoid God's call to preach to his enemies, God sent a great storm to threaten the very existence of the ship on which he was traveling. Jonah realized that his only hope was to cast himself on God's mercy, and he instructed the sailors to throw him overboard into the raging sea. This is where the story becomes a little "fishy." God created a large fish to swallow His rebellious missionary. In the digestive system of the fish—I can't imagine it—Jonah decided that going to Nineveh was a better option.

The narrative continues with a miraculous story of a city that turned to God. From the king in sackcloth and ashes with his face to the ground, to Nineveh's inhabitants all the way down the social ladder—even including the animals—the entire city fasted in repentance and prayer. At the end of the story, Jonah clearly shows that he didn't want the people of Nineveh to repent. He wanted God to destroy them; he thought they deserved it.

Even with an unwilling preacher and a hard message, the violent city of Nineveh repented and turned to God. Our God has always responded with grace and mercy when people repent, whether they have embraced the God of Abraham, Isaac, and Jacob in the past or have always been godless and wicked. God redeemed and spared the entire population of Nineveh as they humbled themselves, prayed with passion and repentance, and turned to Him.

Can you imagine the king of Nineveh sitting in the dust and calling for everyone to fast? When you read the story in Jonah 3:1–10, can you picture the mayor of your city calling out to God in similar humility and repentance? What would happen if the president of the United States, his cabinet, and the Congress would follow this example?

Revival in history is predictable; the pattern is given in 2 Chronicles 7:14. If we do our part, God will do His! As Psalm 145:13 says, God is "faithful to all his promises and loving toward all he has made." It is all about Nineveh-style, dust-driven humility, the passionate pursuit of no-excuses-holiness, a deep longing for intimacy with God, seeking His face, and seeking His presence. It is repentance, repentance, and repentance.

There is no room for pride. There can be no room for satisfaction with the way things are, for "business as usual." The church is too often satisfied with fast food entertainment, junk food business, and everything but seeking God's presence in passionate prayer, and repentance. Obedience is the only way to please God. It is the pathway to His covenant blessings and promises.

Who prevents God from moving in revival? It is not drug dealers, criminals, prostitutes, gamblers, or government. It is God's people—you and me. It was easier to convert pagan Nineveh than religious Nazareth. It is easier to reach non-Christians with Christ's love and truth than to recycle a professing, comfortable, satisfied Christian who has a form of godliness but no power and impact in his community! Familiarity and comfort breed contempt—"Oh, He's just Joseph's kid. He helped his dad in the shop!"

In Jonah 1, the captain and sailors on Jonah's ship were filled with panic and fear because the storm was about to destroy their ship and their lives. As they cried out to their gods, the weather-beaten veterans of the sea noticed that Jonah was not in the prayer meeting. He was sound asleep below the deck. The desperate sailors awakened the sleeping missionary and said, "Hey, man, we're going down. *Pray!* And, by the way there are some things we need to know. Who is responsible for making all this trouble?"

Jonah had to come clean. He explained that he was running from God and the responsibility He had given him. This was the reason God had sent the storm. Since 2 Chronicles 7:14 is addressed to God's people, we must also face the questions the fearful sailors asked Jonah. Our lost world is asking, "Church of Jesus Christ, why are you sleeping? We are going down and are about to die!"

Do I need to rehearse the statistics of our post-Christian nation? Let me remind you—no Ten Commandments, no manger scenes, threats to biblical marriage, the unraveling of the family, the addiction of our municipalities to gambling revenue, corporate corruption, and a shaky world economy. America can no longer depend on her presumption of security since terrorists have penetrated our borders.

Public education is in chaos. Sensuality saturates our media, and porn is addicting millions of men and women. The clergy and Christians are mocked in the American media. Over forty million abortions have been performed in America. According to a message Kirk Bennett gave in January 2005; one in four babies are being aborted in America. Eighty percent of the Christian church is flat-lined or in decline. The North American continent is the only continent where Christianity is not growing.

Why are we sleeping? Are we depressed because of the surrounding conditions? Do we feel guilt because we know in our heart of hearts that we are living in disobedience to God? Have we lost hope? Are we angry because God has called us to this generation? Have we forgotten that God will answer if we ask? Is the storm bad enough to awaken the church? Is it bad enough to motivate her to call out to God in repentance, to abandon her disobedience and to passionately seek His face?

People are asking, "Who is responsible for making all the trouble in the world?"

Our answer to them must be the same as Jonah's: "We are responsible. We are to be the light and the bearers of God's truth. We are to be the radical redemptive agents of God's kingdom, pushing back the darkness of the enemy with obedience to the Great Commandment and Great Commission. We are to love you and share the Good News—the gospel—with you. We are to release the power of God and push back Satan's agenda through prayer.

You can know God personally. You can have an abundant life and know the peace of God. You can go to heaven. We are to be unified so you can look at us as a people and see the second incarnation of Jesus Christ, that God the Father really did send Jesus, His Son. We are sorry that we have stood in open defiance to our Savior's prayer in John 17:20–23. He wanted us to be mobilized across our cities to meet the needs of people instead of building larger and larger governments to do it. We repent.

Again, the world asks us, "Church of Jesus Christ, who are you? What is your country, and who are your people? Where do you come from? What do you do?"

This question forces us to reflect on our identity. Are we really Christians—followers of Jesus Christ? Is there enough evidence to convict us? Who are the people to whom we really belong? Are we distinct from the culture, in the world but not of it? Are we part of the culture, or are we a counterculture? Is there enough visible fruit of the Holy Spirit in our lives to raise curiosity about our love for Christ? Will we pray to our God and ask Him to spare the desperate people in the throes of the storms of life.

These are penetrating questions, and it is time to answer them. It is time to still the storm and save the ship before she goes down. It is time to repent—to pray to our God who answers. It is time to make some radical changes. It is time for revival.

THE CITY WHERE YOU LIVE

And now, we must discuss a third, most important city: the city where you live. What will happen in the places where we live? Will they be like Nazareth or Nineveh? The tale is ours to tell; we must decide.

God is calling the church to unified, passionate prayer and repentance, and this raises a significant question for us. Will we lay aside our personal agendas to embrace the truth that there is only one church, composed of many congregations, in a given geographical area? The New Testament letters teach this important principle by addressing their greetings to the church in an area or a city.

And we face similar questions. Will we unify so that our cities will know the Father sent the Son? Or, will we continue by our actions and choices to perpetuate the tragic fact that the church has been one of the most divided institutions in American culture? How long will God allow His people to stand in open defiance to Jesus' prayer for unity?

Will we join the growing remnant that is being intentional about area-wide unity, even national and international unity, in prayer and repentance? Will we join those who are breaking out of the religious and cultural boxes of the church to passionately seek God's presence, to see revival and Great Awakening sweep the nation?

In West Texas, playa lakes dot the landscape. These shallow, unconnected lakes are normally dry and barren because the area usually receives little rainfall. They do little to change the climate of the region, but only reflect it. For instance, after a good rainfall, they are full of water and provide nourishment for thirsty creatures and birds for a brief time. However, they soon become dry again. When congregations in a city or a region function independently of each other, they are very similar to the playas in Texas. They provide life only until the next dry spell. The atmosphere of the area is unchanged, merely a reflection of the current climate conditions.

On the other hand, ocean currents called gyres are full of life and impact the climates of the entire globe, especially those in their immediate proximity. My friends, it is time for the churches across the United States to turn from the lifestyle of being isolated lakes that only reflect what is going on in the godless, lifeless culture. Instead, we must begin flowing together as a gyre, a current of the Holy Spirit that transforms the spiritual climate of our regions, our nation, and even the world. It is time for the church to move in ocean currents of unity and the Holy Spirit's presence.

We know how revival happens. The ten characteristics of revival are consistent throughout all history. If we do our part, God will certainly do His. He will respond to our passionate prayers for revival as we seek His face. He will honor our humility and repentance and mobilize us to transform the world in which we live. I urge you to join with others who are gathering in prayer for revival. Another great firestorm will sweep through our land.

Appendix I

Litany of Dedication:
Declaring Jesus as King Over Rockford October 2002

A s MEMBERS OF the citywide church of Rockford, Illinois, we are gathered at our city's crown jewel, the Coronado. In this place of coronation, we declare that Jesus Christ, the eternal Son of God, is Lord over Rockford. Together we crown You, Lord Jesus, as King over our city. We beseech You, Lord Jesus Christ, to come in your manifest presence. May Your kingdom come and Your will be done in Rockford as in heaven. For Thine is the kingdom, and the power, and the glory forever. Amen!

REVISED FOR AN AREA-WIDE PRAYER RALLY IN THE CORONADO THEATER IN APRIL 2005

We, the area-wide church of Rockford, Illinois, gathered at our area's crown jewel—the Coronado, the place of coronation—declare that Jesus Christ, the eternal Son of God, is Lord over the Rockford area. Together we crown You, Lord Jesus, to be King over our city. We beseech You, Lord Jesus Christ, to come in Your manifest presence. May Your kingdom come and Your will be done in the Rockford area as it is in heaven. Bring revival to Your church. Bring an area-wide Great Awakening, with thousands coming to faith in Christ. Transform, O God, the greater Rockford area for Your kingdom's sake, for Thine is the kingdom, and the power, and the glory forever. Amen!

Appendix II

Rockford Renewal Ministries: Who Are We?
A Fourteen-Point Strategy

The vision of Rockford Renewal Ministries is a sweeping revival of the church of Jesus Christ in the city of Rockford, Illinois and a Great Awakening across the city, accomplished by effectual, fervent prayer and personal and corporate holiness.

The Mission of Rockford Renewal Ministries is to call the church of Jesus Christ across the city to repentance and to seek God with humble prayer for revival and a Great Awakening according to 2 Chronicles 7:14. The results shall be personal and corporate righteousness, people, and congregations on fire for God and His kingdom, and dramatic social change—the transformation of the city.

WE EXIST TO SERVE...

Jesus Christ

Prayer is an expression of our total dependence on a God who loves us extravagantly. Every area of Rockford Renewal Ministries (RRM) will passionately seek to serve Jesus Christ and fulfill His kingdom purpose.

The City

1. Monthly citywide prayer gatherings—Greater Rockford in Prayer and Praise (GRIPP)

2. Bi-weekly prayer meetings at City Hall and School Board offices

3. Monthly prayer at the jail and in the courthouse

4. Lighthouses of Prayer—neighbors praying for neighbors

5.   Prayer team praying daily

6.   A city-focused servant leadership team of pastors

The Church

1.   Preaching in local churches and for retreats on prayer, revival, repentance, and requested topics

2.   Weekly prayer meeting for revival at RRM office

3.   Maintaining a citywide prayer list

4.   Weekly prayer with gifted intercessors

The Christian Leaders

1.   Fellowship dinners with church leaders

2.   Pastoral counseling

3.   Pastors' prayer summit

4.   Redemptive transformational projects as God directs

DEFINITION OF REVIVAL

Revival is a spontaneous spiritual awakening by God the Holy Spirit among His people. It comes in answer to their humble prayers as they passionately seek His face, and repent of their sins. The awakening results in deepened intimacy with God, passion for Him, holy living, evangelism, and citywide or area-wide transformation, expressed through social reform.

Appendix III

Tips on Prayer

1.   Prayer is 98 percent discipline and hard work. You need learning and skill to use this strategic weapon effectively. The other 2 percent is sheer joy!

2.   Time, sleep, and location are three beastly barriers to prayer. You need to set aside a time when you can be awake, choose a quiet place without distractions, and follow a strategic plan for your prayer time.

3.   Five beastly barriers to *answered prayer* are: motives—James 4:3; impatience with God's timing—Isa. 55:8–9; sin—Ps. 66:18–20; lack of faith—Heb. 10:23, 35–39; 11:1–2,6; Rom. 4:16–22; failure to abide in intimacy with Christ—John 15:5–8.

4.   Everyone will have a different prayer plan. As my brother, Chas, once told me, "Don't make a principle out of your experience; let God be as original with others as He has been with you." When your plan no longer works, change it.

5.   As a fundamental approach to prayer, begin with *adoration* or worship. Praise God for who He is. Think and pray these scriptures: Isa. 40; 1 Chron. 16; Psalms; the seven thousand promises in the Bible. For example, "You have created the heavens and the earth by your great power and outstretched hand. Nothing is too difficult for you." (See Jeremiah 32:17.) Or, "I can do everything through [You] who gives me

strength" (Phil. 4:13). Names of God are wonderful to use in worship. Also, rehearse God's attributes and what He can do: "You are all powerful, you can bring revival, healing, help, save, restore, solve my xyz problem or need."

6. Go to *confession* next. Think specifically about the past day or recent days, and confess your sins to God. Confess through the fruit of the Holy Spirit in Gal. 5:22–23. Confess through the beatitudes in Matt 5:3–12. Think through the terrible triangles of the Bible: The world, the flesh, and the devil. Renounce them in Jesus' name; renounce the lust of the eyes, the lust of the flesh, and the pride of life. I find it helpful to ask the Holy Spirit to show me: *thoughts* that need to be confessed, *attitudes* that were out of line with His truth, and *things I said* that were out of line. I ask the Lord to reveal *things I did* that were wrong and *things that I didn't do.* I review yesterday to confess when I was *relying on myself* rather than Him.

7. Now come to God with *thanksgiving* for every good thing that comes to mind. You won't have enough time for this.

8. Finally, bring your *supplication* to God. Ask! Concentrate on character. Pray Eph. 1:16; 3:16; Phil. 1:9.

9. Make sure you apply the blood of Jesus by faith as in the Exodus: to your *body*—the tent you live in; to your *soul*—your conscious and sub-conscious mind, your emotions and will; and your *spirit*—your control center, where God resides. You do this by faith as it was done in the dedication of the priests and the tabernacle in Exodus and later, the temple (2 Chron. 6–7). Revelation 12:11 says that the saints defeated Satan by the blood of the Lamb—the Lamb of God slain before the foundation of the world, the word of their testimony (perhaps the affirmation that Jesus is Lord), and they didn't love their lives even to the point of death. Declare this: "Jesus, You are

Lord! I shall not love my life even to death. Satan is defeated!"
Ask for a hedge of protection like Job had in Job 1:10. "I ask,
Lord, that the promised angels of Psalm 34:7; 91:9–12; and
Isaiah 37:21–36 would be reinforced around me."

10. Pray through the spiritual armor given to us in Ephesians
    6:10–18. For example, "Lord, I take the *sword of the Spirit*,
    the Word of God. Give me great skill today in using the
    Word as Jesus did in the wilderness: 'It is written...' Holy
    Spirit, remind me of your truth. Speak your rhema word to
    me throughout the day. I hold high the *shield of faith* today,
    my shield, against every dart Satan sends—curses, demons,
    incantations, ceremonies, subtle half truths" (author's empha-
    sis). Continue praying through the rest of the armor: the *belt
    of truth*, which speaks of integrity, no cover-up; the *breast-
    plate of righteousness*—the wonderful gift of His righteous-
    ness, the *helmet of salvation*, which protects our thoughts
    with biblical perspective—who we are, to whom we belong,
    the reason God leaves us here after salvation; and finally our
    feet shod with the *gospel of peace*, which prepares us to walk
    it into our world each day. With each piece of armor I add
    scripture that comes to mind. For example, "Faith is being
    sure of what we hope for and certain of what we do not see."
    (Heb. 11:1), and "Without faith it is impossible to please
    God" (Heb. 11:6).

11. Praying through lists can be very boring, but it is critically
    important. Significant prayer concerns include churches,
    friends and family, missionaries, principalities and powers
    in the city and area, and government officials. Try to pray
    through lists when you are doing an activity such as working
    out on the treadmill (paste lists to the wall), walking, or com-
    muting to work.

12. One of the most effective ways of praying is to write a letter
    to God, and reflect on your life. You can actually write out

A.C.T.S. (see tips 5–8). After this, be sure to stop and ask God to speak to you. As you listen to Him, write down your impressions or the things you see. Don't doubt, but test what you hear with biblical truth. If it is unusual, check it with another mature, trusted Christian.

13.   If you are concerned about special needs, you can pray at designated times: at every stop light or at a certain common intersection, at the ninth hole on the golf course, during long trips in the car, or as you exercise.

14.   Learn about different kinds of fasting. As you practice it, it will enrich your prayer life and help you focus on Christ and the things that are important to Him.

15.   If you are married, set aside time to pray with your spouse; this is one of the secrets of intimacy. Many Christians meet with a small prayer group or a prayer partner. Praying with others is exciting and powerful. Accountability can help you stay focused on Christ, and it is sometimes essential to breaking old patterns.

GUIDELINES FOR PRAYER

Group prayer can quickly become routine and boring. The following guidelines are intended to help group prayer be a dynamic, life-giving experience:

- Listen for the Holy Spirit's direction.

- Pray short prayers so many can pray.

- Allow for silence—and listen.

- Be long on praise and worship.

- Stay with a subject until the Holy Spirit is finished with it.

- Pray brief passages of Scripture.

- Lead in song as the Holy Spirit leads you.

- Be sensitive to the diversity of gifts, volume, and worship style.

- Pray in agreement with others as they pray.

- Blend songs and prayer together.

- Give announcements about coming events before or after your prayer time, not in your prayers.

- Instead of listing requests before prayer, worship and pray with harp and bowl (Rev. 5:8). Unless the group needs to know about something in detail, individuals can bring their requests to God as they are led. Others can join in praying for these concerns.

Appendix IV

Breaking Spiritual Strongholds and Generational Curses

I F YOUR SPIRITUAL journey is extremely difficult, you may have some spiritual house cleaning to do. I have found it very helpful to review my personal history and the patterns of struggle in my life, and I encourage you to do the same. You may be able to identify spiritual strongholds the enemy has established in your life.

Strongholds may develop from the lies of our culture and the world. For example, we may be influenced by the false value that we need to be a certain physical size to be happy. We ourselves are a second source of deceit if we have internalized false statements that others tell us about our identity. Finally, Satan wants to destroy us, and he lies to us daily about many things.

We must test every influence, regardless of its source, against the truth of Scripture. For example, I may think I can't do anything well. However, the Bible promises that I can do all things through Christ who strengthens me (Phil. 4:13), and I must replace my false belief with biblical truth. When we identify the deceitful patterns and lies that trouble us, we must renounce them in the name of Jesus Christ. We must write down or speak out the truth of God's Word, renouncing and casting away any perpetuating demons in the name of Jesus Christ.

Can you identify patterns of oppression and bondage from past generations? How about sensuality, drug or alcohol problems, divorce, child abuse, rage and anger, codependency, and failure to set boundaries with people? These are more than likely generational curses. Identify them, and write them down. Repeat the same process we outlined above for deliverance and victory over spiritual strongholds. For instance, if you struggle with anger, remember what Paul said in Ephesians 4:26–27: "In your anger do not sin. Do not let the sun go down while you are still angry. And do not give the devil a foothold."

I suggest that you find a few fellow believers who are people of prayer, wise and mature in Christ, able to hear God speak, and active in the ministry of spiritual gifts such as discernment and knowledge. Set aside some hours to pray with them, and ask God to show you what generational curses or spiritual strongholds are at work in your soul. Take careful notes so you can refer back to them later.

The following approach to prayer will help you be victorious in this spiritual warfare. Modify it as the Holy Spirit leads you. Always do strategic warfare praying with a group of other believers who are confident of their faith in Christ and His protection.

1. Bind Satan, principalities, and powers from your location and within you. By faith, apply the blood of Jesus Christ to yourself—body, soul, and spirit—and to all prayer partners, beware that some demons use the name, *Jesus*, to fool or deceive us. Put on the full armor of God from Ephesians 6:10–18. Pray through each part of the armor.

2. Renounce each stronghold or curse by name, and break it in the name of Jesus Christ, the eternal Son of God who came in human flesh.

3. Renounce and break all negative soul ties to anyone involved—such as a parent or former sexual partner—from inception forward to the third and fourth generation.

4. Cover the curse or stronghold with the Satan-, death-, and hell-defeating blood of Jesus Christ from inception to the third and fourth generation.

5. Bind up and cast all associated or perpetuating demons, principalities, and powers out to the feet of Jesus or wherever He wants them to go. He knows what to do with them.

6. Cleanse each place that strongholds or demons have occupied or influenced in your soul or body. Do this by faith in Christ and the power of His blood. Ask and thank God for soul healing, and follow through by asking the Holy Spirit to fill the place that was formerly occupied by evil.

7. As you do this for each stronghold or generational curse, one at a time, replace each work of evil with biblical truth. For example, if it was a stronghold of anger, replace it with God's patience and peace. If it was a stronghold of sensuality, replace it with God's purity.

Seven Steps to Freedom, a work and prayer booklet written by Dr. Neal Anderson, is an excellent tool for breaking generational curses and other strongholds. For most people, the booklet is only a brief introduction, and they find it very helpful to read Neal's book, *The Bondage Breaker,* before working through the booklet. Information on this material is available on the Internet under Freedom In Christ.

Appendix V

Truth That Sets Us Free

M Y MISSION IS to know God intimately, love Him passionately, trust Him implicitly, enjoy Him thoroughly, and obey Him completely. God has commissioned me to serve Him radically, joyfully, restfully, happily, and peacefully, as a redemptive agent in this broken world and as a prophet to the nations and my city, speaking the words He places in my mouth and balancing ministry, home life, and recreation.

God has not only given me this mission, but He has also spoken directly to my heart about the way I should fulfill it. He has said, *Bob, My son, enjoy this life to which I have called you. My way is not hurry. My way is not worry. My way is not busy, but peace and joy in My Spirit. "The mind controlled by the Spirit is life and peace" (Rom 8:6).*

I rejoice in this gracious word from God. And I rest in the fact that I am lavishly loved, radically redeemed, graciously forgiven, imperially empowered, generously gifted, freed from my past to follow Jesus, and abundantly blessed. I work out of waiting, serve out of solitude, and lead out of listening.

As I consider the desperate need for revival in our cities and our nation, I am encouraged by God's faithfulness to change lives through the ministry of His Word. We are called to battle the spiritual darkness of our world just as Jesus did when He was tempted in the wilderness. He fought the enemy with the Word—the *logos* and also the *rhema*—which was and is alive and powerful and sharper than any two-edged sword (Heb. 4:12). We are also called to engage the enemy in battle through passionate prayer, as Jesus did when He sweat blood in the garden. Prayer is our work; ministry is our reward.

256

The Word of God is our primary offensive weapon for close-in spiritual warfare, and by it, we take every thought captive "to make it obedient to Christ" (2 Cor. 10:4–5). God's Word manages our mind and emotions with truth that sets us free from fear or fretting. The verses below have strengthened my faith in the face of impossible situations. I pray that they will also give you renewed hope in God's promise to send revival as we earnestly seek His face.

> The Lord is faithful to all his promises and loving toward all he has made.
>
> —*Psalm 145:13*

> Let us hold unswervingly to the *hope we profess*, for he who promised is faithful.
>
> —*Hebrews 10:23, Author's emphasis*

> For the word of God is living and active. Sharper than any double-edged sword, it penetrates even to dividing soul and spirit, joints and marrow; it judges the thoughts and attitudes of the heart. Nothing in all creation is hidden from God's sight. Everything is uncovered and laid bare before the eyes of him to whom we must give account.
>
> —*Hebrews 4:12–13*

> Praise be to the Lord, who has given rest to his people Israel just as he promised. Not one word has failed of all the good promises he gave through his servant Moses.
>
> —*1 Kings 8:56*

> May God himself, the God of peace, sanctify you through and through. May your whole spirit, soul and body be kept blameless at the coming of our Lord Jesus Christ. The one who calls you is faithful…he will do it.
>
> —*1 Thessalonians 5:23–24*

> What I have said, that will I bring about; what I have planned, that will I do.
>
> —*Isaiah 46:11*

He who is the Glory of Israel does not lie or change his mind; for he is not a man, that he should change his mind.

—1 Samuel 15:29

As for God, his way is perfect; the word of the Lord is flawless. He is a shield for all who take refuge in him.

—2 Samuel 22:31

Perfect love drives out fear.

—1 John 4:18

Appendix VI

Firestorms and Their Characteristics

OLD TESTAMENT FIRESTORMS are discussed in chapter 4. Twelve moves of God can be found in the Old Testament, and they are listed below:

OLD TESTAMENT REVIVALS

1. Jacob: Gen. 35:1–15
2. Moses: Exod. 32–33
3. Samuel: 1 Sam. 7:1–13
4. Elijah: 1 Kings 18
5. Joash: 2 Kings 11–12; 2 Chron. 23–24
6. Hezekiah: 2 Kings 18:4–7; 2 Chron. 29–31
7. Josiah: 2 Kings 22–23; 2 Chron. 34–35
8. Asa: 2 Chron. 15:1–15
9. Jehoshaphat: 2 Chron. 17:6–9; 20
10. Zerubbabel, Haggai, Zechariah: Ezra 5–6
11. Ezra and Nehemiah: Neh. 8:9; 12:44–47
12. Jonah in Nineveh: the Book of Jonah

New Testament firestorms are discussed in chapter 5. Eight moves of God can be found in the New Testament, and they are listed below:

NEW TESTAMENT REVIVALS

1. Awakening under John the Baptist: Matt. 3:1–12
2. The revival at Pentecost: Acts 2:1–4, 14–47

3. The revival in the church: Acts 4:23–37
4. The revival that grew out of fear: Acts 5:1–16
5. The revival that grew out of persecution: Acts 7:54–8:25
6. The revival with Cornelius and the gentiles: Acts 10:23–48
7. The Pisidian Antioch revival: Acts 13:44–52
8. The revival at Ephesus: Acts 19:1–20

Five great firestorms in post-biblical history are discussed in chapters six, eight, and ten. They are listed below:

POST-BIBLICAL REVIVALS

1. The First Great Awakening: 1726–1756
2. The Second Great Awakening: 1776–1810
3. The New York City Prayer Meeting Revival: 1857–1858
4. The Welsh Revival of 1904
5. The Azusa Street Revival: 1906–1909

Ten themes have characterized the firestorms of biblical and post-biblical history. They are listed below:

1. Revival occurred in times of personal or national crisis and great spiritual need, in times of deep moral darkness, and spiritual decline among God's people Israel or His church.

2. Revival began in the heart(s) of one or more consecrated servants of God, who became the agent(s) God used to lead His people back to faith in Him and obedience to Him.

3. Prayer was central to revival. Leaders called out to God in prayer, passionately seeking His face in repentance and in the confession of personal and national sins. In many instances, they led God's people to do the same.

4. Revival rested upon the powerful proclamation—preaching and teaching—of the law of God and His Word. Many revivals were the result of a return to Scripture.

5.   Revival in the Old Testament reflected the work of God the Father to awaken His people Israel to a restored relationship with Him, to obey Him and serve His purpose. Revival in the New Testament and post-biblical history reflected the work of the Holy Spirit in miracles and the equipping of people for ministry. It resulted in the spread of the gospel and the growth of the church.

6.   Revival was marked by a return to the worship of God.

7.   Revival led to the destruction of idols and ungodly preoccupations and also to separation from personal and corporate sin.

8.   Revival brought a return to the offering of blood sacrifices in the Old Testament and a concentration on the death, resurrection, and return of Jesus Christ—celebrated in the Lord's Supper—in the New Testament.

9.   Revival resulted in an experience of exuberant joy and gladness among God's people.

10. Revival was followed by a period of blessing and area-wide transformation that produced social reform.

Appendix VII

The Good News: The Message of the Church

G OD'S PEOPLE HAVE always struggled with the problem of drifting into the life of the surrounding culture. However, in recent times, theological and philosophical perspectives have aided and abetted the pattern of drift in our understanding of the gospel. Some have tried to reshape clear biblical teaching on the very nature of man and re-define the gospel, the message of the church. In response to this, I have urged the church to return to the Great Commission (Matt. 28:19–20; Acts 1:8), saying that the mission of the church is more about *going* into the world with God's love and the gospel than *coming* to church.

I believe it is important to review the church's message—the gospel—and mankind's need for redemption as taught in the Bible. Without a clear biblical understanding, we will not present a clear message. In fact, if we err in our understanding and presentation of the gospel, there will be no redemption. Although we must communicate God's truth in a way that cultures can understand, we must never change the truth of the Word of God.

Re-thinking the gospel has taken a variety of forms. Toward the end of the 1800s evolution began to shape the thinking of many, and there was a growing hope and optimism that people and societies could become better and better. World wars, the brutality of dictatorial regimes, depressions, the hideous Holocaust, the exposing of unthinkable torture under Chinese communism and so much more have forever dashed the dreams of changing human nature. Liberal thought and teaching has been unable to change the sinful and selfish hearts of people.

It confirms the appraisal of God's Word. The prophet Jeremiah asked,

"Can the Ethiopian change his skin or the leopard its spots?" (Jer. 13:23). No! And, apart from the transformation of the gospel, the human heart remains the same. It is "beyond cure," or as the King James Version says, "desperately wicked." (Jer. 17:9). The psalmist declared, "The wicked will not stand in the judgment...the way of the wicked will perish." (Psalm 1:5–6).

New theological and philosophical perspectives have detracted from the Great Commission. Some denominations teach Universalism with its false hope that everyone will make it to the good side of God and into His heaven. This removes the responsibility of people to make important choices, and it certainly discredits Jesus' teaching about hell. It rejects the biblical truth that "all have sinned and fall short of the glory of God" (Romans 3:23).

Universalism has required readers of the Bible to take pen knife in hand and remove Romans 6:23 from the Bible: "For the wages of sin is death, but the gift of God is eternal life in Christ Jesus our Lord." It deletes the promise of John 1:12, "Yet to all who received him [Jesus], to those who believed in his name, he gave the right to become children of God." Eternal salvation "is by grace...through faith—and this not from yourselves, it is the gift of God—not by works, so that no one can boast" (Eph. 2:8–9). One who tries to get to heaven in "some other way, is a thief and a robber" (John 10:1).

Another ungodly perspective is Annihilationism, which denies God's eternal nature to punish sin. In spite of what the Bible says, we hear the question, "How could a loving God send someone to hell for eternity?" Biblically we know that mankind is condemned already, and God has provided salvation (John 3:18).

In more conservative circles, Hypercalvinism has stated that God chooses who goes to heaven and who goes to hell, thus taking all responsibility from people. Psychological efforts have detracted us from the necessity of hearing the gospel and responding to it with faith. Many other hopeful approaches, including the human potential movement and therapeutic efforts to improve self-esteem as the answer to man's condition, have watered down man's basic sinfulness. Only through the gospel can mankind's sinful nature be redeemed.

Different forms of liberation theology, sometimes blended with

Marxism, have substituted a socialistic solution to the evils of mankind for redemption. Time has proven that they do not work. Socialistic efforts against injustice, inequity, and inequality have simply replaced one approach with another without solving anything.

Finally, the more extreme ecumenical movement has promoted a new tolerance that bemoans any attempt to convert people to saving faith in Christ. "Let's just all live and love together in peace and not try to change anyone's beliefs," it says. In other words, forget the Great Commission, the gospel, and what the Bible says. It is time to ask what the Bible says about this. Paul warns in Romans 1:18: "The wrath of God is being revealed from heaven against all the godlessness and wickedness of men who suppress the truth by their wickedness."

Let's begin with mankind's basic need and call it being lost, or as I would have said during my youth ministry years, "You are on your way to hell in a handbasket and receiving Jesus as your Savior is your only hope. You need to be saved!" Jeremiah could not have been more clear about the condition of the human heart when he wrote, "The heart is deceitful above all things and beyond cure" (Jer. 17:9). All have sinned and the wages of sin is death, eternal separation from God.

The ugliness, violence, exploitation, selfishness, and greed of mankind can be credited to the fall of Adam and Eve in the Garden of Eden. Ever since then, sin has separated us from God. Our visible, recognizable beauty and value can be credited only to God's image in us, even though it is terribly defaced. The message of the Bible is that only Jesus Christ can radically change the human heart, and He does it through conversion.

WHAT IS CONVERSION?

Conversion—eternal salvation—occurs when we hear the truth about our lost condition, acknowledge it, and embrace the gospel, the Good News of eternal salvation through Jesus Christ. We are redeemed by personally trusting in Jesus' death and resurrection as the payment that was required for our salvation.

Most people do not need to be convinced of their need. They know internally that they cannot even live up to their own standards, not to mention God's holiness. However, those who take a defensive position and are snookered with pervasive humanism, need to hear the bad news of their depravity and sin and the condemnation that results. When they are invited to receive God's gift of salvation through Christ's payment of their sin, they must make a decision. They must receive God's gift of salvation or reject it. Some, unfortunately, decide to wait and lose the opportunity to decide.

The decision to receive Christ as Savior results in a changed life, sometimes rather suddenly and sometimes more slowly. It begins the life of spiritual growth and sanctification that Paul the Apostle described when he shared his commitment to growth in his letter to the Philippian church. Speaking of knowing Christ and His power, Paul said:

> Not that I have already obtained all this, or have already been made perfect, but I press on to take hold of that for which Christ Jesus took hold of me...Forgetting what is behind and straining toward what is ahead, I press on toward the goal to win the prize for which God has called me heavenward in Christ Jesus. All of us who are mature should take such a view of things.
> —*Philippians 3:12–15*

Paul gave us two essentials of conversion in Acts 20:21: "I have declared to both Jews and Greeks that they must turn to God in *repentance* and have *faith* in our Lord Jesus" (author's emphasis). Turning from sin in repentance and turning to God in faith are required for conversion. The need for repentance is woven throughout Scripture, and Jesus declared in Luke 13:3, "Unless you *repent*, you too will all perish." The need for *faith* in God's gracious provision is explained in Ephesians 2:7–9 as well as many other scriptures.

Conversion comes from the Hebrew verb, *shubh*, and the Greek verb, *epistrepho*, both meaning "to turn or return." The simple verb, *strepho*, which means "to turn," is used by Jesus in Matthew 18:3 where He says, "I tell you the truth, unless you change and become like little children, you will never enter the kingdom of heaven." *Epistrepho*, "to turn about" or "to turn toward" is used in James 5:19–20 to describe the action of turning a sinner from the error of his way. It is also used in other places like Matthew 13:15, Mark 4:12, and Luke 22:32. The Greek noun *epistrophe* is rendered "a turning about" in Acts 15:3, and it expresses the requirement to turn from sin and to faith in Christ.[1]

Some have debated if conversion is individual or corporate. Although, a group of individuals can come to faith in Christ at the same time, the writings of the apostle John and the apostle Paul show that it is a personal act. For instance, you may have memorized John 3:16–17, and you will readily recognize the personal nature of conversion in these verses: "Whoever believes in him [Jesus] shall not perish but have eternal life." John also says that if you do not believe you are condemned.

When Paul wrote to the Ephesian church, he described what Jesus has done for us as "incomparable riches of his grace, expressed in his kindness to us in Christ Jesus" (Eph. 2:7). He continued and said that it is "by grace you have been saved, through faith—and this not from yourselves, it is the gift of God—not by works, so that no one can boast" (Eph. 2:8–9). Paul is also writing about individual conversion. And his individual story of conversion is repeated three times (Acts 9:1–9; 22:3–21; 26:4–20) making it a significant example of personal conversion.

Conversion is as individual as birth, and Jesus likens it to birth in John 3:1–8. This text gives the popular description of conversion, as being "born again." Paul likens it to creation or re-creation in 2 Corinthians 5:17: "Therefore, if anyone is in Christ, he is a new creation; the old has gone, the new has come!"

Conversion combines God's sovereignty and human responsibility in a divine creative tension. "Whoever believes in the Son has eternal life" (John 3:36; 5:24) is blended in a divine matrix with, "In him we were also chosen, having been predestined according to the plan of him who works out everything in conformity with the purpose of his will" (Eph 1:11). These truths are vital expressions of biblical truth. To embrace one and neglect the other is to choose an unbalanced extreme.

THREE ESSENTIALS

Conversion has, in my opinion, been inadequately explained in many presentations of the gospel. This creates confusion for a person who is responding to an invitation to receive the gift of salvation provided by Jesus Christ. A simple response, "Yes, I know I am a sinner; I accept the gift" does not give the new convert a very strong foundation for launching his life as a follower of Jesus. I fear that it contributes to situations in which people claim to follow Jesus but never look, act, or talk like He has made a difference in their lives.

Many never get out of discipleship diapers, and I believe they may be illegitimate children of God. They somehow understand that God loves them because of what Jesus did at the cross, but they have never committed themselves to the obedience that is the source of God's blessings, the covenant promises of Deuteronomy 11 and 28 and texts like Joshua 1:1–8.

As we noted above, the apostle Paul talked about two essentials of conversion in Acts 20:21: Turning from sin in repentance and turning to God in faith. However, repentance and faith alone are not complete. One must also embrace:

> The incomparable riches of [God's] *grace*, expressed in his kindness to us in Christ Jesus. For it is by *grace* you have been saved, through *faith*—and this *not from yourselves*, it is the *gift of God*—not by works, so that no one can boast.
> —*Ephesians 2:7–9, Author's emphasis*

In no way can a person work their way to a right relationship with God or pay their own way to heaven. Apart from Christ Jesus we are eternally condemned to separation from God in hell. Romans 3:27–28 says,

> Where, then, is boasting? It is excluded. On what principle? On that of observing the law? No, but on that of faith. For we maintain that a man is justified by faith apart from observing the law.

When God opens our spiritual eyes to understand and agree with the truth of our eternal condemnation and the provision of God's mercy and grace to save us, we are faced with the three essentials of conversion. One, we must turn from sin in repentance; two, turn to God in faith; and three, make a *commitment* to follow Christ as Lord. The word *commitment* comes from the Greek word, *pisteuo*, which is used ninety-eight times in John's gospel, and it is so very vital in conversion.[2] Many people want eternal life and forgiveness without commitment to Christ and His redemptive purpose. As a result, they embrace the love of God without following through in obedience to His Word and a life of growth and discipleship.

Faith in Christ is the action of receiving God's gift of mercy through commitment to Christ. Please, let's not allow people to call themselves Christians—Christ followers—until they have come face to face with God through faith in Jesus Christ. It is so important that they see their sin and falleness, and personally repent—turn from their self-life to follow Jesus and serve Him in a life of growth. Yes, growth will be a challenging journey, but genuine conversion will result in the pursuit of God and His will and way.

The contemporary mind struggles with God's wrath against unrighteousness, but it is a principle that Paul clearly taught in the first five chapters of Romans. He showed how God laid the sin of Adam and Eve on all people of all time, but he didn't stop there. He went on to tell how God, in grace and mercy, also laid all the sin of fallen mankind on Jesus Christ when He suffered and died on the cross. Jesus, the eternal Lamb of God, was killed and sacrificed for the sin of the entire world. Then in grace and mercy God gave the righteousness of Christ to those who receive His gift of salvation.

Jesus died for all of us. It is no wonder the cross of Jesus Christ stands at the apex of redemptive history. It is the watershed at which we all choose our eternal destiny. One slope descends to separation from God and eternity in hell; the other is the path of salvation and eternal life.

Dallas Willard describes conversion and Christian discipleship with fresh, contemporary language in his book, *Renovation of the Heart.*

> The revolution of Jesus is in the first place and continuously a revolution of the human heart or spirit. It did not and does not proceed by means of the formation of social institutions and laws, the outer forms of our existence, intending that these would then impose a good order of life upon people who come under their power. Rather, his is a revolution of character, which proceeds by changing people from the inside through ongoing personal relationship to God in Christ and to one another. It is one that changes their ideas, beliefs, feelings and habits of choice, as well as their bodily tendencies and social relations. It penetrates to the deepest layers of their soul. External, social arrangements may be

useful to this end, but they are not the end, nor are they a fundamental part of the means.

On the other hand, from those divinely renovated depths of the person, social structures will naturally be transformed so that "justice roll[s] down like the waters and righteousness like an ever-flowing stream" (Amos 5:24). Such streams cannot flow through corrupted souls. Conversely, a renovated "within" will not cooperate with public streams of unrighteousness. It will block them—or die trying. It is the only thing that can do so.[3]

How will our family, friends, neighbors, and the entire world know and understand the gospel? We must tell them. We must fulfill the Great Commission. The stakes are very high. The love of Christ and the Word of God compel us: "Spread the Good News—the gospel." Apart from saving faith in Christ, people will spend eternity separated from God and His followers in hell.

For further study of this subject, see David Larson's *The Evangelism Mandate*, p 22.

Notes

INTRODUCTION

1. George Barna, *The Second Coming of the Church* (Nashville, TN: Word, 1998), 6.

2. Elmer Towns and Warren Bird, *Into the Future: Turning Today's Church Trends into Tomorrow's Opportunities* (Grand Rapids, MI: Revell, 2000), 37.

3. George Barna, *The Frog in the Kettle* (Ventura, CA: Regal, 1990), 138.

4. Robert Lewis with Rob Wilkins, *The Church of Irresistible Influence: Bridge Building Stories to Help Reach Your Community* (Grand Rapids, MI: Zondervan, 2001), 23, 25.

5. Edith C. Webster, "Faiths define tolerance," *Rockford Register Star*, November 23, 2002.

6. *The Impossible Dream* from "Man of La Mancha."

7. Jeff Havens, "Violent Crime Rate Dropped 34.6 Percent During Ten Year Period," *The Rock River Times*, vol. 12, no. 32, July 6–12, 2005, 1, 8.

8. Geri Nikolai, "Why Rockford?" *Rockford Register Star: Life and Style*, February 1, 2004, 1g–5g.

1—THE RUMBLING IN THE DISTANCE

1. Robin Mark, *Revival in Belfast*, compact disc, © 1998 Daybreak Music, LTD (adm in the US and Canada by Integrity's Hosanna! Music)/ASCAP c/o Integrity Media, Inc., 1000 Cody Road, Mobile, AL 36695.

2. Dr. Meg Meeker, *Epidemic: How Teen Sex Is Killing Our Kids* (Washington, D. C.: LifeLine Press, 2002.

3. Steve Hudson, personal letter to author, April 16, 1999.

4. Robert Lewis with Rob Wilkins, *The Church of Irresistible Influence: Bridge Building Stories to Help Reach Your Community*, 23, 213.

5. Britt Minshall, *Renaissance or Ruin: The Final Saga of a Once Great Church* (Baltimore, MD: Renaissance Institute Press, 1994), vi–vii.

6. Robert R. Kopp, *Fifteen Secrets for Life and Ministry* (Kirkwood, MO: Impact Christian Books, 2004), 83–85.

7. Bill Bright, *The Coming Revival: America's Call to Fast, Pray, and 'Seek God's Face'* (Orlando, FL: W Life Publications, 1994), 19.

8. Gregory R. Frizzell, *Returning to Holiness: A Personal and Church-wide Journey to Revival* (Memphis, TN: The Master Design. 2000), xvi.

9. Rhonda Hughey, *Desperate for His Presence: God's Design to Transform Your Life and Your City* (Minneapolis, MN: Bethany House, 2004), 20.

10. Ibid., 14.

11. Nancy Leigh De Moss, "A Passion for Holiness," *Spirit of Revival*, September 2004, 21.

12. Statistics published by Traditional Values Coalition, P.O. Box 97088, Washington, D.C. 20090-7088.

13. National Right to Life statistic is available online at www.nrlc.org/ abortion/index.html.

14. Bob Griffin, "The Muscle of Freedom," *Rockford Register Star*, Publisher, Fritz Jacobi, Editorial Editor, Wally Haas, November 2, 2004, 9A.

15. Campus Crusade for Christ *News Room*, http://www.demossnewspond .com/ccci/presskit/history.htm, 1.

16. Ed Silvoso, *That None Should Perish: How to Reach Entire Cities for Christ Through Prayer Evangelism* (Ventura, CA: Regal Books, a division of Gospel Light, 1994), 13.

17. Ibid.

18. Ibid.

19. Ibid., 16.

20. David Bryant, *The Hope at Hand: National and World Revival for the Twenty-First Century* (Grand Rapids, MI: Baker Book House, 1995), 15.

21. Brian H. Edwards, *Revival! A People Saturated With God* (Durham, England: Evangelical Press, 1990), 73–74.

22. Ibid., 73.

23. Ibid., 84.

24. Ibid.

25. Jim Cymbala, *Fresh Wind, Fresh Fire: What Happens When God's Spirit Invades the Hearts of His People* (Grand Rapids, MI: Zondervan Publishing House, 1997), 25–26.

26. Dutch Sheets, *Intercessory Prayer: How God Can Use Your Prayers to Move Heaven and Earth* (Ventura, CA: Regal Books, 1996), 11–12.

27. Susan Childress, "Prayer Yields Bountiful Harvest," *Christianity Today*, vol. 39, no. 37, June 19, 1995, 39.

28. Bill and Pam Malone, "God Is Moving in the San Francisco Bay Area," *Pray!*, issue 5, March/April 1998, 9.

29. Jeff King, "Rockin' With the Holy Ghost," *Charisma*, vol. 23, no. 4, November 1997, 78–81.

30. *Pray!*, vol. 2, no. 5, issue 8, September/October 1998, taken from front cover.

31. Henry T. Blackaby and Claude V. King, *Fresh Encounter: Experiencing God in Revival and Spiritual Awakening* (Nashville: Broadman and Holman, 1996), v.

32. "The Lausanne Covenant For World Evangelism," *Lausanne Covenant*, 1974, 1989, 1. For more information, visit www.lausanne.org.

33. Billy Graham, Mission America brochure.

34. John Quam, "A Time of Harvest for America—Some Harvest Indicators," *Mission America Monthly*, vol. 11, no. 11, February/March 1998 newsletter, 3.

35. For a thorough coverage, pro and con, of Mel Gibson's *The Passion of the Christ*, see http://www.beliefnet.com/index/index_525.html.

36. Jeff Havens, "Violent Crime Rate Dropped 34.6 Percent during Ten-Year Period," *The Rock River Times*, vol. 12, no. 32, July 6–12, 2005, 1, 2, 8.

3—TRACING THE STORM PATTERN

1. Jim Stewart, CBS *Evening News*, Washington, D.C., January 6, 2005.

2. Hughey, *Desperate for His Presence: God's Design to Transform Your Life and Your City*, 69–79.

3. Ibid., 79.

4. Ibid., 93.

5. George Barna, *The Year's Most Intriguing Findings*, Barna Research Online, December 17, 2001, www.barna.org/FlexPage.aspx?Page=BarnaUpdate&BarnaUpdateID=84).

6. Hughey, *Desperate for His Presence: God's Design to Transform Your Life and Your City*, 110.

7. Walter Kaiser, *Quest for Renewal* (Chicago: Moody, 1986), 9.

8. Dr. J. J. Edwards, "O. T. 101: Israel's Faith and History," seminary notes, 1968, 9–17.

9. George Ladd, *The Gospel of the Kingdom* (Grand Rapids, MI: Wm. B. Eerdmans Publishing Company, 1959), 114.

10. Nicholson and Lee, eds., Francis Thompson, "Hound of Heaven," *The Oxford Book of English Mystical Verse*, (New York: Bartleby.com, 2000), 239.

11. W. E. Vine, *An Expository Dictionary of New Testament Words* (Old Tarpan, NJ: Fleming H. Revell Company, 1966), 146–147.

12. David Larsen, *The Evangelical Mandate: Recovering the Centrality of Gospel Preaching* (Westchester, IL: Crossway Books 1992), 171–172.

13. Stephen F. Olford, *Heart-Cry for Revival* (Westwood, N.J.: Fleming H. Revell, 1962), 68.

14. Arthur Wallis, *Rain From Heaven*, (Minneapolis, MN: Bethany Fellowship, 1979), 17.

15. Blackaby and King, *Fresh Encounter: Experiencing God in Revival and Spiritual Awakening*, 23.

16. Thomas Ashbridge, *Why Revival Tarries* (London: Pickering and Inglis, 1945), 15–18.

17. J. Edwin Orr, *The Second Evangelical Awakening in Britain* (London: Marshall, Morgan, and Scott, 1949), 118–119.

18. Earle E. Cairns, *An Endless Line of Splendor: Revivals and Their Leaders from the Great Awakening to the Present* (Wheaton, IL: Tyndale House Publishers, 1986), 319–321.

19. Ibid., 322.

20. Ibid., 323.

21. R. A. Torrey quote available online at http://www.bible.org/page .asp?page_id=59.

22. Eric W. Hayden, *Spurgeon on Revival* (Grand Rapids, MI: Zondervan Publishing House, 1962), 73–74.

23. Lewis Drummond, *Eight Keys to Biblical Revival* (Minneapolis, MN: Bethany House Publishers, 1994), 189–190.

24. Edwards, *Revival! A People Saturated With God*, 31, 73–74.

25. Elana Lynse, *Flames of Revival* (Wheaton, IL: Crossway Books, 1989), 47–48.

26. Olford, *Heart-Cry for Revival*, 80.

27. James Burns, ed., *The Laws of Revival* (Wheaton, IL: World Wide Publications, 1993), 23–24.

28. Ibid., 54.

4—OLD TESTAMENT FIRESTORMS

1. Wallis, *Rain From Heaven*, 32.

2. Orville J. Nave, *Nave's Topical Bible* (Nashville, TN: The Southwestern Company, 1962), 113.

3. Text note on Genesis 32:28, *NIV Study Bible* (Grand Rapids, MI: Zondervan Bible Publishers, 1985), 56.

4. Kaiser, *Quest for Renewal*, 13.

5. Ibid., 13–14.

6. Ibid., 14.

7. Ibid.

8. Ibid., 14–15.

9. Ibid., 15.

10. Drummond, *Eight Keys to Biblical Revival*, 7–8.

11. Wilbur Smith, *Nine Characteristics of Great Revivals in the Old Testament: The Glorious Revival Under King Hezekiah* (Grand Rapids, MI: Zondervan, 1937), 7–8.

12. Wilber Smith, *The Glorious Revival*, 7–8 and Walter Kaiser, *Quest for Renewal*, 15–16.

13. Edwards, *Revival! A People Saturated With God*, 18, 30.

14. Elana Lynse, *Flames of Revival*, 23–28.

15. Wallis, *Rain From Heaven*, 101–102.

5—NEW TESTAMENT FIRESTORMS

1. Mission America telephone conference call, *City Impact Round Table*, interview with George Otis, Jr., February 8, 2005, Mission America Coalition: a collaborative movement of Christians promoting unity, evangelism, and revival; P.O. Box 13930, Palm Desert, CA 92255, page 8; Email: infor@missionamerica .org; Phone: 760-200-2707; Contact: Carolyn O'Brian, info@cityreaching.com.

2. Malcolm McDow and Alvin L. Reid, *Fire Fall: How God Has Shaped History Through Revivals* (Nashville: Broadman and Holman Publishers, 1997), 69.

3. Lyle Shaller, "Jesus for Peoria," *The Community Builders Foundation*, June 2002, 3.

4. Blackaby and King, *Fresh Encounter: Experiencing God in Revival and Spiritual Awakening*, 58.

5. Arthur Wallis, *Rain From Heaven*.

6. Olford, *Heart-Cry for Revival*, 67–76.

7. Ibid., 79–87.

8. George Otis, Mission America telephone conference call.

9. E. D. Head, *Revivals in the Bible*, (Fort Worth, TX: Southwestern Baptist Seminary, 1951), 15–40.

6—Great Storms of History: Characteristics 1–3

1. Edward Gibson, *The Decline and Fall of the Roman Empire* (New York: Washington Square Press and Simon and Schuster, 1970).

2. Patrick J. Johnstone, *Operation World—Europe* (Grand Rapids, MI: Zondervan, 1993), 60.

3. Chuck Colson, *Breakpoint*, December 30, 2004.

4. Cairns, *An Endless Line of Splendor: Revivals and Their Leaders From the Great Awakening to the Present*, 32, 83.

5. Mary Stewart Relfe, *Cure of All Ills* (Montgomery, AL: League of Prayer, 1988), 71.

6. Cairns, *An Endless Line of Splendor: Revivals and Their Leaders From the Great Awakening to the Present*, 196–197.

7. Frank Bartleman, *Azusa Street: The Roots of Modern-day Pentecost* (South Plainfield, NJ: Bridge Publishing, 1980), ix.

8. Ibid., xx.

9. Richard M. Riss, *20th Century Revival Movements in North America* (Peabody, MA: Hendrickson Publications, 1988), 47.

10. McDow and Reid, *Fire Fall: How God Has Shaped History Through Revivals*, 184–185.

11. Ibid., 184, 204.

12. Henry Johnson, *Stories of Great Revivals* (London: The Religious Tract Society, 1906), 21–22.

13. Ibid., 22.

14. Ibid., 22–23.

15. Ibid., 23.

16. Warren A. Candler, *Great Revivals and the Great Republic* (Nashville: Publishing House of the M. E. Church, 1904), 43–45.

17. Winke Pratney, *Revival* (Springfield, Pa.: Whitaker House, 1983), 111.

18. McDow and Reid, *Fire Fall: How God Has Shaped History Through Revivals*, 228.

19. Ibid.

20. Candler, *Great Revivals and the Great Republic*, 164, 167.

21. Ibid., 169.

22. J. Edwin Orr, *The Fervent Prayer: The Worldwide Impact of the Great Awakening of 1858* (Chicago: Moody Press, 1974), 1.

23. Candler, *Great Revivals and the Great Republic*, 210.

24. Orr, *The Fervent Prayer: The Worldwide Impact of the Great Awakening of 1858*, 1–2.

25. Cairns, *An Endless Line of Splendor: Revivals and Their Leaders From the Great Awakening to the Present*, 147.

26. J. Edwin Orr, *The Second Great Awakening in America* (London: Marshall, Morgan and Scott, 1952), 83.

27. Johnson, *Stories of Great Revivals*, 348.

28. McDow and Reid, *Fire Fall: How God Has Shaped History Through Revivals*, 276.

29. George T. B. Davis, *When the Fire Fell* (Philadelphia: The Million Testaments Campaigns, 1945), 66–67.

30. Bartleman, *Azusa Street: The Roots of Modern-day Pentecost*, x–xi.

31. Ibid., 18–19.

32. Ibid., 20.

33. Relfe, *Cure of All Ills*, 65.

34. Ibid., 66.

35. Ibid.

36. McDow and Reid, *Fire Fall: How God Has Shaped History Through Revivals*, 282–283.

37. Cairns, *An Endless Line of Splendor: Revivals and Their Leaders from the Great Awakening to the Present*, 31–33.

38. McDow and Reid, *Fire Fall: How God Has Shaped History Through Revivals*, 167–168.

39. Edith L. Blumhofer and Randall Balmer, *Modern Christian Revivals* (Chicago: University of Illinois Press, 1993), 84.

40. McDow and Reid, *Fire Fall: How God Has Shaped History Through Revivals*, 229–231.

41. Ibid., 231.

42. Robert Bakke, *The Concert of Prayer: Back to the Future* (Minneapolis, MN: The Evangelical Free Church of America, 1993), 14–15.

43. McDow and Reid, *Fire Fall: How God Has Shaped History Through Revivals*, 235–239.

44. Cairns, *An Endless Line of Splendor: Revivals and Their Leaders From the Great Awakening to the Present*, 148–150.

45. Relfe, *Cure of All Ills*, 47–49.

46. Ibid.

47. Ibid., 45.

48. McDow and Reid, *Fire Fall: How God Has Shaped History Through Revivals*, 255.

49. Cairns, *An Endless Line of Splendor: Revivals and Their Leaders From the Great Awakening to the Present*, 194–197.

50. McDow and Reid, *Fire Fall: How God Has Shaped History Through Revivals*, 277.

51. Ibid., 276.

52. Riss, *20th Century Revival Movements in North America*, 47.

53. Ibid., 49.

54. Ibid., 51–52.

55. Edwards, *Revival! A People Saturated With God*, 73–74.

56. Ibid., 73–84.

57. Pratney, *Revival*, 68.

58. Ibid., 70.

59. Wesley Duewel, *Revival Fire* (Grand Rapids, MI: Zondervan, 1995), 52–54.

60. Ibid.

61. McDow and Reid, *Fire Fall: How God Has Shaped History Through Revivals*, 205.

62. Johnson, *Stories of Great Revivals*, 24.

63. Relfe, *Cure of All Ills*, 27.

64. Ibid.

65. Ibid., 28.

66. Pratney, *Revival*, 112–114.

67. McDow and Reid, *Fire Fall: How God has Shaped History Through Revivals*, 231.

68. Ibid., 229.

69. Cairns, *An Endless Line of Splendor: Revivals and Their Leaders From the Great Awakening to the Present*, 92.

70. Ibid., 178–179.

71. Ibid., 178.

72. Bartleman, *Azusa Street: The Roots of Modern-day Pentecost*, ix.

73. Ibid., 8–9.

74. Ibid., 13.

75. Ibid., 36.

76. Ibid., 47.

77. Ibid., 58.

78. Cairns, *An Endless Line of Splendor: Revivals and Their Leaders From the Great Awakening to the Present*, 188–189.

79. Wesley Duewel, *Revival Fire*, 180–181.

80. Richard Dresselhaus, "Three Miles from the Coffee," Enrichment (Summer 2004), 36.

7—PRAYER: FANNING THE FLAMES OF INTIMACY WITH GOD

1. E. M. Bounds quote available online at www.cybernation.com/ quotationcenter/ quoteshow.php?type=author&id-1078.

2. Ibid.

3. Martin Luther quote available online at www.cybernation.com/ quotationcenter/ quoteshow.php?type=author&id-1078.

4. E. M. Bounds quote available online at www.cybernation.com/ quotationcenter/ quoteshow.php?type=author&id-1078.

5. Edwards, *Revival! A People Saturated With God*, 73–74.

6. E. M. Bounds quote available online at www.cybernation.com/ quotationcenter/ quoteshow.php?type=author&id-1078.

7. Oswald Chambers, *My Utmost for His Highest*, (New York: Dodd Mead and Company, 1935), 291.

8. Dr. Martin Lloyd Jones quote available online at www.ravenhill.org/index, Maxims 3.

9. E. M. Bounds quote available online at www.cybernation.com/ quotationcenter/ quoteshow.php?type=author&id-1078.

10. Author's paraphrase of story taken from http://www.tlta.com/publications/ downdate/WorkSmarterNotHarder.pdf.

11. Dutch Sheets, *The River of God* (Ventura, CA: Regal Books, 1998), 194.

8—GREAT STORMS OF HISTORY: CHARACTERISTIC 4

1. Orr, *The Second Great Awakening in America*, 19–20.

2. Ibid., 130.

3. Ibid., 154.

4. Ibid., 19–64.

5. Ibid., 155.

6. Cairns, *An Endless Line of Splendor: Revivals and Their Leaders From the Great Awakening to the Present*, 194–197.

7. Relfe, *Cure of All Ills*, 95.

8. Davis, *When the Fire Fell*, 65.

9. Ibid., 72–73.

10. McDow and Reid, *Fire Fall: How God Has Shaped History Through Revivals*, 280–281.

9—THE WORD OF GOD: AN AMAZING STRATEGIC WEAPON

1. Henry Ward Beecher quote available online at www.cybernation.com/ quotationcenter/quoteshow.php?type=subject&id=137&page=1.

2. Ibid.

3. Martin Luther, "A Mighty Fortress Is Our God," *Great Hymns of Faith* (Grand Rapids, MI: Zondervan, 1969), 36.

10—GREAT STORMS OF HISTORY: CHARACTERISTICS 5–10

1. McDow and Reid, *Fire Fall: How God Has Shaped History Through Revivals,* 225–226.

2. Relfe, *Cure of All Ills*, 23.

3. Pratney, *Revival*, 106–107.

4. Johnson, *Stories of Great Revivals*, 192–193.

5. Candler, *Great Revivals and the Great Republic*, 88–89.

6. Ibid., 100.

7. Ibid., 189.

8. Pratney, *Revival*, 115, 134–135.

9. Relfe, *Cure of All Ills*, 35.

10. McDow and Reid, *Fire Fall: How God Has Shaped History Through Revivals*, 247.

11. Ibid., 247–248.

12. J. Edwin Orr, *The Second Evangelical Awakening*, 20.

13. Ibid., 66.

14. Candler, *Great Revivals and the Great Republic*, 222.

15. J. Edwin Orr, *The Second Evangelical Awakening*, 114–115.

16. Ibid., 116.

17. Davis, *When the Fire Fell*, 72–73.

18. Pratney, *Revival*, 178.

19. Bartleman, *Azusa Street: The Roots of Modern-day Pentecost*, ix.

20. See www.wesleycottage.ukonline.co.uk/methodism%20-%20the%20history.htm.

21. Pratney, *Revival*, 107.

22. Edwards, *Revival! A People Saturated With God*, 140–141.

23. Pratney, *Revival*, 137.

24. Edwards, *Revival! A People Saturated With God*, 132.

25. Ibid., 132, 140.

26. Ibid., 116–17.

27. Ibid., 118.

28. Ibid., 116–117.

29. Orr, *The Fervent Prayer: The Worldwide Impact of the Great Awakening of 1858*, 5.

30. Bartleman, *Azusa Street: The Roots of Modern-day Pentecost*, 64.

31. Mel Gibson, *The Passion of the Christ*, New Market Films, Icon Distribution, Inc., 2004.

32. McDow and Reid, *Fire Fall: How God Has Shaped History Through Revivals*.

33. Ibid.

34. Edwards, *Revival! A People Saturated With God*, 108.

35. Ibid.

36. Duewel, *Revival Fire*, 65–66.

37. Relfe, *Cure of All Ills*, 28–29.

38. Cairns, *An Endless Line of Splendor: Revivals and Their Leaders From the Great Awakening to the Present*, 97.

39. Bartleman, *Azusa Street: The Roots of Modern-day Pentecost*, 80.

40. *Braveheart*, Twentieth Century Fox Distribution, Paramount Pictures, 1995 (Marquis Film, The Ladd Company, Icon Productions).

41. Candler, *Great Revivals and the Great Republic*, 50.

42. Ibid., 179.

43. Orr, *The Second Great Awakening in America*, 41–42.

44. Riss, *20th Century Revival Movements in North America*, 38.

45. Davis, *When the Fire Fell*, 74.

46. Ibid., 74, 78.

47. Bartleman, *Azusa Street: The Roots of Modern-day Pentecost*, 56.

48. Riss, *20th Century Revival Movements in North America*, 5–7.

49. "Transformations," © 1999, The Sentinel Group, www.transformnations .com, Global Net Productions.

50. "The Quickening," © 2003, The Sentinel Group, www.transformnations .com, Global Net Productions.

51. Relfe, *Cure of All Ills*, 20–22.

52. Ibid., 23.

53. Candler, *Great Revivals and the Great Republic*, 87–100.

54. McDow and Reid, *Fire Fall: How God Has Shaped History Through Revivals*, 225–226.

55. Relfe, *Cure of All Ills*, 35–36.

56. McDow and Reid, *Fire Fall: How God Has Shaped History Through Revivals*, 247–248.

57. Candler, *Great Revivals and the Great Republic*, 150.

58. Relfe, *Cure of All Ills*, 49.

59. Ibid., 62.

60. Ibid., 87–94.

61. Orr, *The Second Great Awakening in America*, 156–157.

62. Orr, *The Fervent Prayer: The Worldwide Impact of the Great Awakening of 1858*, 176.

63. Ibid.

64. Riss, *20th Century Revival Movements in North America*, 40.

65. Johnson, *Stories of Great Revivals*, 370.

66. Pratney, *Revival*, 191.

67. Bartleman, *Azusa Street: The Roots of Modern-day Pentecost*, ix.

68. Pratney, *Revival*, 194.

69. George Otis, Jr., unpublished teaching notes, recorded in Hughey, *Desperate for His Presence: God's Design to Transform Your Life and Your City*, 196.

70. David Wilkerson, January 17, 2005, letter.

71. McDow and Reid, *Fire Fall: How God Has Shaped History Through Revivals*, 297.

11—A TALE OF THREE CITIES

1. Bonaro W. Overstreet, *Hands Laid Upon the Wind* (New York: Norton, 1955), 15.

2. Charles Dickens, *A Tale of Two Cities*, (New York: Sheldon and Company, 1863), 7.

3. Meg Meeker, *Epidemic: How Sex Is Killing Our Kids* (LifeLine Press: Washington, D.C., 2002).

4. Patrick M. Scamlon, "Cheating, Writing, and Arithmetic: A New Epidemic of Fraud Is Sweeping Through Our Schools," *U.S. News and World Report* (November 22, 1999), 16.

5. Angie Cannon article available online at www.usnews.com/usnews/news/articles/991206/archive_003643.htm.

6. See National Right to Life web site at www.nrlc.org/abortion/index/html.

7. Alan Keyes, Speech given at the Rockford, Illinois airport, September 21, 2004.

8. Tommy Tenney, *The God Chasers* (Shippensberg, PA: Destiny Image Publishers, Inc, 1998).

APPENDIX VII

1. W. E. Vine, *An Expository Dictionary of New Testament Words*, (Old Tarpan, NJ: Flemin H. Revell Co, 1940), 239.

2. Ibid., 211.

3. Dallas Willard, *Renovation of the Heart: Putting on the Character of Christ* (Colorado Springs, CO: Nav Press, 2002), 15.

Selected Bibliography

Anderson, Leith and Elmer Towns. *Rivers of Revival*. Ventura, CA: Regal Books, 1997.

Anderson, Neil. *The Bondage Breaker*. Eugene, OR: Harvest House Publications, 2000.

———. *A Way of Escape: Freedom From Sexual Strongholds*. Eugene, OR: Harvest House Publications, 1994.

———. *Victory Over the Darkness: Realizing the Power of Your Identity in Christ*. Ventura, CA: Regal Books, 2000.

Autrey, C. E. *Revivals of the Old Testament*. Grand Rapids, MI: Zondervan, 1960.

Avant, John, Malcolm McDow, and Alvin Reid, eds. *Revival: The Story of the Current Awakening in Brownwood, Ft. Worth, Wheaton, and Beyond*. Nashville: Broadman and Holman, 1996.

Baker, Ernest. *The Revivals of the Bible*. Capetown, South Africa: Miller Publishing, 1906.

Barna, George. *The Frog in the Kettle*. Ventura, CA: Regal Books, 1990.

———. *The Second Coming of the Church*. Nashville: Word Publishing Group, 1998.

Bartleman, Frank. *Azusa Street: The Roots of Modern-day Pentecost*. South Plainfield, NJ: Bridge Publishing, 1980.

Blackaby, Henry T. and Claude V. King. *Fresh Encounter: Experiencing God in Revival and Spiritual Awakening*. Nashville: Broadman and Holman, 1996.

Blumhofer, Edith L. and Randall Balmer. *Modern Christian Revivals*.

Chicago: University of Illinois Press, 1993.

Bready, John Wesley. *England: Before and After Wesley: The Evangelical Revival and Social Reform*. New York: Russell and Russell, 1971.

Bright, Bill. *The Coming Revival: America's Call to Fast, Pray, and 'Seek God's Face,'* Orlando, FL: W Life Publications, 1995.

Bryant, David. *The Hope at Hand: National and World Revival for the Twenty-First Century.* Grand Rapids, MI: Baker Book House, 1995.

Burns, James. ed. *The Laws of Revival,* by Tom Phillips. Wheaton, IL: World Wide Publications, 1993.

Cairns, Earle E. *An Endless Line of Splendor*. Wheaton, IL: Tyndale House Publishers, 1986.

Candler, Warren A. *Great Revivals and the Great Republic*. Nashville: Publishing House of the M. E. Church, 1904.

Cho, Paul Y. *Prayer: Key to Revival*. Dallas: Word Publishing, 1984.

Coleman, Robert E. *The Coming World Revival.* Wheaton, IL: Crossway Books, 1995.

Cymbala, Jim. *Fresh Wind, Fresh Fire: What Happens When God's Spirit Invades the Hearts of His People*. Grand Rapids, MI: Zondervan Publishing House, 1997.

———. *Breakthrough Prayer: The Secret of Receiving What You Need From God.* Grand Rapids, MI: Zondervan, 2003.

Damazio, Frank. *Seasons of Revival: Understanding the Appointed Times of Spiritual Refreshing*. Portland, OR: B. T. Publishing, 1996.

Davis, George T. B. *When the Fire Fell*. Philadelphia: The Million Testaments Campaigns, 1945.

Drummond, Lewis. *Eight Keys to Biblical Revival*. Minneapolis, MN: Bethany, 1994.

Duewel, Wesley. *Revival Fire*. Grand Rapids, MI: Zondervan, 1995.

Dye, Colin. *Revival Phenomena*. Tonbridge, England: Sovereign World Publishing, 1996.

Edwards, Brian H. *Revival! A People Saturated With God*. Durham, England: Evangelical Press, 1990.

Emerson, Michael O. and Christian Smith. *Divided by Faith: Evangelical Religion and the Problem of Race in America*. New York, NY: Oxford University Press, 2000.

Fereday, William Wollreidge. *Josiah and Revival*. Kilmarnock, Scotland: J. Ritchie Publishers, 1940.

Finney, Charles G. *Lectures on Revivals of Religion*. Cambridge, MA: Harvard University Press, 1960.

Finney, Charles G. and Louis Gifford Parkhurst, Jr., eds. *Principles of Revival*. Minneapolis, MN: Bethany House, 1987.

Foster, Richard J. *Prayer: Finding the Heart's True Home*. San Francisco, CA: Harper, 1992.

Frangipane, Francis. *The Three Battlegrounds: An In-depth View of the Three Arenas of Spiritual Warfare: The Mind, the Church and the Heavenly Places*. Cedar Rapids, IA: Arrow Publications, 1989.

Frizzell, Gregory R. *How to Develop a Powerful Prayer Life*. Memphis, TN: The Master Design, 1999.

———. *Returning to Holiness: A Personal and Church-wide Journey to Revival*. Memphis, TN: The Master Design, 2000.

Gillies, John. *Historical Collections of Accounts of Revival*. Edinburgh, UK: Banner of Truth Trust, 1981.

Goetzman, Martha. *Anomalous Features in the Chicago Prayer Meeting Revival as Revealed in Contemporary Newspaper Accounts*. M.A. Thesis, Trinity Evangelical Divinity School, 1985.

Hardman, Keith J. *Seasons of Refreshing: Evangelism and Revival in America.* Grand Rapids, MI: Zondervan, 1994.

Hayden, Eric W. *Spurgeon on Revival.* Grand Rapids, MI: Zondervan Publishing House, 1962.

Henson, Al. *Practical Theology of Revival.* Canadian Revival Fellowship. Cassette, 1998.

Hempy, Robert W. *A Comparative Study of Selected Revivals in America.* M.Div. thesis, Western Evangelical Seminary, 1960.

Hughey, Rhonda. *Desperate for His Presence: God's Design to Transform Your Life and Your City.* Minneapolis, MN: Bethany House, 2004.

Hunt, Alfred Leedes. *Evangelical By-paths: Studies in the Religious and Social Aspects of the Evangelical Revival of the Eighteenth Century and a Reply to Its Critics.* London: Charless J. Thynne and Jarvis, 1927.

Johnson, Henry. *Stories of Great Revivals.* London: The Religious Tract Society, 1906.

Kaiser, Walter. *Quest for Revival.* Chicago: Moody, 1986.

Kilpatrick, John. *When the Heavens Are Brass: Keys to Genuine Revival.* Shippensburg, PA: Revival Press, 1997.

Kopp, Robert R. *Fifteen Secrets for Life and Ministry.* Kirkwood, MO: Impact Christian Books, 2004.

Ladd, George. *The Gospel of the Kingdom.* Grand Rapids, MI: Wm. B. Eerdmans Publishing Company, 1959.

Larsen, David L. *The Evangelism Mandate: Recovering the Centrality of Gospel Preaching.* Westchester, IL: Crossway Books, 1992.

Lewis, Robert and Rob Wilkins. *The Church of Irresistible Influence: Bridge Building Stories to Help Reach Your Community.* Grand Rapids, MI: Zondervan, 2001.

Lloyd-Jones, Martyn G. *Revival*. Westchester, IL: Crossway Books, 1987.

Lutzer, Erwin W. *Flames of Freedom*. Chicago: Moody Press, 1976.

Lyrene, Edward Charles. *The Role of Prayer in American Revival Movements, 1740 to 1860*. PhD diss., Southern Baptist Theological Seminary, 1985.

McDow, Malcolm and Alvin L. Reid. *Fire Fall: How God Has Shaped History Through Revivals*. Nashville: Broadman and Holman Publishers, 1997.

McKenna, David L. *The Coming Great Awakening: New Hope for the Nineties*. Downers Grove, Ill.: InterVarsity Press, 1990.

Minshall, Britt. *Renaissance or Ruin: The Final Saga of a Once Great Church*. Baltimore, MD: Renaissance Institute Press, 1994.

O'Connor, Elizabeth. *Journey Inward, Journey Outward*. Washington, D.C.: Potter's House Books, 1968.

Olford, Stephen F. *Heart-Cry for Revival*. Westwood, NJ: Fleming H. Revell, 1962.

Orr, J. Edwin. *The Fervent Prayer: The Worldwide Impact of the Great Awakening of 1858*. Chicago: Moody Press, 1974.

———. *The Second Great Awakening in America*. London: Marshall, Morgan and Scott, 1952.

———. *The Second Evangelical Awakening*. London: Marshall, Morgan and Scott, 1964.

———. *The Flaming Tongue: The Impact of Twentieth Century Revivals*. Chicago: Moody Press, 1973.

Owens, Jimmy and Carol. *Heal Our Land: Securing God's Blessing on America*. Grand Rapids, MI: Zondervan, 1997.

Phillips, Tom and Mark Curshall. *Revival Signs*. Gresham, OR: Vision House Publishing, 1995.

Pratney, Winke. *Revival*. Springfield, PA: Whitaker House, 1983.

Randall, Christie J. *The Revival Under Hezekiah*. M.A. Thesis, Trinity Evangelical Divinity, 1991.

Ravenhill, Leonard. *Revival God's Way: A Message for the Church*. Minneapolis: Bethany House Publishers, 1986.

———. *Why Revival Tarries*. Minneapolis: Bethany Fellowship, 1959.

Rhee, Yoon-Ho. *Towards a Theory of Revival: A Case Study of the Biblical and Korean Revivals*. M.A. Thesis. Fuller Theological Seminary, 1988.

Riss, Richard M. *20th Century Revival Movements in North America*. Peabody, MA: Hendrickson Publications, 1988.

Relfe, Mary Stewart. *The Cure of All Ills*. Montgomery, AL: League of Prayer, 1988.

Roberts, Richard Owens. *Revival*. Wheaton, IL: Richard Owen Roberts Publishers, 1982.

Shearer, John. *Old Time Revival: How the Fire of God Spread in Days Now Past and Gone*. London: Pickering and Inglis, 1930.

Sheets, Dutch. *Intercessory Prayer: How God Can Use Your Prayers to Move Heaven and Earth*. Ventura, CA: Regal Books, 1996.

Silvoso, Ed. *That None Should Perish*. Ventura, CA: Regal Books, 1994.

Smith, Timothy L. *Revivalism and Social Reform: American Protestantism on the Eve of the Civil War*. Baltimore: Johns Hopkins University Press, 1980.

Smith, Wilbur. *Nine Characteristics of Great Revivals in the Old Testament: The Glorious Revival Under King Hezekiah*, Grand Rapids, MI: Zondervan, 1937.

Smyth, Charles and Hugh Eggerton. *Simeon and Church Order: A Study of the Origins of the Evangelical Revival in Cambridge in the Eighteenth Century*. Cambridge: University Press, 1940.

Sprague, William B. *Lectures on Revivals of Religion.* Edinburgh, UK: Banner of Truth Trust, 1978.

Thornbury, John F. *God Sent Revival: The Story of Asahel Nettleton and the Second Great Awakening.* Grand Rapids, MI: Evangelical Press, 1977.

Towns, Elmer and Warren Bird. *Into the Future: Turning Today's Church Trends into Tomorrow's Opportunities.* Grand Rapids: Revell, 2000.

Wagner, C. Peter. *Prayer Shield: How to Intercede for Pastors, Christian Leaders and Others on the Spiritual Front Lines.* Ventura, CA: Regal Books, 1995.

————. 1995. *Praying With Power: How to Pray Effectively and Hear Clearly From God.* Ventura, CA: Regal Books. (See other books in this series by C. Peter Wagner, published by Regal: *Warfare Prayer*; *Breaking Strongholds in Your City*; *Churches That Pray*; *Engaging the Enemy: Wrestling With Dark Angels*.)

Wallis, Arthur. *In the Day of Thy Power: The Scriptural Principles of Revival.* London: Christian Literature Crusade, 1956.

Walton, Harold W. *A Study of the Principles in Revival.* Abstract, D.Min. Project, Trinity Evangelical Divinity School, 1995.

White, Tom. *City-wide Prayer Movements: One Church, Many Congregations.* Ann Arbor, MI: Vine Books Servant Publications, 2001.

Whittaker, Colin C. *Great Revivals.* Springfield, MO: Gospel Publishing House, 1984.

Whittaker, Donald S. *The Theology of Revival of Jonathan Edwards.* M.A. Thesis, Trinity Evangelical Divinity School, 1973.

Wilkerson, David. *America's Last Call.* Lindale, TX: Wilkerson Trust Publications, 1998.

Willard, Dallas. *Renovation of the Heart: Putting on the Character of Christ.* Colorado Springs, CO: Nav Press, 2002.

Woods, Arthur Skevington. *The Indistinguishable Blaze: Spiritual Renewal and Advance in the Eighteenth Century.* Grand Rapids, MI: Eerdmans, 1960.